Educational Technology in Changing Society

Educational Technology in Changing Society

Editor

Rajarshi Roy

SHIPRA

ISBN: 978-81-7541-599-7

First Published in India in 2011

Educational Technology in Changing Society

Published by:
SHIPRA PUBLICATIONS
LG 18-19, Pankaj Central Market,
I.P. Ext., Patparganj, Delhi-110092
Ph. 91-11-22235152, 22236152

Br. Off: 4617/18, Ansari Road, Daryaganj,
Delhi-110002; Ph. 65946453, 9810522367
Email: info@shiprapublications.com
www.shiprapublications.com

Dedicated to

Late Professor Amlan Dutta

The Humanist of the era

and

Late Professor Arati Sen

Educationist

Preface

Educational technology in Indian context is not a unique one, though connotes several meanings in varied dimensions in present academic spectrum. Till date, irrespective of academic expectation, educational technology doesn't have obvious natural boundaries. Though there emerged specified definitions. However much of its claimed territory is inhabited by people, who seek occupational identity within the educational technology territory but lagging with the basic concept of 'instruction'. An overwhelming attempt of domination over the field by the technocrats from multimedia and computer sciences is a common phenomenon now-a-days.

By nature, educational technology aught to be an applied field of study and practice; any application in the area aught to be based on grounded theory. Unfortunately the practices are floating ignoring the theory and trend reveals almost a complete omission of knowledge field. It is to be understood that nether multimedia, nor computer sciences are the synonymous with educational technology, however may contribute (and often contribute) for implementation of the 'principles of instruction', which is considered as the heart of 'educational technology'.

To realize the essence of importance of educational technology, one needs to focus over the purpose of the same in context of curricula-determination, supposed to be followed by curricula-planning, further followed by classroom implementation, mostly through audio-visual and multi-media devices. Instructional technology helps implement curricula planning. In this spectrum, cognition and developing knowledge and consolidation thereof is the ultimate goal. Noteworthy here is the distinction of information and knowledge, which is often ignored in the discourse of educational technology. Till date, educational technology needs to become pre-occupied with the development of rich and interesting environment in which learner can make real decisions about 'what to explore'. It needs to bring out the significance of intellectual interaction and self-initiated exploration.

Here it is worth noting that a field of study is much less rigorous than a discipline. A discipline is usually defined as an organized body of knowledge, which is constantly tested and changed by research. Disciplines are more often found in the sciences although the term covers social sciences and humanities too. Fields are usually found in the areas of applied studies—the professions. Field often draws on disciplines for basic substance. Educational technology aught to be a field of study centering round the discipline 'education' in general and 'instructional methodology' in particular. Deviation of the same from the core will ultimately dilute the concept of 'educational technology' and will lead to sophistication of technology mere and unwanted domination thereof over the core and ignoring the process for developing 'cognition'.

Educational technology emerged in Indian context during late sixties. Emergence of educational technology is a resultant of use of various technical and technological devices and gadgets in the arena of pedagogical setup. As such, it is perceived by a section of people that educational technology is just the application of technology in teaching learning situation. The trend of conceptualizing 'educational technology' provokes a section of educationists to comment that educational technology is the mechanization of educational process. Use of machine in the process of education mostly takes place in three forms.

However the contemporary educational psychologists, irrespective of schools, accept 'teaching' as 'art' and 'science' simultaneously. It is a fact that mere availability of technological devices and use thereof may not help in the process of learning without the basic knowledge of learning-i.e., knowing *how students learn.* In such scenario, learning will not be effective. Therefore, the teacher aught to know how the students learn. Effectiveness of technological gadgets depends upon the knowledge of the teacher about their uses. Modern educational technology aught to emphasis over these very dimensions of learning. These 'techniques of teaching', 'methodology, following which teaching takes place', and 'the task of teaching' together forming the bases of learning. These come under the purview of learning technology. Therefore all these techniques, methods and teaching are supposed to come under the purview of 'educational technology'. These are technology of education, commonly termed as software. Hence, software dimension of education is believed by a section, to be educational technology.

The ultimate aim of educational technology is to improve the pedagogical process. Within a narrower span of time, educational technology deduced a hermeneutic approach of development, often faced by counter questions from different schools of thoughts and disciplines. The field, irrespective of 'dimensions' and 'schools of thought' are engaged in developing the system of education and thereby for betterment of human society. Now days good many instructional designs are in use in varying educational setups. These are the contribution of educational technology. Training psychology, cybernetic psychology and system analysis are the few examples in this context. These dominos of knowledge are helping to control and evaluate teacher's behaviour. Also it contributes a unique concept 'teaching theory', in retrospect with learning theory. Teaching models are the outcomes of this teaching theory only.

The present volume accords contribution from the scholars from various corner of the globe, discusses the pertinent themes and concept, centering round the area, 'Educational Technology', covering the dimensions theory and practices in changing society, which is expected to update the changing concept pertaining to educational technology.

Rajarshi Roy

Contents

PART A
EDUCATIONAL TECHNOLOGY AS KNOWLEDGE BASE

1.

A Conceptual and Definitional Focus of the Meaning of Educational Technology in the 21st Century

Denis Hlynka and Markian Hlynka

This chapter identifies two basic functions of technology in education, provides an overview of what technology (without the education) means, and finally what, therefore, *educational technology* should mean, based on the new definition from the Association for Educational Communications and Technology (AECT, 2008) that focuses and determines the potential pedagogic value of an 'educational technology.'[1]

As we move from technology to educational technology, we (authors are speaking in the first person, as in the classroom) will encounter critical terms including ICT, interactivity, and educational media.

First Considerations

Now, we want you to bring to your chair (or desk) two items, two exemplars of educational technology. They will not be difficult to find at all. We want you to bring a book and a pencil or a pen if you cannot find a pencil. They are closely enough related. And if you can't find a book, you can use this one that you are reading.

You have in front of you two 'educational technologies', a pen(cil) and a book.

Background and Contextual Information

Here is a minimalist definition of the act of teaching/learning: a teacher teaches something to someone using some medium of communication. There are four components:

(*i*) A teacher
(*ii*) A learner
(*iii*) Content (something to teach)

(*iv*) A medium through which one teaches. (spoken language, a text, a blog, etc.)

This is a simple model that has its origins in classic communication theory. David Berlo's 1940 communication model called the SMCR model identified those basic components. Berlo's terms were sender, message, channel, and receiver.[2]

Superimposing Berlo's model onto the above minimalist definition, the sender is the teacher, the receiver is the learner, the message is the content and the channel is the medium of communication.

Contemporary thinking sees Berlo's model as too linear, and this criticism is fair. However, it is not too much of a stretch to add feedback loops or to interchange the role of teacher and student, so that the model becomes consonant with contemporary models.

Furthermore, in today's milieu, certain elements of this basic model may disappear. For example self-learning removes the teacher, or at least the teacher becomes a part of the medium: a book, a video, or a DVD tutorial. Contemporary inquiry models can also easily be adapted into the SMCR model.

The Book

A few paragraphs ago, we asked you to bring to your reading space a book and a pen(cil). Let us first focus on the book. Recall our minimalist model of pedagogy: A teacher teaches something to someone through some medium. So our question is this? Where is the *something*, that is the content or the information that is being taught? Write your tentative answer in the block. (All right, you don't have to write it if you don't want to.)

> *Question one: Given that right now, I am the teacher, you are the learner, the book is the medium of communication, then* **where** *is the content or the information to be taught and learned?*
>
> ______________________________

Easy enough. You probably said 'in the book'. And you are probably correct. So the book is an educational technology that *contains* and disseminates information. Note also that the book is an old technology, not one that we would normally consider under the category of '*new* information technologies'. And yet, what are the 21st century counterparts of the book? Your turn again…

> Question two: What are some 21st century counterparts of the book? Name three:
>
> 1.______________________________
> 2.______________________________
> 3.______________________________

Your answer may have included blogs, wikis, webpages, perhaps even 'more books'. Indeed 21st century books are not really too different from 19th century books; blogs even tend to look like 13th century scrolls (though not typically as elegant and aesthetic), and webpages are … well, still a combination of pictures and texts … and something called links. No huge revolution here. This is nothing stunningly new. Printing was invented centuries ago, and text is still a basic way of communicating. Perhaps the information can be available faster than before, and possibly there is more information out there, and it gets confusing when one tries to distinguish the real from the copy.[3]

So, we have identified a prototype educational technology, designed to store and disseminate information: the book… and any of its contemporary 21st century variants.

The Pen(cil)

It is time to move to our second "educational technology". You should have in front of you a pen or pencil. For the sake of this discussion we shall consider them synonymous, and from now on, we will use the word pencil. If you have a pen, that's fine. It is time to move to a parallel question to the opening one:

> Question three: Given that right now, I am the teacher, you are the learner, the pencil is the medium of communication, then where is the content or the information to be taught and learned?

Something has happened. Where *has* the information gone? Where is it? It is *not* in the pen. Some might argue that it is in the teacher's head; others might argue that it is in the learner's mind. (The former are called cognitivists; the latter are constructivists.) But the pencil is somehow a different kind of technology than the book. **The pencil holds no inherent content.** Now, we need to modify and re-ask the second question.

> Question Four: What are some 21st century counterparts of the pencil? Name three:
> 1.____________________
> 2.____________________
> 3.____________________

In other words, our search is for technologies to assist in *communication*, rather than provide *information*. What did you answer? Blogs, twitters, cell phones (mobile technologies) or older technologies such as the telephone, the walkie-talkie and the telegraph? Indeed 21st century twitters (tweets?) are not really too different from the 19th century telegraph; cell phones are not much more than modern telephones. There is no huge revolution here either.

So, we have now identified a second prototype educational technology, this time designed for *communication* purposes: the pencil... and any of its contemporary 21st century variants. Some writers use the phrases "productivity software" and "authoring systems" to capture the essence of technology for communication.

The above discussion has suggested that educational technologies have two fundamental functions: information and communication. The book example shows technologies that primarily exist to provide information. The pencil example shows that technologies that carry no 'permanent' content but exist to assist in communication. Information technologies require a writer, or an artist to produce the information that becomes the content. Communication technologies do not need a writer. We are all instantaneous 'writers' when we use communication technologies.

Canadian theorist Harold Innis was one of the first in the 1950s who captured this distinction in another way. He argued that technologies are either time-biased or space-biased. Innis was one of the first to theorize about the importance of technologies on society. In two books, *The Bias of Communication (*1949*)* and *Empire and Communication* (1950), Innis posited that technologies bias the nature of empires and civilizations.

> *Concentration on a medium of communication implies a bias in the cultural development of the civilization concerned either towards an emphasis on space and political organization or towards an emphasis on time and religious organization.* (p. 170)

A time-biased society tended to focus on communication over time, over years, to focus on permanence. Books are the prime example, but also architecture. A space-biased society is an all-at-once society. The radio, the telephone, and the television are all biased in favour of communicating over distance.

Innis' work took us up to only 1950, at which point radio was the dominant medium of western society. He concludes *The Bias of Communication* with the following provocative statement:

> *The bias of communication in paper and the printing industry was destined to be offset by the bias of radio. Democracy, which in the words of Guizot sacrificed the past and the future to the present, was destined to be offset by planning and bureaucracy.*

To unravel Innis' last statement: Guizot, the noted French statesman and politician and 22nd Prime Minister of France during the years 1847-48 worried that democracy was a thing of the present, which sacrificed both past and future for a volatile present. Innis ironically suggests that radio too will once again shake things up with a resulting focus on planning and bureaucracy. From the view of the first decade of the 21st century we can only remark how prescient Innis was!

Today Innis might argue that today we live in a society that uses *both* space-bound and time-bound technologies. As one or another takes prominence in a given situation, the potential impact changes.

Going back to our initial discussion, it can be argued that the book favours a time-bound bias (information); the pencil allows immediate communication, which is space-biased. But what effect will the space-bound and instantaneous 21st century phenomena of the internet, the blog and the tweet have, first on society, and then on education? For example, will *Wikipedia*, fifty years from now, have the same permanence, as did the original encyclopedia of Diderot and D'Alembert? Diderot's encyclopedia (1751) and D'Alembert's famous accompanying preface were the first attempts at an encyclopedia that captured all knowledge. In Diderot's preface of 1851 D'Alembert explained the aim of the enlightenment and its encyclopedia as providing nothing less than a record of all knowledge:

> *The work whose first volume we are presenting today has two aims. As an encyclopedia it is to set forth as well as possible the order and connection if the parts of all human knowledge*[4]*. As a reasoned dictionary ... it is to contain the general principles that form the basis of each science and each art, liberal and mechanical, and the most essential facts that make up the body and substance of each.*

While today's Wikipedia boasts being developed by 'the wisdom of the crowd', D'Alembert's contributors were considerably more carefully chosen, resulting in his words as "the work of a society of men of letters". The credibility of Diderot and D'Alembert's work thus places them in the domain of time-biased, permanent technology for information. Wikipedia, contrarily, starting from a similar assumption of a comprehensive encyclopedia of all knowledge, nevertheless fits more comfortably as a space-biased communication system. In other words, we are arguing here that the encyclopedia of 1751 was essentially time-biased, while the contemporary encyclopedia of our time, Wikipedia, is essentially space-biased! It is a slippery distinction.

At this point, two caveats are in order. Our time is one of convergence. This means that some technologies perform both functions (information *and* communication) fairly equally. Blogs ultimately contain both, *information* that is used to *communicate.* But that doesn't change the nature of the issue. In other words, the functions of communication and information are not mutually exclusive. It is also to be noted that communication is two-way, while information is one-way.

The second caveat is this. The above discussion of technology used for information and for communication presents us with a new dilemma. It implies, at least indirectly, that technology is a tool, an object, a thing. As we shall see below, while the tool definition of technology may be a common sense one, it is also misleading.

What is ICT?

If there are information technologies to provide information, and communication technologies to provide communication, the functions become blurred when we combine them into the term "information and communications technologies". It is easy to see why the designation ICT standing for information and communications technologies is so often used: it captures those two distinct functions of technology.

In general, the term ICT, however convenient, should be avoided, if only on the grounds of lack of understanding by the general public. ICT is not a word, but a set of initials. As such it can stand for whatever one wants. Indeed, ICT also stands for the time zone *Indo China Time.* It also stands for the Malaysian *Island College of Technology*, the *Institute for Counter Terrorism*, the *International Campaign for Tibet,* and a USA first-nations magazine titled *Indian Country Today*! In other words, *our* use of the initials ICT is not an exclusive one. Educational technologists do not *own* the initials ICT. Thus, the term becomes jargon understood only by insiders. Jargon is convenient to insiders (admittedly "information and communications technologies" is a mouthful), but nevertheless it locks out the general public from understanding.

Introducing Interactivity into the Mix

One often hears that a defining characteristic of a new information technology is that it is interactive. However, one needs to be careful before making such a generalization.

Contemporary pedagogic theory indeed seems to place a high value on interactivity. Information is deemed to be traditionally one-way, most notably in the concept and phrase "mass communications." (Note the slippage as information becomes communication!) Therefore, it is often stressed that a critical element of the *new* information and communication technologies is that they provide the potential for interaction. Constructivist theory, inquiry modes of learning, project based learning, and the analysis/synthesis mode of procedure all rely on a back and forth question/answer technique.

On the other hand, one might argue that the component of interactivity is NOT inherent in the technology. Print can be made interactive by the insertion of questions. Film and television have several techniques to make those media at least pseudo-interactive. Even in the clearly one-way movies of the 1930s, it was not uncommon for an actor to literally step out of character and turn to address the movie audience.[5] Since the technology was one-way sender to receiver only, then creative attempts to make it interactive were employed. An artist always works with his material as effectively as possible. If that material is not inherently interactive, the artist searches for ways to make it so. Today, radio and television constantly exhort the audience to email, telephone a comment, twitter or otherwise ask a question.

In other words, interactivity is a stylistic method to give a passive audience an opportunity to be a part of the discourse. It is not really an automatic or built in feature of a technology. One task of an effective teacher is to creatively involve the audience, and to turn an inherently one-way lecture into a two-way conversation. Thus, this is not an automatic characteristic of new information technologies.

Interactivity, in short, is nothing more than a narrative technique. Modern computer games take this concept to its limit.

Defining Technology

We have examined technology as information and as communication. Having made that point clear, it is now necessary to distance ourselves from that focus. It is necessary because such a focus implies that technology is a thing, a tool. On the one hand, there is no doubt that the idea of technology as a tool is the common definition of technology. Ask a random person for a definition of technology and they will most likely say that it is a tool. Oddly, if one looks for a dictionary definition of technology, one finds no hint of the "tool" definition.

Kenneth Clark, introducing his 1969 television series *Civilization* began by admitting an inability to define his subject: "What is civilization? I don't know. I can't define it in abstract terms – yet. *But, I think I can recognize it when I see it*, (italics mine) and I am looking at it now. " In a like manner, it is not simple to define technology, let alone educational technology. We think that we can recognize educational technology when we see it, and that is part of the problem.

Webster's Third International Dictionary provides three definitions for technology. The first, "terminology of a particular subject" we can safely ignore as not being relevant to our discussion. The second, "the science of the application of knowledge to practical purposes" or "applied science" is one we will encounter regularly, and again and again. Note that the common tool definition is just barely hinted at here. The third Webster definition is

> *'the totality of the means employed by a people to provide itself with the objects of material culture.'*

Similarly, the Oxford American repeats the "science of the application of knowledge" definition. This classic oft-quoted definition seems to belong to John Kenneth Galbraith (1967):

> *"the systematic application of scientific or other knowledge to practical tasks."*

There is an interesting minor discrepancy between these similar statements with respect to the use of the word scientific. Galbraith says "scientific or other knowledge"; the Webster definition quoted above says "science of the application of knowledge", while Oxford says "science of the application of..." The critical question revolves around the issue of whether technology follows science, or whether it follows *any* kind of knowledge.

Philosopher Frederick Ferre (1995) sidesteps the issue and defines technology as

> *'practical implementations of intelligence'.*

Ferre adds a caveat that is an important one to remember for educational technologists: to 'respect ordinary usage, while tightening looseness.'

Val Dusek (2006) argues that there are three 'characterizations' (rather than definitions) of technology: technology as hardware, as rules, and as system. Dusek suggests that his "consensus definition" focuses on the complexity of technology as

> *'a complex of hardware, knowledge, inventors, operators, repair people, consumers, marketers, advertisers, government administrators and others'.*

As we will see shortly, this definitional exploration is quite congruent with the latest AECT (2008) definition of "*educational* technology" which will be discussed below. Finally, Dusek notes that a tools definition sees technology as neutral, while a systems definition moves technology into a non-neutral position. As he states: "When one includes advertising, propaganda, government administration and all the rest, it is easy to see how the technological system can control the individual rather than the other way around as in the case of simple tools". (page 36).

Canadian scholar Ursula Franklin in her 1989 *Massey Lectures* broadcast on the national Canadian Broadcasting Corporation under the title of *The Real World of Technology* presented a similar broad understanding of the essence of technology. The series introduction, by host Lister Sinclair, state in part:

> *In these* Massey Lectures, *Dr. Franklin is discussing technology, not as gadgets, but rather as a whole set of social and cultural arrangements characterized by production based rules for social control, by pervasive mechanization, by mass production, with rigid divisions of labour, and by an associated political mindset, all bundled together in a single social system.*

Segue from Technology to Educational Technology

Once we delimit our focus to information technologies and communication technologies, one final delimitation is necessary: education / pedagogy. That is, our interest is technology in the service of education. The danger is in defaulting educational technologies to the common, but limiting, tools approach. Educational technology can be 'seen' most easily as hardware: the motion picture film, radio, television, video, and most commonly, computers. Indeed, the common use of the term 'computers in education' when one really means 'technology in education' is a serious and unnecessary re-focusing of educational technology.

Defining Educational Technology

The above discussion sets the stage for an inclusive definition of educational technology. The international Association for Educational Communications and Technology (AECT) is perhaps the most significant organization to regularly have concerned itself with defining the field. AECT has produced major definitional documents in 1994 and 2008.

The 1994 definition states:

> *Instructional Technology is the theory and practice of design, development, utilization, management and evaluation of processes and resources for learning.*

Their latest 2008 definition is the following:

> *Educational technology is the study and ethical practice of facilitating learning and improving performance by creating, using, and managing appropriate technological processes and resources.*

This most recent definition contains several significant components. First, it is both a study and a practice. What the definition avoids is the ever-so-common tool definition. By deliberate omission, educational technology is not a tool, or at least *not only* a tool. The tool definition is extremely limiting and ultimately demeans and delimits the potential of technology in education. The AECT definition captures the "not only a tool" qualification by refocusing technology as a study and a practice.

The second part of the definition suggests the purpose of educational technology: 'facilitating learning and improving performance'. This is absolutely critical to a clear definition. The third part of the AECT definition captures the process component of 'creating, using, and managing'. In other words it describes *how* one facilitates learning and improves performance. Finally, the fourth component of the AECT definition identifies the end goal of working with 'technological processes and resources'.

For those who might balk at such a process definition that sees educational technology as an entire system, as opposed to hardware or 'ICTs', it needs to be reiterated that, as shown above, formal definitions of technology do not focus on the concept of technology as tool, but instead focuses on system and process dimensions. In short, the AECT definition is fully congruent with formal definitions of technology itself.

The definition is, however, not without its controversies. Most significant is the ethical bias of the definition. AECT has determined that educational technology is a positive force, and therefore, must be an *ethical* practice and use *appropriate* resources and processes. Conversely, one might argue that it is still an 'educational technology', even if used unethically. One cannot guarantee that merely using "educational technology" will automatically be ethical.

Is it *Educational Media* or *Educational Technology*?

One more definitional hurdle needs exploration. Historically the term *media* was more common, and *educational media* the common term for technology in education. For example, Marshall McLuhan, who changed the way we look at technology, preferred the term *media*. His classic work was titled *Understanding Media*; his most remembered aphorism was 'The medium is the message'; his most delightful pun was 'The medium is the massage'. It would seem that the terms *educational media* and *educational technology* are essentially synonymous, with the latter simply being the more contemporary terminology. However, there is an implied expansion as one moves from media to technology that may signal an increased function of the referent. It does seem that 'educational media' focuses unambiguously on the 'tool' definition concept while educational technology allows for a system or process definition. It would seem that a medium is something you work with or on, often as an artist. A technology is an enabler, something you work through.

Oddly, the more and more popular term ICT takes us right back to the narrower *tool* definition. (As has already been noted above, the generic set of initials ICT are commonly used to abbreviate 'information and communications technology'. This term is society-wide, and refers to technology in its broadest sense in any field, education being only one. That leaves educators having to 'add back' the pedagogic component, which gives us such awkward terms as *ICT in education* and *ICT literacy*. All of which results in confusion.)

To summarize the argument: *Educational media* implies tools for teaching/learning; *educational technology* is a system in which one defines, develops and evaluates instruction in a systematic way, while *ICT* takes us back to tools as a component for society (not limited to education), which in turn leads us to "ICT in education" which is probably synonymous for 'educational media'. This takes us back full circle to where we started!

Conclusion: Who cares?

Today's society is in a hurry. It is a society that seems to value products and performance above all else. We are admonished to "just do it." But a fast-paced society is not necessarily a thinking society. Nor is change synonymous with progress. Philosophers and academics have long advocated the necessity for thinking out logically and clearly what we do and why. The speed of reaction, the instant globalization of information dissemination, and the confusion between marketing cant and thoughtful analysis all lead to a society of information overload.

Canadian Marshall McLuhan's four laws of media[6] are only one way of examining media and technology kaleidoscopically and holistically as one examines what each medium enhances, obsolesces, retrieves and reverses into.

Author T.S. Elliot was *not* thinking of information overload when he wrote his now famous poem *The Rock* (1934), but he captures therein, in two short lines, the dilemma facing all educators:

> Where is the wisdom we have lost in knowledge?
> Where is the knowledge we have lost in information?

This is not only the paradox but also the promise of contemporary educational technology. It is a promise that has so far fallen short.

REFERENCES

Association for Educational Communications and Technology (2008). Definition. In A. Januszewski and M. Molenda (Eds.), *Educational Technology: A definition with commentary.* (pp. 1-14). New York: Lawrence Erlbaum Associates.

Benjamin, W. *The work of art in an age of mechanical reproduction.* London: Penguin Books.

Clark, Kenneth (1969). *Civilization.* London: British Broadcasting Corporation and John Murray.

D'Alembert, J. (1963). Preliminary Discourse to the Encyclopedia of Diderot. Indianapolis: The Library of Liberal Arts. p. 4.

Dusek, V. (2006). *Philosophy and Technology.* Oxford: Blackwell Publishing.

Elliot, T.S. *The Rock.* London: Faber and Faber.

Ferre, F. (1995). *Philosophy of Technology.* Athens: University of Georgia Press.

Galbraith, J. (1967). *The New Industrial State.* New American Library

Hlynka, D. (2009). Just do it. *Educational Technology*: 49(2), March-April. 50-52.

Hlynka, D. (2008). Educational Technology: A definition for the 21st century. *Educational Technology,* 48(6). pp. 48-50.

McLuhan, M., and McLuhan, E., *The Laws of Media*: *The new Science*. Toronto: University of Toronto Press.

Sinclair, L. (November 1989). Introduction to the Massey Lectures. Canadian Broadcasting Corporation. [Audiotape]

NOTES

1. Hlynka, D. (2008). Educational Technology: A definition for the 21st century. *Educational Technology* 48(6). pp. 48-50.
2. Many visual designations of this model are available online. Search <berlo SMCR> using *Google Images* to find several representations of this model.
3. See Walter Benjamin, *The work of art in an age of mechanical reproduction.* Available online.
4. Emphasis of the authors. It is interesting to compare this with the proposed almost identical purpose of *Wikipedia* 'Wikipedia's purpose is to act as an encyclopedia, a comprehensive written compendium that contains information on all branches of knowledge' (at Wikipedia:Purpose).
5. See for example, the 1937 film *Git Along Little Dogies* starring Gene Autry has Autry as a real personality stepping out of his fictional character (also named Gene Autry!) and asking the live audience in the theatre watching the movie to join in a sing-along. To help out, the lyrics of the song are placed under the screen. In another example, the *Crimson Pirate* (1952) begins with Burt Lancaster, in character as Captain Vallo, addressing the film audience directly. All of this is simply a narrative technique aimed at engaging the audience more directly.
6. See McLuhan, M., and McLuhan, E., *The Laws of Media*: *The New Science.*

2.

Platforms for Education: The Enhanced Home and School

Bruce Joyce** and **Emily Calhoun

Scenes

****

Charlie

Fifteen year-old Charlie is perched on a high stool in front of a shelf he has made to hold his computer, accessories, and three or four opened books. Above the shelf is a bookcase on whose shelves sit a number of potted plants, labeled according to treatments.

Charlie is taking a BSCS-based advanced-placement course, a distance offering by a state university. He lives in a small Georgia town and goes to a high school, which serves about 75 students in each grade. Last summer the biology teacher resigned for personal reasons and the district officials have not yet found a suitable replacement. Thus, Charlie is taking the course. The district has not yet decided whether to accept distance courses, so Charlie is taking it for college credit, which, if necessary, he can transfer to the school.

The potted plants are part of his course-related project. Tomato plants in his family's vegetable garden have not been healthy or yielding well. He is experimenting with a number of variables – soil, fertilizer, water – in an attempt to find an optimal mix. The plants currently on his shelf migrate to other environments – an ultraviolate center, the center of a fountain, — ... Charlie's room has become a platform on which he seeks learning.

We will meet our enterprising Charlie later.

***

Nancy

Nancy's pleasant home has a number of fine attributes and one really distinctive feature – her inquiry center. As in many American households, family life is often centered around the eat-in kitchen center and the 'family room,' where fireplace and television device, comfy sofas, chairs, plush carpet, and pillows welcome the kids and parents and visitors.

The living room in many houses has become a bit extraneous. When she and her husband looked for a house, Nancy lobbied for a big kitchen with room for a big dining table. And she lobbied for an outsized family room with a pass-through from the kitchen.

She likes to study and is constantly involved in inquiries with conventional and cyberspatial resources. But she likes to be near her little tribe rather than a separated space in a spare room. She turned the often-unused 'living room' into her space platform. Print books fill the shelves on one wall. In the center is a big old Victorian oak table where her computers, monitors, video machines, and printers hold sway.

Nancy Olson is a high school science teacher. As we look into her world, she is, like Charlie, studying BSCS materials at distance with resources provided by another state university. She and her colleague, Judy, are revamping their science offerings. Part of their motivation in studying at distance is to estimate the potential of online and distance offerings for the students in their school. Thus, they are both strengthening their in-classroom courses and preparing the way for their students to learn from a combination—a set of hybrid courses.

Nancy and Judy will also look in on us later.

***

Mary

Mary Bishop's sixth grade classroom is populated by more than 1000 fiction and non-fiction books. On the third week in October she is focusing the students on writing titles. She has selected 30 books and, using the covers, the students are classifying their titles. When they have built a number of categories they will practice generating some of their own, emulating the styles of the published authors.

In this unit, the print medium is central. When writing, the students will use their laptops and networked printers, but cyberspace will not be an avenue until the time comes to access newspapers and libraries and extend their categories.

Without strong literacy skills, students cannot profit from the cyberspace revolution. Mary epitomizes the kind of teaching that is essential if the promise is to be fulfilled. Another hybrid environment is created.

She will look in on us later as we develop our theme.

***

Tom and the Countries of the World

Tom's yearlong course, for students from Grade Nine through Grade Twelve, provides a foundation for global understanding. This year he has started the students on 20 countries he has selected. The students classify countries on demographic variables, using databases, among others the excellent CIA source. Then they examine the web-pages belonging to cities in those countries. Their first task is to develop hypotheses about relationships among variables in the databases. For example, 'Is GNP or GDP related to fertility?'

As they learn about apparent relationships within the 20 countries, they will expand the base to include others in order to test their hypotheses.

Tom represents schooling where information and communication technology enhance the core curriculum areas. Like the others, he will look in on us as we explore that dimension of our inquiry – the creation of hybrid schools.

Authors' note

In our workshops and courses, our close colleagues and we have been using these databases for 25 years. The major innovations that have emerged over that quarter of a century are the availability of information made available by cities and towns around the globe and the ability to make contact with people who live in them. The venerable pen pal has come of age with a vengeance.

***

The Young Lady from Iran

'The young woman seated next to us at the sushi bar exuded a vaguely exotic air; her looks and style, we thought, made it likely that she was not American'.

"But then she spoke in perfect American English, even ending her declarative sentences in that rising lilt of many young Californians'.

'As it turns out, however, she wasn't from these parts after all; she was born in Iran and spoke only Farsi until her arrival here two years ago. What classes, we wondered, had she attended to learn the language so well?'

" 'I didn't,' she said. I used Rosetta Stone.' "

Eric A. Taub. (2010), 'The Web Way to Learn a Language', *The New York Times*. Thursday, February 28, p. B-10.

The chapter in the form of an article-note goes on to discuss various language programs on DVD's, online, and, sometimes, with combinations of contact with native speakers and instructors. Our Young Lady epitomizes how much skill in self-education will determine the futures of our Global Citizens – folks who are growing up literally everywhere.

***

Windows on the World

Charlie, Nancy, Mary, Tom, and the Lady from Iran have used their environments as platforms from which they access learning opportunities.

Homes and schools are windows on the world and always have been. Not only do they teach and enculturate, they help us peek out beyond our immediate surroundings. School curricula have given us a place to stand and tools for inquiring when school days are over. The school library has gifted us immeasurably. The home is a laboratory where we practice inquiring, socializing, and loving. And the home takes us beyond its boundaries and leads us down the street to the churches and stores and sights that are somewhere out there.

Before about 1880 the outside world came into home and school in the experiences brought there by people who had been across their borders and through books, magazines, and newspapers. By the mid-1700 those avenues provided a considerable amount. We have always been impressed that, by the time they were twenty-five years old, Hamilton, Madison, and Jefferson had read *everything in print in the English* language. They approached the drafting of the Constitution with the print part of the culture in their heads! Libraries gave them their windows on the world. From their time, not only has there been a veritable explosion in print media, but the development of new technologies has opened new and powerful avenues between the Big World and home and school. These trails have been constructed by the arrival of telephone, record player, radio, television, computer, and mobile devices. In the process they have been broadened, paved digitally, and turned into boulevards with two-way traffic. Now school and home are not just recipients but interactive entities – parts of the Big World in their own right. As this paragraph is being written, a terrible crisis in Haiti has resulted in a call for donations by the Red Cross. More than 200 million dollars has been pledged in the week just past and 21 million of that was raised through a texting initiative! As part of the effort, a group of 20 nine and ten year-olds raised their contribution in the old-fashioned way. They set up a hot cocoa stand in their neighborhood and sold enough to send a $1300 check to the Red Cross.

Steadily, home and school have evolved into what we can now see are platforms for learning. From them we can access information, receive instruction, and communicate. These platforms are not being fully utilized as yet, but there are considerable amounts of use in many homes and schools and the potential is enormous. New learning has infected many ordinary happenings.

*** *Authors' Note* ***

The other day we realized that there have been just three weddings in the last three years where one party was a member of our family or a close friend. In two of them the new partners met in cyberspace. In one case they lived on different continents and met on an online motorcycle club. In the other, they met people who lived a short distance away but wouldn't have encountered in person. The third met by smiling at each other in a restaurant. That noted, they gathered the small wedding party in a lovely setting in another country – a setting that they had found perched in cyberspace.

*** ***

In these homely examples, the new partners *learned*, the members of the wedding parties *learned*, and a circle of friends *learned.* Among the learning was awareness of the force of new ways of making friends and becoming lovers. The new partners were explorers, leading their friends to the New World. Our home, our family, was the intimate setting – the new platform floating in its own corner of cyberspace.

The Three Big Changes

Of all the changes that are impelling the elaboration of home and school into platforms, three stand out. First, the cyberspace library has come to town. Growing as if magically by amazing leaps an incredible bound, a massive database has appeared at every doorstep. Second, formal instructional opportunities are appearing and maturing into sites where you can find a huge range of courses and curricula. Third, interactive communication devices and organizations are crossbreeding at an expanding rate, increasing one's ability to enter other environments and act on them. Just about the time you learn to use your cell phone you have to welcome the next generation. And new habits are springing up.

Let's look at our reconstituted platforms and consider how our New Libraries, New Courses, and New Communication Tools fit into them.

We need to remember that the development of fine schooling is still a matter of creating a vibrant learning society, which is the base where its hybrids are created.

The New Libraries

We don't need to enumerate here all the positive features of the process of inquiry with backup from Google and siblings. Websites, articles in

Wikipedia, maps of everywhere, scientific studies – vast amounts of informed and off-the-wall opinion – await our queries. Our hydra-headed cellphones whiz us into outsized informational warehouses staffed by sophisticated cyber-assistants. And we need to remember that more and more of the holdings of conventional libraries and museums are now lined up in these New Warehouses. The Congressional Library and the libraries of our greatest universities and cities now crawl into our laps, often with greater ease and efficiency than they used to when we had to visit them personally.

Self-education opportunity has dropped in on us in the form of a massive, enveloping, multimedia-tongued, and hungry creature. And, because of that.

Cyber-home schooling is beginning to thrive. There used to be a saying that your neighborhood school taught all the kids the same stuff, but their homes differed greatly in the amounts and quality of what was learned there, which is why everybody did not finish at the same place. The coming of ICT can exacerbate those differences hugely. Conversely the levelling of the playing field has never been more within reach. 20 January, 2010, the *New York Times* [Tamar Lewin. Children Awake? Then They're Probably Online p. A-1, A-3] reported a study by the Kaiser Family Foundation indicating that the average United States schoolchild spends about seven and a half hours per day using some form of electronic media or device – up from six and a half hours, five years ago. Significantly, media often fills what would have otherwise been 'dead time'. While waiting in the car for their parents to conclude an errand, the children listen to music, speak to their friends, take and send pictures, receive and send text, write and search with their laptops, and read e-books. Thinking of those parents – and *their* parents, the Baby Boomers are beginning to retire and many have lived their entire adult lives in a post-Walkman world. They cannot remember a time when libraries of music were not with them.

The Kaiser study did not include adults, but at work and at home, time connected to electronic media is remarkable. Complaints about television offerings are legion, but we are more impressed by opportunities to learn than by the schlock. Today, the last day of January, the Turner Classic Movies channel announced that, leading up to the Academy awards, it would show outstanding films from the beginning of talkies to now – 93 fine movies in all, three a night. The history of film is there to be enjoyed – and to be studied in courses on the literature of film.

How to use the New Libraries is critical and becoming more so by the minute. How to develop questions, search for relevant material, learning how to organize it once it is found, and becoming skillful in drawing conclusions and taking actions.... Learning how to learn has jumped to the head of the educational objectives list.

The New Courses

The cyberspace school grows apace. Resource-based educational opportunities – self-education through the use of structured materials – have been growing since the days of the correspondence school and mail order offerings. There have been some dramatic jumps, as the development of the GED, the invention of the Open University, the assembly of multimedia packages. Sesame Street recently celebrated its fiftieth birthday. More quietly than the rise of the New Library, the New School is creating itself.

In a course, instructional materials or instructors lead the student through activities designed to build certain kinds of knowledge and skill. The term 'curriculum' derives from the Roman word for course in the sense of a closed track, generally round or oval, although it can be linear as in cross-country racing or marathoning. Courses can be very highly structured or can use sets of inductive or problem-solving exercises. Use of the library can be an integral part of them. We now have campus-based, house-based, hybrid, and distance-based courses in an improvised concert with one another.

An enormous number of resource-based courses are currently available. The ones relevant to elementary and secondary education include variations of the common core subjects and a much larger range of other content than the staff of any physical school site could possibly offer. Many educators have been skeptical about their effectiveness compared to face-to-face instruction. We will not summarize the relevant research here except to comment that many students learn quite well from a considerable range of courses. They should not be dismissed out-of-hand. A fine review by Clardy (2009) provides a balanced description of the literature that should, at the least, alleviate some of the worrisome questions that are raised. A number of others are included in the references.

Post-secondary education has been a good address for resource-based courses with content both familiar and unfamiliar. The *New York Times* Knowledge Network is dazzling in the range and sophistication of offerings available to all of us.

Professional Development is a humble example of the coming world. Not long ago nearly all professional development was instructor-based or self-instruction by groups of teachers – professional learning communities. Today on this desk are catalogues indicating 78 online courses from ASCD, 100 from public broadcasting, and 20 from a consulting firm. Thus far the hybrid is less seen than either the cyber course or the within-setting varieties.

The development of the New Courses combines with the New Library to present a situation where a large part of the core education of many students in, say, Grade Four to Grade Sixteen can be accomplished effectively through them. Interestingly, government policies did not lead to their development. Once the means were at hand, the New Courses developed. Were policymakers to set out to consolidate them and commission more, the New School would come into existence. That is what happened when the Open University in the UK was developed and caused a tremendous increase in the proportion of students in higher education. American Colleges and Universities are offering considerable numbers of distance courses. Some private entrepreneurial universities are now advertising entire programs and even curricula in clinical areas, such as teaching. Imagine online pre-service teacher education. We have a feeling that hybrids are a better option, but a great deal of entrepreneurial and technical imagination is out there now.

Communication Devices and Basic Application Software (apps)

Without the physical devices and software the New Library and New Courses would not exist. Think of a student's room as a carrel, furnished with an IPOD, a Droid, a laptop, a satellite video connection, a TV and a wall of bookshelves, a desk, a couple of very comfortable chairs, and a bed. And, some of the devices and basic apps have had an enormous impact on living, interacting, and working and enlarged the places where electronic activity can take place. A major equity question will be whether we move, probably through schools, to provide all students with what they need. The equipment for Charley's room needs to come with registration. Nancy's equipment needs to be delivered to her the first day on the job.

Pervasive Themes and Issues: Perennials and New Shoots

Considering the promise inherent to this century reopens some long-term issues in education and brings some new arrivals as well. The following two need continuous attention in this book and in the coming years. They call out for serious inquiry, will not be resolved quickly or casually, and will not creep quietly away on their own.

An old unresolved question is sharply redefined by the application of information and communication technology to education – what has to be taught by a face-to-face teacher and what can a student learn as well through independent inquiry?

No simple answer will emerge here. How well students learn to teach themselves will be a major factor. Both children and adults have tremendous individual differences in this area. (Imagine how Jefferson and Hamilton stood out in self-educating capacity.) Schooling can affect those differences. We *can* help people learn how to learn. Within schools, the hybrid course is probably the next logical stage of development. But good self-educators have always roared ahead and they now have afterburners.

The important question is not whether instructor-led classes, hybrids, on distance means are the best choices for all purposes. The best mix for a given school needs to be the focus. Good learning can take place with all options. However, the school as a platform needs to be a vibrant society.

A difference between school and home has also been heightened by the power of the developing technologies. The school is a very important center of the neighborhood and town. But the home has greater maneuverability. Developing access to distance courses makes a good example. If the biology department of a high school decides it would like to increase access to a distance provider, there are layers of decision-makers to work through and consensus from the rest of the faculty may have to be achieved. The home can simply call it up and register.

If you want to start a movement in your community, you can do it easier from the home. That is why charter schools are so popular. They entice us to Just Do It. But most current charter schools are depressingly ordinary. We need to find out how to bring the maneuverability of the home to the business of collective education.

REFERENCES

Clardy, Alan (2009). *Distant, On-Line Education: Effects, Principles, and Practices*. ERIC: Ed 506182.

Clary, Renee & Wandersee, James (2009). Can teachers 'learn' in an online environment? *Kappa Delta Pi Record*. 46(1), 34-38.

Kulik, C. & Kulik, J. (1991). Effectiveness of computer-based instruction. *Computers in Human Behavior*. Vol.7, 75-94.

Sizemann, T., Kraiger, K., Stewart D., & Wisher R. (2006). The comparative effectiveness of web-based and classroom instruction: A meta-analysis. *Personnel Psychology*. Vol. 59, 623-664.

Tallant-Runnels, M., Tomas, J., Lan, W., and Cooper, S. (2006). Teaching Courses online: A review of the research. *Review of Educational Research*. 76(1), 93-135.

Zhao, Y., Lei, J., Jan, B., Lai, C., & Tan, H. (2005). What makes the difference? A practical analysis of research on the effectiveness of distance education. *Teachers College Record*. 107(8), 1836-1884.

3.

Designing Effective Online Courses with First Principles of Instruction

Theodore W. Frick, Joyce Hwee Ling Koh and Rajat Chadha

Online courses are becoming a popular mode of learning. The proliferation of Web 2.0 tools present exciting possibilities to change paradigms of education, especially for students who do not perform well in traditional face-to-face courses (Christensen, Johnson & Horn, 2008).

These developments raise the following critical questions:

> Is there one best theory to guide the design of online instruction?
> Is there one best tool for online instruction?

This chapter addresses these questions by proposing that effective online instruction is not attained through the use of one best instructional theory or tool. It can, however, be achieved by embodying a set of fundamental principles for online instruction. These "*First Principles of Instruction*" (Merrill, 2002, 2007a) are applicable regardless of the medium of instruction. In addition to discussing examples of how the *First Principles of Instruction* can be applied to both online and face-to-face instruction, this chapter also presents the Teaching and Learning Quality (TALQ) survey, an instrument designed to evaluate training courses according to these *First Principles*.

Different Perspectives of Effective Instruction

Developments in the field of learning psychology have influenced how we design instruction. Between the 1950s and 1970s, behaviorism defined learning as a behavior that could be shaped by environmental stimuli. In the 1980's, cognitivist views of learning shifted our focus from environmental stimuli to learner cognition, while the 1990's saw the advent of constructivist theories that advocate learner responsibility for constructing their own learning. What does each of these perspectives recommend?

Behaviorism

B.F. Skinner's model of operant conditioning was a behaviorist theory that had immense impact on education. Operant conditioning postulated that voluntary behavior could be strengthened or weakened by controlling the environmental antecedents and consequences following the behavior (Driscoll, 2000). A central idea in operant conditioning advocates that complex behavior could be broken down into simpler components and then learned incrementally through the process of shaping (Burton, Moore & Magliaro, 1996; Skinner, 1996). When applied to instruction, reinforcers and inhibitors of learning behaviors could be designed and executed as a series of stimuli to shape desired learning outcomes.

Operant conditioning influenced the development of an instructional methodology called Programmed Instruction. This was a series of self-paced learning materials where learning content were presented to students in short segments. Students answered questions after completing a segment, and were given immediate feedback. They would be allowed to proceed to new material if their answers were correct, but redirected to remedial explanations for wrong answers (Heinich, Molenda & Smaldino, 1999; Reiser, 2001).

Cognitivism

Behaviourist theories were concerned about the relationship between environmental stimuli and learner behaviors. Learner cognition was considered as a 'black box' that need not be understood (Driscoll, 2000). Cognitive psychologists argue against the assumption that learners are passive recipients of environmental stimuli. Rather, students' cognition and thinking impact how they learn. In particular, cognitive psychology theories such as *Schema Theory* and *Network Models* propose that learners have a system of knowledge organization, either as schemas or as a network of nodes and links (Bruning, Schraw, Norby & Ronning, 2004). Learning occurs when knowledge is assimilated, encoded, and can be effectively retrieved from long-term memory.

Cognitivist theories guided the development of several instructional theories that address the cognitive processes involved in learning. One example is Gagné's nine events of instruction, which are comprised of activities that instructors can use to stimulate internal cognitive processes such as attention, retrieval and reinforcement (Gagné, Briggs & Wager, 1988). Examples of these events are gaining the attention of students, stimulating recall of prerequisite learning and providing feedback about performance correctness. While Gagné's theory dealt with an overall view of the instructional process, other theories addressed complex cognitive operations that involved algorithms or heuristics. An example may be the

Algo-heuristic Theory of Instruction (Landa, 1983), which proposed that unobservable cognitive processes could be analyzed into a 'level of elementariness' that they could be understood and performed in a standardized way by a student without error. These processes could be combined to derive algorithms and heuristics for problem-solving.

Constructivism

The 1990's saw a rising concern that the education system was too focused on rote instruction with students as passive recipients (Airasian & Walsh, 1997; Perkins, 1991). Constructivist views of learning propose that reality is in the mind of the learner, and learning is a process whereby learners construct meaning from the ways in which they perceive and interpret their experiences (Jonassen, 1991).

Several instructional theories sought to describe learning environments that support and mediate active learning of students. Grabinger (1996) proposed that rich environments for active learning (REALs) should use realistic problems and authentic assessment, promote student responsibility and initiative for learning, encourage cooperative learning, and provide generative learning activities that promote argumentation and reflection. These basic principles were also embodied by Hannafin, Land and Oliver (1999). Their conception of *Open Learning* Environment included providing students with concrete experiences through problem contexts, and stimulating self-directed learning by supporting the process of problem conceptualization, metacognition, and problem-solving with information tools. Jonassen (1999) also described a theory for desiging constructivist environments that provide authentic problems, learner selectable information and tools. However, his model emphasizes the use of related cases and worked examples as cognitive scaffolding, and supporting learning through modelling, and coaching.

How to Design Effective Online Learning?

With such a proliferation of instructional models, one may wonder if there is one best way to approach the design of online instruction that could increasingly involve the use of Web 2.0 tools. In an online environment, learning occurs within what Garrison, Anderson, and Archer (2000) termed a '*community of inquiry*' where teachers and students interact to construct knowledge. Effective instruction occurs when the community attains 'deep learning' (i.e. focused on meaning and understanding), as opposed to 'surface learning' (i.e. focused on information recall) (Scouller, 1998). Deep learning has also been understood as cognitive presence or critical thinking (Garrison et al., 2000).

Salmon (2004) developed a five-step model for effective e-learning moderation. It is primarily focused on managing student access, ownership, and knowledge construction as they learn through the online platform. This model provides a good start to the effective management of online learning experiences. But, there are few other instructional theories related to online or Web 2.0 platforms. What principles can be used for effective online instruction? Can principles from behaviorist, cognitivist, and constructivist perspectives apply?

The First Principles of Instruction

The *First Principles of Instruction* were developed by David Merrill in an attempt to identify the common features underlying various instructional theories (Merrill, 2002, 2007a, 2007b). It describes the fundamental principles of effective instruction, and provides a unifying view of different instructional perspectives. The *First Principles* were derived through theoretical analysis of major instructional theories (Merrill, 2002). The five fundamental principles described in Merrill (2002) and Merrill (2007a) are summarized in the following section:

1. Task-centered principle

Learning is promoted when learners engage in tasks from the real-world, are taught the whole task, and learn tasks in progressive order of complexity.

The task-centered principle first proposes that instruction should be anchored upon real-world problems or tasks. This emphasis on authentic learning contexts has been advocated in various instructional theories that have been influenced by constructivist perspectives. Problem-based learning (PBL), for example, is a method where students learn knowledge and skills through the process of problem-solving (Albanese & Mitchell, 1993). Students engaging in PBL are not taught basic skills but seek and learn appropriate knowledge as they engage in problem-solving. Merrill (2007a) emphasized the *First Principles* to have a 'problem-centered approach' (Merrill, 2002; p. 45), but advocates teaching learners directly how to solve problems. The *First Principles* also recommend a *whole task* approach to instruction (Merrill 2007b; Van Merriënboer, Clark & de Croock, 2002), as opposed to teaching tasks as distinct parts. Learning how to solve parts of a problem did not imply that learners could synthesize their knowledge to perform the task effectively. A *whole task* approach ensures that the knowledge of individual task-components are integrated towards problem-solving. Tasks should also be taught in progressive levels from simple to complex. This corresponds to the recommendations of the Elaboration Theory (Reigeluth, 1999) and the 4C/ID model (van Merriënboer, 1997).

2. Activation principle

Learning is promoted when learners are prompted to share or demonstrate prior knowledge and experiences; and provided with a structure to organize new knowledge

The Activation principle is consistent with the postulations of cognitivist theories. When students share or demonstrate prior knowledge, their existing schemas and memory networks are instantiated, which helps them to assimilate new knowledge with their pre-existing structures of understanding. Bransford, Brown and Cocking (2000) found that students are better able to master new concepts when teachers engaged their initial understanding at the onset of teaching. Network Theory also proposes that information is retrieved through the process of spreading activation along one's hierarchical knowledge network (Bruning et al., 2004). Learners with more extensive networks of knowledge are capable to search and retrieve information more efficiently. If learners have limited prior knowledge or experience with the content, they need to be provided with structures of knowledge to help them form schemas of what they will be learning. Examples of such structures are advanced organizers (Ausubel, 1963). They help students develop cognitive structures to organize new content they are learning.

3. Demonstration principle

Learning is promoted when the information and portrayals of demonstrations are consistent.

Merrill (2007a) described five types of component skills that could be involved in task mastery: information-about (facts related to the task), parts-of (parts of a task entity), kinds-of (different classes of a task), how-to (procedures and steps of a task), and what-happens (conditions, and consequences of actions). Successful demonstrations occur when there is consistency between the information and portrayals of a component skill (Gagné, 1985; Merrill, 1994). For example, explaining and demonstrating the steps of a task will teach learners "how-to", but not "what-happens"; which is more suitably taught by providing information and enactments with scenarios and case studies. Effective instruction of task performance occurs when information and portrayals are consistent with the component skill. Without this consistency, learners will be left to learn task performance through their own discovery.

4. Application principle

Learning is promoted when students apply what they learned through a varied sequence of tasks that is consistent with its task component. Application needs to be supported with corrective feedback, and coaching needs to be gradually withdrawn to facilitate independent performance.

Practice and feedback have been prescribed in various instructional theories (Bereiter & Engelmann, 1966; Gagné et al., 1988). A particularly successful behaviorist model is Direct Instruction where students are taught through systematic presentation of learning content, guided practice, feedback, and independent practice. It was found to have positive impact on student achievement, engagement and affect (Magliaro, Lockee, & Burton, 2005). In the Application principle, Merrill (2007a) recommended that effective practice occurs when learners practice solving a series of tasks or problems of varying complexity. This ensures that learners are being exposed to the range of task complexities they are required to master. It also requires that practice be consistent with the task component that is being mastered. For example, asking learners multiple choice questions about the steps of a task will help them review their knowledge of 'information-about', but does not provide practice that facilitates mastery of 'how-to'. Therefore, consistency between information, portrayals, and applications of task components is also required for effective instruction.

The Application principle further emphasizes that feedback should be corrective—i.e. where errors are pinpointed with suggestions for correction. It is more effective than merely telling learners if they are right or wrong. This corresponds with the constructivist theory of minimalism, where learners are taught to recognize and correct their errors while working on authentic problems (Carroll, 1990). Another important aspect of the Application principle is the need to foster mastery by diminishing coaching gradually. This is synonymous with the idea of scaffolding (Wood, Bruner, & Ross, 1976), where experts help novices to master specific tasks they cannot originally perform without assistance—i.e., tasks which are in the learner's zone of proximal development (cf., Vygotsky, 1978). This is done by controlling the level of support and assistance until novices are able to master and perform the entire task independently (Puntambekar & Hubscher, 2005).

5. Integration principle

Learning is promoted when learners explore how their newly gained knowledge and skills can be personally useful.

Constructivist views of learning propose that humans are active agents, who desire to make sense of their world (Perkins, 1991). The Integration principle proposes that effective instruction occurs when learners are able to find personal meaning in what they learned. One way of helping learners integrate knowledge is through personal reflection. Learners should be challenged to explore personal applications beyond what was learned in class. Peer discussions and critique can also be used to stimulate the process of integration. Social constructivists such as

Vygotsky (1978) postulated that learning occurs through social interaction. Several instructional methods, such as reciprocal teaching (Palinscar & Brown, 1984) and the Learning Together Model (Heinich et al., 1997), are examples of instructional methods that use social experiences to enhance learning.

Research on First Principles of Instruction

Thomson/NETg conducted an experimental study in which they investigated the relationship between all five *First Principles of Instruction* and student learning achievement (Thomson, 2002). Instructional designers from NETg applied *First Principles of Instruction* to revise an existing e-learning Excel course to a new scenario-based course. In the revised course, Excel commands were taught in the context of scenarios similar to real-world problems that included five spreadsheet problems.

NETg recruited 128 volunteer participants from among their customers. Participants were divided into three groups: a scenario-based group ($n = 49$), the existing e-learning group ($n = 49$), and a control group ($n = 30$) which did not receive any instruction.

The existing e-learning course illustrated Excel commands and operations in a typical didactic approach. This part of the existing e-learning course was also accessible to the scenario-based course group. The difference in the scenario-based course group was that Excel commands were taught in context of five authentic problems. This part of the course was designed following the *First Principles of Instruction*.

Following instruction, learners took a post-test on three Excel tasks. Differences in group means on the post-test were statistically significant ($p < 0.001$). In the scenario-based course that used *First Principles of Instruction* the group mean was 89 per cent, whereas the group mean for the existing instruction was 68 per cent, and the control group scored 34 per cent on average. Furthermore, the time required by the scenario-based course group to complete the post-test was considerably less than that of the existing e-learning based course group (29 vs. 49 minutes, $p < 0.001$).

In a subsequent descriptive-correlational study, Frick, Chadha, Watson, Yang and Green (2008) collected data from 140 students enrolled in 89 different courses at several U.S. universities. They found that student ratings of instructor use of *First Principles of Instruction* were correlated significantly ($p < 0.0005$) with student self-reported academic learning time ($r = 0.682$), learning progress ($r = 0.823$), mastery of course objectives ($r = 0.341$), satisfaction with the course ($r = 0.830$), and student ratings of overall instructor and course quality ($r = 0.867$).

In a somewhat larger study, Frick, Chadha, Watson and Wang (2010) collected data from 193 students enrolled in 111 different courses at multiple postsecondary institutions. Similarly, they reported very high Spearman correlation coefficients between student ratings of instructor use of *First Principles of Instruction* and student self-reported academic learning time ($r = 0.670$), learning progress ($r = 0.833$), mastery of course objectives ($r = 0.344$), satisfaction with the course ($r = 0.850$), and student ratings of overall instructor and course quality ($r = 0.890$). All correlations were statistically significant at $p < 0.0005$.

In the most recent study of 464 students enrolled in 12 different courses at a large Midwestern U.S. university, Frick, Chadha, Watson and Zlatkovska (2009) reported similar highly significant correlation coefficients ($p < 0.0005$) between the student ratings of instructor use of *First Principles of Instruction* and student self-reported academic learning time ($r = 0.583$), learning progress ($r = 0.725$), satisfaction with the course ($r = 0.778$), and student ratings of overall instructor and course quality ($r = 0.774$).

In this study, *instructors* also rated their students according to their mastery of course objectives. These ratings were based on student performance in those instructors' classes and were typically based on test scores, projects, papers, etc. Frick et al. (2009) found that if students agreed that their instructors used *First Principles of Instruction* and they also agreed that they experienced academic learning time (ALT), those students were about 5 times more likely to be independently rated by their instructors as having achieved a *high level of mastery* of course objectives. Perhaps even more significant was the finding that when students did not agree that their instructors used *First Principles* and also did not agree that they experienced ALT, they were about 26 times more likely to be independently rated at a *low level of mastery* by their instructors.

Two of the studies conducted by Frick et al. (2008; 2010) included students from online and face-to-face classes. Approximately one-third of the respondents in each study rated courses that they had taken online, compared with two-thirds who had rated face-to-face courses. There were no significant differences (ANOVAs) between online and face-to-face respondent groups on student ratings of instructor use of *First Principles of Instruction,* student ALT, satisfaction, learning progress, or ratings of overall quality. Nor were there any significant associations (Chi-Squares) between course setting (online verses. face-to-face classes) and other demographics such as gender, year in school, and course grade. In short, course setting had no statistically significant association with other variables measured in those two studies.

In the three descriptive-correlational studies conducted by Frick et al., items on the various scales were randomly mixed on the survey instruments so that students knew neither what the scales were nor which items were associated with each scale. Each scale consisted of 2 to 5 items, and internal consistency reliabilities of these scales were reported to be generally high (Cronbach alpha coefficients). The survey instrument is referred to as the Teaching and Learning Quality (TALQ) scales.

Chadha (2009) has further studied these scales by investigating agreement of ratings among students within a class and the dependability of these TALQ measures. Based on his findings, he recommends the course evaluation items listed in Table 3.1. Students respond to each item on a Likert scale (Strongly Agree, Agree, Undecided, Disagree, Strongly Disagree). These items should ideally be randomly ordered within the overall course evaluation instrument so that students should not be aware of the scales being used.

Items from each scale (e.g., academic learning time, activation) are then averaged to form a scale score (cf. Frick, et al. 2008). Note that several items are worded negatively as a check on whether students are reading the items carefully, and should be reverse-scored before combining into the respective TALQ scale. If reverse-scoring is not practical, then one should avoid the negatively worded items, or modify the wording to make them positive.

TABLE 3.1: Recommended TALQ scale items

Scale	*Items*	*Notes/Comments*
Global Instructor and Course Quality Scale	• Overall, I would rate the quality of this course as outstanding. • Overall, I would rate this instructor as outstanding. • Overall, I would recommend this instructor to others	Use all 3 items for best scale reliability.
Student Satisfaction Scale	• I am very satisfied with how my instructor taught this class. • I am dissatisfied with this course. • This course was a waste of time and money. • I am very satisfied with this course.	Use 2 or 3 of the original 4 items. Note that the middle two items are stated negatively and would need to be reversed-scored before combining into a scale.
Academic Learning Time Scale	• I did not do very well on most of the tasks in this course, according to my instructor's judgment of the quality of my work.	Use all 4 items. The 1st item must be reverse-scored before combining with the remaining items to form a scale score. Note that the

Scale	*Items*	*Notes/Comments*
	• I put a great deal of effort into this course. • I frequently did very good work on projects, assignments, problems and/or learning activities for this course. • I spent a lot of time doing tasks, projects and/or assignments.	2nd and 4th items measure student engagement separately from student success in course tasks on the 1st and 3rd items.
Learning Progress Scale	• Compared to what I knew before I took this course, I learned a lot. • I learned a lot in this course. • Looking back to when this course began, I have made a big improvement in my skills and knowledge in this subject. • I learned very little in this course. • I did not learn much as a result of taking this course.	Use 2 of these items. Note that if the last 2 items are chosen, they must be reverse-scored before combining into a scale.
Authentic Problems Scale	• I was expected to perform a series of increasingly complex authentic problems in this course. • I was expected to solve authentic problems or to complete authentic tasks in this course. • In this course I was expected to solve a variety of authentic problems that were organized from simple to complex.	Use all 3 items from this scale.
Activation Scale	• I engaged in experiences that subsequently helped me learn ideas or skills that were new and unfamiliar to me. • In this course I was able to recall, describe or apply my past experience so that I could connect it to what I was expected to learn. • My instructor provided a learning structure that helped	Use at least 3 items on this scale. Note that if the last item is used it must be reverse-scored before combining with others to form this scale.

Scale	*Items*	*Notes/Comments*
	me to mentally organize new knowledge and skills. • In this course I was able to connect my past experience to new ideas and skills I was learning. • In this course I was not able to draw upon my past experience nor relate it to new things I was learning.	
Demonstration Scale	• My instructor demonstrated skills I was expected to learn in this course. • Media used in this course (texts, illustrations, graphics, audio, video, computers) were helpful in learning. • My instructor gave examples and counter-examples of concepts that I was expected to learn. • My instructor did not demonstrate skills I was expected to learn. • My instructor provided alternative ways of understanding the same ideas or skills.	Use all 5 items of this scale. Note that the 4th item needs to be reverse-scored before combining with others to form this scale.
Application Scale	• My instructor detected and corrected errors I was making when solving problems, doing learning tasks or completing assignments. • I had opportunities to practice or try out what I learned in this course. • My instructor gave me feedback on what I was trying to learn.	Use all 3 items.
Integration Scale	• I had opportunities in this course to explore how I could personally use what I have learned. • I see how I can apply what I	Use any 3 items.

Scale	*Items*	*Notes/Comments*
	learned in this course to real life situations. • I was able to publicly demonstrate to others what I learned in this course. • In this course I was able to reflect on, discuss with others, and defend what I learned.	

An Example of Application of *First Principles* to a Graduate-Level Course

Next, we describe an example of a course, which has been redesigned around *First Principles of Instruction*, R690: Application of Research Methods to IST Issues. This course is intended for Ph.D. students in Instructional Systems Technology (IST), to be taken early in their program. *The 2008 syllabus to this course is provided online at*:

https://www.indiana.edu/~istr690/frick08fall/index.html (Frick, 2008a).

The goal of R690 is to help graduate students to "learn disciplined inquiry in IST through first-hand experience—i.e. by doing representative research tasks and critiquing research done by others. The objectives of this course are to:

1. Conduct interviews for need-assessment (qualitative method).
2. Do content analyses (qualitative method).
3. Conduct usability evaluations (qualitative and quantitative methods, problem diagnoses).
4. Write a report describing needs assessment, results, usability evaluation, results, and recommendations (for client and instructor).
5. Analyze existing survey data with SPSS (quantitative methods, tool skills).
6. Critique research reports done by others." (Frick, 2008a, n.p.)

The reader should note that the objectives of this class are described as *tasks* that students are expected to do. Through these tasks, students are expected to learn about different kinds of research methods and important criteria for judging the adequacy of research. While understanding is important, it is connected to these tasks. These tasks determine the structure of the course instead of topics such as qualitative research methods in IST, quantitative methods, content analysis, statistical package for social sciences (SPSS), chi-square, *t*-tests, etc. The instructor has identified specific resources that students are expected to read on a weekly basis outside of class. Students are expected to apply knowledge from these resources to tasks that they are expected to do.

The following elaborates the course's use of *First Principles of Instruction*:

Students in R690 are expected to conduct *Authentic Tasks*—typical of research in IST—, which are organized from simple to complex. The first authentic whole task students are expected to do is to conduct disciplined inquiry for a need-assessment and analysis. In this task students as a whole class led by the instructor create interview questions related to the area of need. For example, in 2007-2008, the IST Department was redesigning its website and wanted to know what the target audience expected to find there and what they would want to do on the website. In this case, the IST Department was the client.[1]

Next R690 students are expected to conduct interviews with members of the target audience in which the questions are asked and interviewee responses are further probed. Students work in pairs so that one is asking the questions and follow-ups while the other takes detailed notes on the respondent's answers. Students used to conduct interviews with at least two real interviewees each. Each student then writes up the results of his or her two interviews as a report. Thus, this is a whole task in disciplined inquiry, and it is authentic since the results are used by a client who needs such a needs assessment to be performed. It is a meaningful, real-world task.

These interview reports are further analyzed in class by caryingout a content analysis in an activity led by the instructor. Individual responses to each interview question are cut and pasted onto individual 3x5 cards. Students discuss their findings as they do this activity sitting around a table. The instructor then leads a card-sort activity—similar to the classic game, *Concentration*—in which cards containing commonalities are grouped. Students take turns reading the responses on their cards and then the group quickly tries to identify which pile it belongs to (via rapid free association). The piles 'emerge' as common themes or patterns in the interviewee responses.

The second authentic task that students are expected to do is to conduct a usability test. They must first create usability tasks based on the results of the prior needs assessment (e.g., that the target audience would do on a website that is being evaluated). These usability tasks are formed during a class activity in which the results of the previous content analysis (the various piles from the card sort activity) are utilized. Then students must design the usability study and carry it out with at least two members of the target audience. Students again work in pairs so that one can administer the test while the other takes detailed notes on an observation form.

Students are then expected to write a team report in which the results are combined which identifies major problems with the product and makes recommendations for possible improvements to minimize the problems observed. This, too, is a whole task that is authentic.

The needs assessment and usability evaluation tasks require mostly qualitative methods.

The third task in this course requires students to use quantitative methods for analysis of findings in a research study that was previously completed by a former IST Ph.D. student in his or her dissertation. R690 students are provided with a number of research questions that require use of descriptive and inferential statistics for analysis via SPSS; and they are expected to each independently write a report that provides the results of the analysis and the conclusions drawn from the results. Each student is given a subset of the real data that had been previously collected, so he or she will not necessarily obtain the exactly the same results as found in the original study.

The final task in this course is to identify and critically evaluate a published research study in an area of interest to each student. The student is expected to critique the study as one would do if reviewing it for a journal editor, applying criteria that are typically required by research journals for such reviews. Each student critique is written as a report that describes the research study, applies relevant criteria to the study, and then draws conclusions based on the application of the criteria. Thus, this R690 course is structured around these four authentic, whole tasks that are arranged in increasing complexity.

In this R690 course the *Activation Principle* is exemplified in the following ways: For example, in the very first class student teams conduct mini-research projects in which they are given a specific research task, carry it out, and report their findings to the whole class. This is to give the students a common experience that they can connect with later activities in the course. Each mini-research project exemplifies different kinds of knowledge outcomes from disciplined inquiry. As another example of activation, when students are getting ready to do the SPSS data analysis tasks, the original author of the research study makes a presentation to the class. Students also read the research report as a further means of activation so that they will be able to connect the SPSS tasks they are expected to do with this completed research study. As a further kind of activation, the instructor provides a conceptual structure (advance organizer) for types of knowledge that results from research, so that students can connect findings in research reports they read with this conceptual model.

In the R690 class, an example of the *Demonstration Principle* is a video that students watch which illustrates how to conduct a usability test. The instructor also models how to do a content analysis, which is done as a group activity in which the results from student interviews are subjected to a card-sorting procedure in order to identify categories and trends. He further demonstrates the use of SPSS and various descriptive and inferential statistical functions for carrying out the data analysis tasks. The instructor not only shows them how to use SPSS itself, but also models how to interpret the results based on the data analyzed. When students are expected to conduct research critiques, the instructor models the application of evaluation criteria repeatedly in classes in which research studies are critiqued through whole-class discussion. Students are also expected to read critique reports that past students have written, which serve as further models of critiques.

For the *Application Principle*, students are expected to conduct interviews for the needs assessment and to write a report. The instructor provides feedback via e-mail when their reports are submitted electronically and when he grades them. For the usability evaluation, students often initially practice a usability test with the instructor acting as the "subject" so that he can provide feedback on how well they conducted the usability test. Students then perform the usability tests with real subjects. In the SPSS activity students do the SPSS analysis of their own individual (and unique) data sets in which they answer a series of research questions. The instructor provides feedback two ways:

1. After students have written their reports, he shows them a model report he has written so that they can compare their results with his results.
2. He also provides individual written feedback when he grades their reports.

Students practice doing research critiques during numerous class discussions when research studies are jointly critiqued, and the instructor provides feedback on their critical thinking in class (as well as models critical thinking). Students also apply what they have learned when they do their individual critiques and write them up. The instructor provides detailed feedback when he grades their critiques. These are all examples of the *Application Principle*.

The *Integration Principle* is illustrated in this class in a number of ways. In the very first class, student teams make presentations to the rest of the class on the findings from their mini-research projects. In the part of the course where they are doing the critiques, each student is assigned a time slot in a class session in which he or she is expected to present a summary of the study being critiqued via a short PowerPoint presentation to the class. Everyone in the class is expected to have read the study prior to class. The student then leads the discussion of the study, while the instructor also contributes additional insights and criticisms of the study. Students are also expected to integrate what they learn in the R690 class as they participate in external research groups led by faculty in the department (these groups are conducting research studies, mentored by those faculty members).

In summary, this R690 course has been designed on the basis of *First Principles of Instruction.* This course had been designed originally around Problem-Based Learning (PBL) and taught this way for about 12 years. R690 was redesigned in 2006 with *First Principles of Instruction* in mind. Although the R690 course has historically received very good ratings in student course evaluations, ratings have been even higher since the redesign.

Considerations for Conversion of R690 to an Online Course

Next, the authors provide an example of what it would take to convert an existing face-to-face course to an online course that utilizes *First Principles of Instruction.* Since R690 is already designed around *First Principles*, the challenge is to determine ways in which current face-to-face activities can be accomplished in an online learning environment. Planning for this conversion is described next.

First, the R690 class already has a website that is online (see Frick, 2008a). The first author has previously created a template in Adobe Dreamweaver, which is easy to use and update. He either uses Dreamweaver or Adobe Contribute to edit the web pages associated with the R690 course which uses the course template[2]. This course website includes the syllabus, the course schedule, a list of resources (with restricted access), and links to Google Groups (a free online tool) for document sharing and asynchronous discussion among students when working on tasks. The distance version of R690 is expected to use a similar course website.

Indiana University currently provides a content management system called Oncourse. Two aspects of Oncourse are used in R690: the drop box and the grade book. The drop box is where each student can electronically submit a deliverable, such as the report on the results of the interviews she or he did or his or her research critique. Each Oncourse drop box is private in that only the student and his or her instructor can view it. The Oncourse grade book provides a student roster and allows the instructor to enter a list of assignments to be graded in the class. Thus, the instructor can easily award points or letter grades to each item for each student and can provide feedback in an adjacent text box. The grade book is also private in that a student can only see his or her own grades and instructor feedback.

Google Groups is planned for asynchronous discussion because of the excellent way it is integrated with a wiki (called Pages in Google Groups), a document sharing area (called Files), and e-mail among students in the group.

Indiana University also provides Adobe Acrobat Connect for use by instructors and students. Acrobat Connect (formerly Macromedia Breeze Meeting) allows for synchronous interaction with voice and video via each participant's webcam. Another extremely important feature is that the instructor (and also students) can share their computer screens—thus everyone in the group can see that user's computer screen, which could be displaying a PowerPoint presentation, a word processing document, a web page, etc. Group meetings in Acrobat can also be recorded for archival purposes, so those who cannot attend in real-time can view the meeting at a later time. Acrobat Connect also provides a back channel for Internet chat to occur, which is also useful if there are audio problems, or if students have comments or questions and do not want to interrupt the ongoing video demonstration or audio discussion.

In R690, a class presentation or demonstration could be done live in Acrobat Connect and recorded. Anecdotally, the instructor has found it more convenient to make movies or podcasts with TechSmith's Camtasia, since the quality of audio and video is better and these can be easily edited and combined[3]. For example, a movie demonstrating the SPSS data analysis tasks could be made. During the live demonstration in class, the instructor could run Camtasia to capture his voice and the computer displays. Then the captured audio and video could be edited and put online. This could then be viewed online by students not only in the face-to-face class, but also in the distance version. In summary, current class sessions in R690 where there is an instructor presentation or demonstration can be recorded as podcasts or movies.

For R690 class activities in which students carry out a task with instructor coaching, a somewhat different approach will be needed for the online version. For example, the R690 card-sorting activity that is done as a group for content analysis of interview results would not lend itself to capture by Camtasia. Here it would make sense to have someone record this face-to-face class activity with a digital camcorder when this card-sort activity is undertaken. This way, online students could watch it (*Demonstration Principle*).

However, students would not be able to participate actively in the card-sort themselves (*Application Principle*) when just watching the online video. This card-sorting activity might be conducted synchronously online by a combination of Acrobat Connect and Microsoft Word. For example, the class could be participating synchronously in Connect, while the instructor is sharing his computer screen. On his computer screen could be a Word document. In Word, text boxes could be created for each pile as they emerge. Students could take turns reading to the group an item on their 3 × 5 card (or paste it into the chat line, so everyone can see the item in chat). Everyone would look at the Word document and then decide which pile (text box) it should go in.

If this card-sorting activity could not be done synchronously, then it could be done asynchronously via Google Docs. Google Docs allows a group to share and edit together a single document online. Some protocol would need to be developed so that students could add their 3 × 5 cards to various piles or stacks. Alternatively, each student could get all the 3 × 5 'cards' from everyone and do the card-sorting activity by himself or herself. Then each student would post a document (e.g., in Google Groups) that would show the results of his or her card-sort. Students could then compare their results by examining each other's documents and discuss the similarities and differences asynchronously in the Discussions area of Google Groups.

For the research critique classes, each student would post (in PDF format) the research article to be discussed in the Files section of Google Groups, or just attach it to a Discussions topic that is viewable by the class, or e-mail it to the instructor who would then in turn upload it to the course website and make a hyperlink to it. Students in the class would be expected to read the article before the critique session would begin.

Since each student is expected to make a presentation and lead the critique, that student could make a PowerPoint presentation ahead of time and then make the presentation in Acrobat Connect by sharing his computer screen. Alternatively, the student could record his or her voice over the PowerPoint presentation and capture it with Camtasia. The recording could then be uploaded to the course website so everyone in the class could view it.

The in-class critique and discussion of each research report is an important activity that normally is done in the last third of the R690 course. This could be accomplished via synchronous discussion in Acrobat Connect. Alternatively, the Discussions feature of Google Groups could be utilized so that an asynchronous written discussion of that research article could occur. Some kind of structure and protocol for participation in the critique session would need to be created. The instructor would need to participate regularly in the discussion board in order to provide important feedback to students with respect to their application of criteria used in critiques.

In summary, the above description should give the reader an idea of how an existing face-to-face course that has been designed with *First Principles of Instruction* could be converted to an online course. Next, an existing online course that utilizes *First Principles* is described.

An Existing Online Course Designed around *First Principles of Instruction*

The first author has also designed and taught an online course, R547: Computer-Mediated Learning. See the syllabus (Figure 3.1).

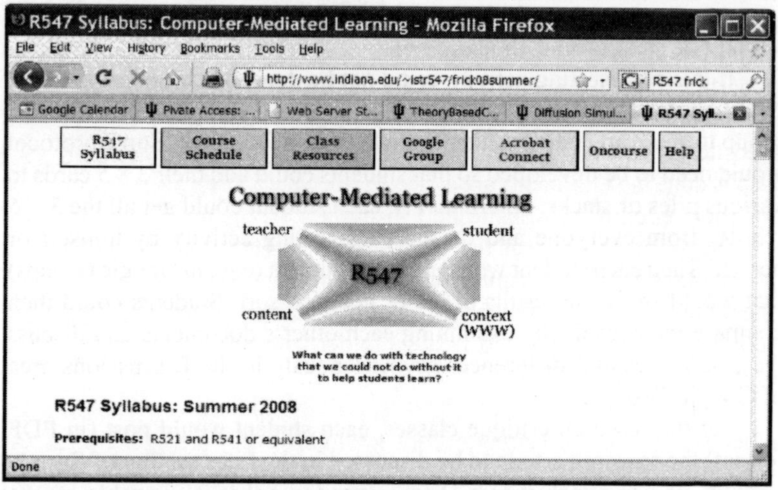

Fig. 3.1. Online course syllabus for R547: Computer-Mediated Learning
https://www.indiana.edu/~istr547/frick08summer/index.html (Frick, 2008b)

The primary goal of R547 is for students to develop an e-learning product themselves that is a real-world project, i.e., it will be used online by others for purposes of learning. An example of such a product is an e-learning product made by a student in 2006: http://mentor.ucs.indiana.edu/~frick/r547/2006/creditcards/menu.htm (Frick, 2006). The R547 distance student was working for a company that counselled their clients on how to understand statements from creditors (e.g., a credit card billing statement a client has received). The e-learning product s/he developed in R547 was then used by her company as part of training for the counsellors who worked with clients.

The student e-learning products in R547 are expected to incorporate *First Principles of Instruction*. This requirement can be understood by viewing the syllabus grading criteria at https://www.indiana.edu/~istr547/frick08summer/#grading (Frick, 2008c).

Sequencing of authentic tasks is accomplished in R547 by two parallel streams. One stream focuses on how to technically put instruction and resources on the web, without worry about the specific content. A second parallel stream has to do with design and development of the learning.

In the technical stream, it begins with the simplest form of Web publishing. Students are expected to convert an existing document that is in Word (e.g., his or her résumé) to PDF format and then to upload it to his or her website. The task is completed when the student sends e-mail to the instructor with a hyperlink to the PDF file, and also adds the hyperlink to the wiki page (in Google Pages) for posting his or her course deliverables. This is the epitome of Web publishing, put a file on one's website and then create a hyperlink that points to it. A more complex task is done next. Students are expected to create a Dreamweaver template for their e-learning website and to build a navigational structure for moving from one part of the site to another. The web pages just have placeholder content or dummy content. The third task is to create a style sheet in CSS and use it as part of their Dreamweaver template. A bonus activity requires students to create a folder with restricted access as part of their website.

In the design stream, students are first expected to determine the objectives of their e-learning product and how they are going to assess student achievement or mastery or those objectives. Students are then expected to create a rapid *paper* prototype of their e-learning product (or the parts that can be done online) that shows evidence of utilization of *First Principles of Instruction.*

The two streams then merge as the student is expected to create a rapid *computer* prototype of his or her e-learning product. The student is subsequently expected to conduct formative evaluation and usability tests of the e-learning product with at least three members of the target audience. The R547 student also evaluates student learning achievement from his or her e-learning product by administering his or her performance assessments as pre- and post-tests, and then computing the differences (i.e., measures of individual student learning gains). Finally, the student is expected to write a final report that summarizes the design process, describes how *First Principles* have been applied, and discusses the formative evaluation and usability testing of the product and results of his or observations. See an example of a final report at https://www.indiana.edu/~istr547/frick08summer/Wendy_R547_FinalReport.pdf (Frick, 2008d). This report describes the objectives of the e-learning product, the performance assessment, how it meets the requirements of *First Principles of Instruction*, the usability evaluation of her product, and the results.

The reader should note that R547 is not a beginning class. It is an intermediate level course, which master's and doctoral students take after core courses in instructional design. Otherwise, the gaps between the tasks would probably be too great for students. The R547 course is taken entirely online and has been taught this way since 2006 when it was offered online, using *First Principles of Instruction.*

Examples of *Activation*, *Demonstration*, *Application* and *Integration Principles* in R547 are listed below:

- *Activation*: initial movie in course overview; students view work by prior students in R547 (see links in syllabus); activation is used in the mini-movies, especially at the beginnings; instructor uses activation techniques when responding to student questions in online discussion in Google Groups.
- *Demonstration*: mini-movies[4] show how to use Acrobat Connect, VPN, Dreamweaver and CSS; demonstrations are abundant in the textbook by Bardzell and Bardzell (see print resources in the syllabus).

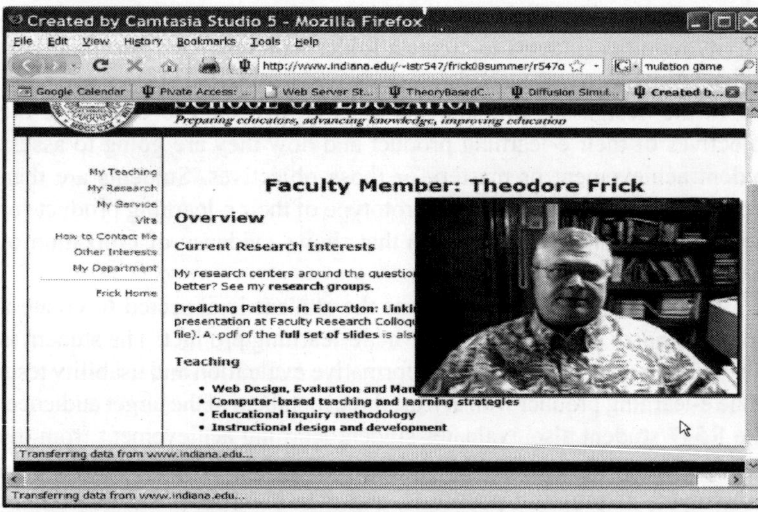

Fig. 3.2: Overview of R547 taught at a distance: Online movie (podcast) with audio and video overlay to introduce the course

https://www.indiana.edu/~istr547/frick08summer/r547overview2008/r547overview2008.html (Frick,2008e)

- *Application*: students create the web deliverables, objectives, assessments, paper and computer prototypes; students conduct formative evaluation of their e-learning products with real subjects; students analyze results of formative evaluation and usability testing and write a summary report.
- *Integration*: students post their deliverables in the Wiki (Google Pages), so other students can view each other's work; students present their final e-learning product in Acrobat Connect to the instructor and students at the end of the course; perhaps most important of all, integration often occurs when students immediately use what they have learned in their jobs[1].

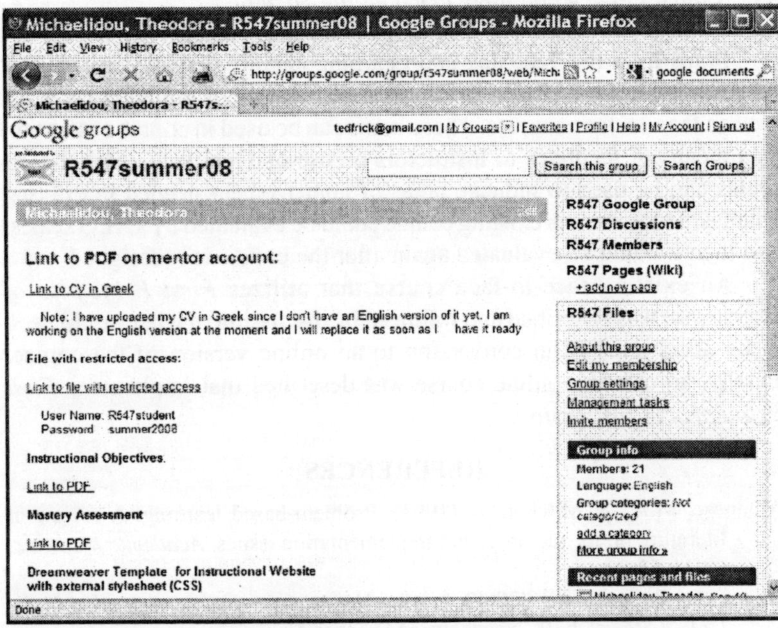

Fig. 3.3. An example of an R547 student posting to her wiki page in Google Groups

An example of links to a student's deliverables that she posted on her Google Page (wiki) is illustrated in Figure 3.3. Everyone in the class can see what other students have done. The Google Group is set up so only students and the instructor in the R547 can see it. While instructor feedback on early versions of a student's deliverable is posted in Google Discussions (so the whole class can benefit from the instructor's comments), the feedback and grade on each deliverable are provided in the Oncourse grade book and which are privately shared between the instructor and each student.

Summary

We have discussed how *First Principles of Instruction* is supported by extant theories of learning and instruction from three different paradigms—behaviorist, cognitivist, and constructivist.

Several empirical studies were reviewed in which *First Principles of Instruction* have been investigated. *First Principles of Instruction* are highly associated positively with student perceptions of overall quality of instruction, satisfaction with the course and instructor, student learning progress, student academic learning time, and student learning achievement. These relationships appear to be consistent, regardless of whether a course is taught face-to-face or online.

Items from the Teaching and Learning Quality (TALQ) scales were listed that can be included on student evaluations of online courses, as well as face-to-face courses. These items can be used in course evaluation as a means of feedback to instructors on use of *First Principles.* TALQ scales can be used to indicate areas of improvement needed in existing courses. Moreover, an existing course could be evaluated by TALQ scales, and then it could be evaluated again after the course is redesigned.

An existing face-to-face course that utilizes *First Principles of Instruction* was described and followed by discussion of what would need to be accomplished in conversion to an online version of the course. Finally, an existing online course was described that implements *First Principles of Instruction.*

REFERENCES

Albanese, M.A., & Mitchell, S. (1993). Problem-based learning: A review of literature on its outcomes and implementation issues. *Academic Medicine,* 68(1), 52-81.

Allen, I.E., & Seaman, J. (2008). *Staying the course – Online education in the United States,* 2008. Needham, MA: Sloan-C.

Airasian, P., & Walsh, M. (1997). Constructivist cautions. *Phi Delta Kappan*, 78, 444-449.

Ausubel, D. (1963). *The Psychology of Meaningful Verbal Learning.* New York: Grune & Stratton.

Bransford, J., Brown, A., & Cocking, R. (2000). *How people learn: Brain, mind, experience, and school* (pp. 3-27; 114-127). Washington DC: National Academy Press.

Bereiter, C. & Englemann, S. (1966). *Teaching Disadvantaged children in the preschool.* Upper Saddle River, NJ: Prentice Hall.

Bruning, R.H., Schraw, G.J., Norby, M.M. & Ronning, R.R. (2004). *Cognitive psychology and instruction* (4th ed.). Upper Saddle River, New Jersey & Columbus, Ohio: Pearson Prentice Hall.

Burton, J.K., Moore, D.M., & Magliaro, S.G. (1996). Behaviorism and instructional technology. In D.H. Jonassen (Ed.), *Handbook of research for educational communications and technology* (pp. 46-73). New York: Macmillan.

Carroll, J.M. (1990). *The Nurnberg funnel: Designing minimalist instruction for practical computer skill.* Cambridge, MA: MIT Press.

Chadha, R. (2009). *Dependability of college student ratings of teaching and learning quality.* Bloomington, in Ph.D. dissertation, Indiana University Graduate School.

Christensen, C., Johnson, C.W. & Horn, M.B. (2008). *Disrupting class: How disruptive innovation will change the way the world learns.* USA: McGraw-Hill.

Driscoll, M. (2000). *Psychology of learning for instruction* (2nd ed.). Boston: Allyn & Bacon.

Frick, T.W. (2006). E-learning product: Understanding creditor statements.

Retrieved August 24, 2009 from: http://mentor.ucs.indiana.edu/~frick/r547/2006/creditcards/menu.htm.

Frick, T.W. (2008a). Syllabus: Application of Research research Methods to IST Issues. Retrieved August 24, 2009 from: https://www.indiana.edu/~istr690/frick08fall/index.html .

Frick, T.W. (2008b). Syllabus: Computer-mediated learning. Retrieved August 24, 2009 from: https://www.indiana.edu/~istr547/frick08summer/index.html.

Frick, T.W. (2008c). R547 grading criteria. Retrieved August 24, 2009 from: https://www.indiana.edu/~istr547/frick08summer/#grading.

Frick, T.W. (2008d). Final report for e-learning product. Retrieved August 24, 2009 from: https://www.indiana.edu/~istr547/frick08summer/Wendy_R547_FinalReport.pdf.

Frick, T.W. (2008e). Screencast of R547 instructor demonstration. Retrieved August 24, 2009 from: https://www.indiana.edu/~istr547/frick08summer/r547overview2008/r547overview2008.html.

Frick, T.W., Chadha, R., Watson, C., & Wang, Y. (2010, in press). Theory-based course evaluation: Implications for improving student success in postsecondary education. In M. Orey, V. McClendon, & R. Branch (Eds.), *Educational media and technology year book.*

Frick, T.W., Chadha, R., Watson, C., Wang, Y., & Green, P. (2008, in press). College student perceptions of teaching and learning quality. *Educational Technology Research and Development.*

Frick, T.W., Chadha, R., Watson, C., & Zlatkovska, E. (2009, in press). Improving course evaluations to improve instruction and complex learning in higher education. *Educational Technology Research and Development.*

Gagné, R.M. (1985). *The conditions of learning and theory of instruction* (4th ed.). New York: Holt, Rinehart and Winston.

Gagné, R.M., Briggs, L., & Wager, W. (1988). Events of instruction. *Principles of instructional design* (3rd ed., pp. 177-197). Orlando, FL: Holt, Rinehart & Winston.

Garrison, D.R., Anderson, T., & Archer, W. (2000). Critical thinking in a text-based environment. Computer conferencing in higher education. *Internet in Higher Education,* 2(2), 87-105.

Grabinger, R.S. (1996). Rich environments for active learning. In D.H. Jonassen (Ed.), *Handbook of Research for Educational Communications and Technology* (pp. 665-692). New York: Macmillan.

Hannafin, M., Land, S., & Oliver, K. (1999). Open learning environments: Foundations, methods, and models. In C.M. Reigeluth (Ed.), *Instructional design theories and models volume II* (pp. 115-140). Mahwah, NJ: Erlbaum.

Heinich, R., Molenda, M., Russell, J., & Smaldino, S. (1999). *Instructional media and technologies for learning* (6th ed., pp. 7-92; 302-331). Columbus, OH: Prentice-Hall.

Jonassen, D.H. (1991). Objectivism versus Constructivism: Do we need a new philosophical paradigm? *Educational Technology Research and Development,* 39(3), 5-14.

Jonassen, D.H. (1999). Designing Constructivist Learning Environments. In C.M.

Reigeluth (Ed.), *Instructional design theories and models volume II* (pp. 215-240). Mahwah, NJ: Lawrence Erlbaum.

Landa, L.L. (1983). The Algo-heuristic theory of instruction. In C.M. Reigeluth (Ed.), *Instructional design theories and models: An overview of their current status* (pp. 163-212). Hillsdale, NJ: Lawrence Erlbaum.

Magliaro, S.G., Lockee, B.B., & Burton, J.K. (2005). Direct Instruction revisited: A key model for instructional technology. *Educational Technology Research and Development,* 53 (4), 41-55.

Merrill, M.D. (1994). *Instructional design theory*. Englewood Cliffs, NJ: Educational Technology Publications.

Merrill, M.D. (2002). First principles of instruction. *Educational Technology Research and Development,* 50(3), 43-59.

Merrill, M.D. (2007a). First principles of instruction: A synthesis. In R.A. Reiser & J.V. Dempsey (Eds.), *Trends and Issues in instructional design and technology*, 2nd ed. Vol. 2. pp. 62-71. Upper Saddle River, NJ: Merrill/Prentice Hall.

Merrill, M.D. (2007b). A task-centered instructional strategy. *Journal of Research on Technology in Education,* 40(1), 33-50.

Reigeluth, C. M. (1999). The Elaboration Theory: Guidance for scope and sequence decisions. In C.M. Reigeluth (Ed.), *Instructional design theories and models volume II* (pp. 425-454). Mahwah, NJ: Lawrence Erlbaum.

Reiser, R.A. (2001). A history of instructional design and technology: Part II: A history of instructional design. *Educational Technology Research & Development,* 49(2), 57-67.

Salmon, G. (2004). *E-moderating: The key to teaching and learning online* (2nd ed.). Routledge Falmer: London

Scouller, K. (1998). The influence of assessment method on students' learning approaches: Multiple choice question examination versus assignment essay. *Higher Education*, 35, 453 472.

Palincsar, A.S., & Brown, A.L. (1984). Reciprocal teaching of comprehension-fostering and comprehension-monitoring activities. *Cognition and Instruction,* 1, 117-176.

Perkins, D.N. (1991). Technology meets constructivism: Do they make a marriage? *Educational Technology,* 31(5), 18-23.

Puntambekar, S., & Hubscher, R. (2005). Tools for scaffolding students in a complex learning environment: What have we gained and what have we missed? *Educational Psychologist,* 40(1), 1-12.

Skinner, B.F. (1996). The science of learning and the art of teaching. In D.P. Ely & T. Plomp (Eds.), *Classic writings on instructional technology* (pp. 199-210). Englewood, CO: Libraries Unlimited.

Thomson. (2002). *Thomson job impact study: The next generation of learning.* Naperville, IL: NETg (http://www.netg.com).

van Merriënboer, J.G. (1997). *Training complex cognitive skills: A four-component instructional design model for technical training*. Englewood Cliffs, NJ: Educational Technology Publications.

van Merriënboer, J.G., Clark, R.E., & de Croock, M.B. (2002). Blueprints for complex learning: The 4C/ID-Model. *Educational Technology Research and Development,* 50 (2), 39-64.

Vygotsky, L.S. (1978). *Mind in society*. Cambridge, MA: MIT Press.

Wood, D., Bruner, J.S., & Ross, G. (1976). The role of tutoring in problem solving. *Journal of Child Psychology and Psychiatry and Allied Disciplines,* 17, 89-100.

NOTES

1. These students typically are working in professional jobs and taking IST distance courses one or two at a time as they seek a certificate and/or a master's degree.

   Each time the course is taught a different real-world client is sought. For example, the previous year the client was our Education Technology Services (ETS) and the website was for the School of Education. During the 2009 fall semester, the client is expected to be the Association for Educational Communications and Technology (AECT), which is redesigning its website.
2. The university provides a web account that he uses for publishing his course website. The university also currently has a site license with Adobe so that tools such as Dreamweaver, Contribute, etc. can be installed on personal computers that faculty, staff and students use while at Indiana University.
3. To see an example of this, go to https://www.indiana.edu/~istr547/frick08summer/r547overview2008/r547overview2008.html (Frick , 2008b). The site provides an overview of an existing online course, R547, Computer-Mediated Learning that was designed and has been taught by the first author. Once these movies have been created, they can simply be uploaded to the course website and hyperlinks can be made in the Resources folder (e.g., see R547 discussion below).
4. R547 mini-movies are viewable at: https://www.indiana.edu/~istr547/frick08summer/resources/index.html. A username (*professor*) and password (*frick*) are required.

4.

Use of ICT and Cognitive Apprenticeship Model to Enhance the Teaching of Biology

Lum Wai Mei

In recent years, cognitive apprenticeship has become increasingly prominent as a model of instruction. This development is attributable to its potential to help solve the educational problems of brittle skills and inert knowledge that often arise with traditional schooling. Cognitive apprenticeship is a collaborative approach to instruction in which tutor and pupil interact to facilitate knowledge construction in the ways, which are most relevant to the learner.

In this chapter, the author discusses how he designs a lesson using the cognitive apprenticeship model and the impact of this lesson on the students' learning. He also discusses how technology could act as a cognitive apprenticeship model and the impact of technology on the students' learning. Lastly, he would look at some of the constraints posed by the cognitive apprenticeship model, based on the literature reviews.

Cognitive Apprenticeship Model in Teaching Biology

For teaching Biology, some problems are encountered when the author taught the topic on diffusion and osmosis. Questions on that topic were given to the students and the students were asked to write down their explanations for their answers. However, the students take a longer time to answer the questions. When this topic is tested for examinations, most of the students did not do very well. Looking at the problems faced, the author decided to design a lesson based on the model of cognitive apprenticeship. Cognitive apprenticeship is a model of learning based on the situated cognition theory. There are six stages of cognitive apprenticeship *(modeling, coaching, scaffolding, articulation, reflection and exploration).* The author included a step-by-step guide as to how the students should answer the questions based on the above topic. Scaffolding to the students by including diagrams in the worksheet was also provided.

What it was observed that the students were able to solve the questions faster and they felt more confident in solving the problems.

	Six stages of cognitive apprenticeship
Modeling	An expert performing a task so that students can observe and build a conceptual model of the processes that are required to accomplish it.
Coaching	Teacher observing students while they carry out a task and offering hints and feedback.
Scaffolding	The supports the teacher provides to help students carry out the task.
Articulation	Getting students to articulate their knowledge, reasoning or problem-solving processes in a domain.
Reflection	Enabling students to compare their own problem solving processes with those of an expert or another student.
Exploration	Pushing students into a mode of problem solving on their own.

Designing Issues for Learning Environments

There are two kinds of *modeling* that are critical to consider in the design of learning environments: (1) modeling of the physical process underlying phenomena by which the teacher want students to understand. (2) Modeling the thought processes underlying expert performance. The benefits of *scaffolding* are that it helps students to accomplish difficult tasks, providing focused help at critical times and only as much help as needed. Teachers have a variety of methods for getting students to *articulate* their ideas and thinking processes (Collins, 1993).

For example, Bereiter and Scardamalia (1987) have students describe their thinking processes while planning an essay. Schoenfeld (1985) has students work in groups to solve difficult math problems, so that they are forced to articulate their thinking to each other. Inquiry teachers (Collins & Stevens, 1983) pose problems and questions for students to get them to articulate and refine their theories. As Brown (1985) has pointed out, programs like Robot Odyssey and Truckin force students to articulate their theories in order to construct robot agents to carry out their plans. *Reflection* involves looking back over one's performance on a task. Examples are Algebraland (Brown, 1985) or the Geometry Tutor (Anderson, Boyle & Reiser, 1985) where the system keeps a record of all the students moves in solving an algebra equation or developing a geometry proof (Collins, 1993).

When the author pose questions to his students during lesson, he use to randomly called upon some students to explain their answers and articulate their thought processes to the whole class. Another teaching approach the author can try out is to get the students into groups of 4. In each group, each student would take turns to explain their answers to the rest of the students in the group. In this case, a lot of social interaction and collaboration among the students is observed.

After getting the students to articulate their thoughts to the other students, the teacher use to present the model answers on the whiteboard. Students were expected to compare their answers with the model answers and to add in whatever information they had missed in their answers.

Designing Effective Learning Environments

The Collins, Brown, and Newman cognitive apprenticeship model is recommended; its four building blocks – content, methods, sequence and sociology – together define an effective learning situation. There are current programs for integrating academic and vocational education and apprenticeships in light of the cognitive apprenticeship models. Apprentices are inducted into a community of expert practice in which the 'teacher' continuously engages in and is a master at the practice being learned. His or her performance constitutes the standard for the apprentice (Berryman, 1991).

Content: Schools usually focus on the concepts, facts and procedures of a subject. Students also need three other areas of content: (1) 'tricks of the trade' – problem solving strategies. (2) Cognitive management strategies – goal setting, strategic planning, monitoring, evaluation. (3) Learning strategies – exploring new fields, getting more knowledge with familiar subject and reconfigure knowledge already possessed (Berryman, 1991).

Methods: Teaching methods should give students a chance to observe, engage in, invent or discover new strategies in context. The teachers help to coach the students – offering hints, feedbacks and reminders and provide scaffolding for students when they learn to carry out tasks (Berryman, 1991).

Sequencing: Learning should be staged so that the learner builds the multiple skills required in expert performance. This requires a sequence of increasingly complex tasks and diverse problem solving (Berryman, 1991).

Sociology: The learning environment should produce the technological, social and motivational characteristics of real world situations where what is being learned will be used. For example, in the real world, people have to work with partners; this model calls for students to work together to solve problems to carry out tasks (Berryman, 1991).

Based on the Collins, Brown and Newman cognitive apprenticeship model, I strongly agree that the learning of a student should be staged in such a way that it progresses from a novice's performance to that of an expert. At the early learning stage of a student when he is just a novice, the teacher serves as a facilitator to guide the student by the modeling, coaching and scaffolding approach. After a period of time, when the student develops the expertise to perform a task on his own, the teacher would slowly remove the support that he has been giving to the student (fading stage). This model is multi-disciplinary and it can apply to all the teaching subjects in the school.

Constructivism

Using a constructivist approach, teachers facilitate learning by encouraging active inquiry, guiding learners to question their tacit assumptions and coaching them in the construction process. This contrast with the behavioralist approach that has dominated education, in which the teacher disseminates selected knowledge, measures learners' passive reception of facts and focuses on behavior control and task completion. A constructivist teacher is more interested in uncovering meanings than in covering prescribed material (Sandra, 1997).

The concept of *situated learning* – that knowledge is created and made meaningful by the context in which it is acquired – is embedded in constructivism. Situated learning results from undertaking authentic activities which are guided by expert practitioners situated in a culture of practice. Experts organize or index their base of constructed knowledge in order to recognize patterns and solve problems in new situations. Through experience, experts amass a rich index of cognitive structures that they can easily recall and use. A constructivist method for helping novices to acquire expertise is cognitive apprenticeship (Sandra, 1997).

Traditional teaching focuses on teacher-lecture and passive transmission of knowledge from the teacher to the students. In view of our education system moving into the 21st century, perhaps the teachers should change their perceptions of teaching and step out of their comfort zone of traditional teaching. The author proposes that the design of the curriculum should be more inquiry-based and authentic (linking to real-world situations) with the incorporation of technology.

Instructional Strategies

The cognitive apprenticeship model employs the following instructional strategies: (1) collaboration (2) reflection (3) student autonomy activities and (4) intrinsically motivating strategies (Dunlap, 1997).

Collaboration: The students in a collaborative group are working closely together; thus students are able to share ideas and perspectives, as well as help each other clarify issues. This is important in helping students develop metacognitive skills (Dunlap, 1997).

Reflection: Reflection is encouraged so students will elaborate on what they have learned (Dunlap, 1997).

Student autonomy: Students can accomplish a task they would not be able to carry out without help (Dunlap, 1997).

Intrinsically Motivating Activities

When students are intrinsically motivated, they are more likely to be more self-determined; they may attempt more problems, focusing on the way to solve the problem instead of finding the correct solution. The self-determination and desire to return to a learning activity is part of lifelong learning. Students take ownership of the problem by assuming the roles of real stakeholders. When students take on the roles of scientists, programmers, historians, etc., their motivation soars because they realize it's their problem' (Stepien & Gallagher, 1993 and Dunlap, 1997).

The author has an example of a science lesson whereby students take on the role of a 'scientist'. The worksheet is as attached (Appendix 1). In this lesson, students are expected to conduct an experiment (effects of light intensity on the rate of photosynthesis). They conduct the experiment using computer simulations, as if they are conducting the 'real' experiment as a scientist. At the end of the experiment, they have to tabulate their results and determine the conclusion of the experiment. The author has conducted this lesson before and what he observes was that even the not-so motivating students became interested in the lesson.

Science experiments conducted by the students are one way to bring the scientific concepts 'alive'. The author feels that students are able to remember these scientific concepts better through their experience of conducting the experiment (authentic learning), rather than recalling concepts from the textbook.

Using Technology — Multimedia

Recent research in the learning sciences coupled with a shift to the situated cognition paradigm in the cognitive sciences has led to a significant rethinking of the nature of learning and cognition and how we can use technology to support learning. Based upon theories of situated learning and cognitive apprenticeship, students are able to engage in social dialog with experts through Internet technologies such as email, email redistribution lists (listservs) and the World-Wide Web (Chee, 1994).

SMALLTALKER is a Macintosh-based multimedia-learning environment for Smalltalk programming. The learning environment supports both concept learning and skill acquisition. The use of various elements of the interface (mouse, windows and text manipulation) is demonstrated to students via movie clips. Students are then coached on the use of the interface in a different problem setting. In the *modeling* stage of cognitive apprenticeship, the movies are accompanied by the expert's voice narration of the instruction. With the use of multimedia, concepts and processes can be 'brought alive', focusing students' attention on the meaning and sense of what they observe. In the *scaffolding* stage, students have the option while they solve the problems, to request help by selecting the button "I'm stuck" from the panel of buttons at the bottom of the screen. The help window lists a set of topics on which assistance on specific aspects of the problem students are attempting is available. Making the activation of the help system the responsibility of students encourages them to take active control of their learning (Chee, 1994).

The author agrees that multimedia is a powerful tool to act as an 'expert' to deliver concepts to the students. Some multimedia such as Smalltalk, even provides help and support to the students when they are 'stuck' at problem-solving.

The stages of cognitive apprenticeship can also be carried out by multimedia, besides the teacher. As what future schools are doing now, students learn independently with the help of multimedia and the teacher acts as a facilitator. Perhaps more and more schools would transform into so-called future schools in the next couple of years.

Examples of multimedia that are used in lessons are downloaded from the MOE website (http://www3.moe.edu.sg/edsoftware/ir/). An example is the interactive resource on the experiment of photosynthesis.

Technology — Computer-based Simulations

Simulations have been used to deliver instruction in educational settings on the basis that they increase the ability of participants to apply what they have learned in the classroom to the real world. For advocates of *situated approaches* to learning, the provision of *authentic activity* in schools is a way to increase cognitive engagement, support meaningful learning and facilitate transfer. One of the strengths of simulation for instructional purposes is its potential to shelter learners from costly forms of natural *feedback* (skidding into a snow bank) and to provide real-time artificial feedback (turn in the direction of the skid) (Lebow, et. al., 1994).

What matters most is not the realism of the simulation or the processing level of the learner, but whether the learner practices what is essential for the transfer situation. Thus, a good test is also a good learning activity and instruction and assessment are inseparable within an authentic learning environment (Lebow, et. al., 1994).

For example, some students are struggling with the concepts of diffusion and osmosis during biology lessons. Perhaps I can let them go through computer simulations (websites are given in Appendix 2) to help them understand the concepts. In the modeling stage of cognitive apprenticeship, the computer simulation acts as the expert. With the use of multimedia, concepts and processes can be 'brought alive', focusing students' attention on the meaning and sense of what they observe. In the scaffolding stage, the students would ask the teacher for help if they have doubts in the lesson. It is assumed that the fading stage is similar to the students taking examinations. When the students are doing their examinations, they are not allowed to refer to any websites or the teacher.

Using Technology — Videos

Situated learning offers an approach to structuring learning experiences that captures both experiential and reflective dimensions of cognition and to enculturating students into authentic practices through activity and social interaction. The major features of video and multimedia computing technology are:

(1) Instruction is anchored in a video-based, problem-solving environment.
(2) Instruction provides multiple perspectives.
(3) Instruction promotes everyday cognition and cognitive apprenticeship.
(4) Information is designed in an embedded format. Based on the theories of situated learning, *cognitive apprenticeship* and cooperative learning, *anchored* instruction made it possible to provide a life-like inquiry situation for teaching several scientific concepts and problem-solving strategies (Shyu & Hsin-Yih, 1997).

Besides using computer simulations to illustrate the concepts of diffusion and osmosis, it is considered that videos are another way to illustrate the concepts, as most of the students of the author are visual learners. The students can learn through multimedia in multiple perspectives (visual, audio, simulation, interactive, collaboration).

Videos are also useful in conducting science practicals. The procedures of an experiment are demonstrated fully by the video itself.

In this case, the video helps in the modeling process of a student. The student looks at the video and conducts the experiment in the same way as what the video (the expert) shows. If the student encounters any difficulty when s/he is doing the experiment, s/he would approach the teacher for assistance (coaching and scaffolding process). After that, s/he would repeat the experiment without the help of video and teacher (fading process).

The Internet as a Tool for the Social Construction of Knowledge

The cognitive apprenticeship model proposes that the design of learning environments reconstruct important attributes of master-apprentice relationships. Among other attributes, 'apprenticeship embeds the learning of skills and knowledge in their social and functional context.' Authentic tasks and meaningful situations are required to bring novices into a culture of expert practice. The social environment provides a set of experiences from which the individual tests understanding and adopts group norms. Based upon theories of situated learning and cognitive apprenticeship, students engage in social dialog with experts through Internet technologies such as email, discussion forums and the World-Wide Web (Farquhar, et. al., 1996).

The author also makes use of discussion forum for the students to pose questions regarding the topic diffusion and osmosis. The students are encouraged to interact and discuss the questions as a class.

Impact on Students' Learning (Life-long Learning)

Just as the format of traditional apprenticeship helps an apprentice learn how to use the tools of the trade, *cognitive apprenticeship* helps students learn how to use the cognitive tools required for lifelong learning by enabling students to acquire, develop and use cognitive and metacognitive tools as they engage in authentic domain activity (Dunlap, 1997).

The students learn to collaborate with one another through group work and social interaction. This is an important life skill that the students would need in the future when they become working adults. In the workplace, they would need to collaborate with their colleagues and business partners.

Impact on Students' Learning (Student Engagement)

With the help of technology and cognitive apprenticeship model infused into the lesson, the students are more engaged and on-task. They are able to solve scientific problems in a shorter time. This contrasts with the traditional teaching method (lecture style, no technology).

A survey (appended in Appendix 3) was conducted on six classes of Secondary two students (total number of students = 246). The survey revealed positive results about the online resources used for the topic (diffusion and osmosis). Majority of the students (85.7%) agreed that the online resources helped them to understand the lecture material. Majority of the students (88.4%) also agreed that they gained a better understanding of what they know about diffusion and osmosis. Apart, 89.1 per cent of the students agreed that they would be able to learn more about diffusion and osmosis on their own because of skill(s) gained from the online resources.

Constraints

Barriers such as time constraints, administrative procedures, community pressures (accountability demands, standardized testing) and lack of consensus on the goals and purposes of education limit teachers' ability to implement constructivist approaches (Parnell, 1996). According to Hyerle (1996), constructivist approaches such as cooperative learning and portfolio assessment are already being used in schools, but most of these 'create the environment for constructivism but do not center explicitly on how an individual learner constructs knowledge' (Kerka, 1997).

As Brown et al. (1989) suggested, conventional classroom tasks frequently lack the contextual features that support transfer from the school setting to the outside world (Kerka, 1997).

REFERENCES

Berryman, Sue E. (1991). Designing Effective Learning Environments: Cognitive Apprenticeship Models. Columbia Univ., New York, NY. Inst. on Education and the Economy.

Chee, Yam San (1994). SMALLTALKER: A Cognitive Apprenticeship Multimedia Environment for Learning Smalltalk Programming. Education Resources Information Center (ERIC).

Collins, Allan (1993). Design Issues for Learning Environments. Center for Technology in Education, New York, NY.

Dunlap, Joanna C. (1997). Preparing Students for Lifelong Learning: A Review of Instructional Methodologies. Education Resources Information Center (ERIC).

Farquhar, John D. and Others. (1996). The Internet as a Tool for the Social Construction of Knowledge. Education Resources Information Center (ERIC).

Kerka, Sandra (1997). Constructivism, Workplace Learning and Vocational Education. ERIC Clearinghouse on Adult Career and Vocational Education Columbus OH.

Lebow, David G. Wager, Walter W. (1994). Authentic Activity as a Model for Appropriate Learning Activity: Implications for Design of Computer-Based Simulations. Education Resources Information Center (ERIC).

Shyu, Hsin-Yih (1997). Effects of Anchored Instruction on Enhancing Chinese Students' Problem-Solving Skills. Taiwan National Science Council, Taipei.

APPENDIX

Effect of Light Intensity on Rate of Photosynthesis

Aim:

1. To investigate the effect of different light intensities on the rate of photosynthesis at 25°C and:
   (a) 0.03% of CO_2
   (b) 0.13% of CO_2

Instructions:

1. Select the % CO_2 to be 0.03%.
   Select the light intensity by moving the slider to different markings.
2. Click on Start Experiment
3. After 1 minute on the stopwatch, record in the table below the Rate of Photosynthesis as given by the Number of Bubbles given off by the water plant.
   N.B. You may click on Stop Experiment if you wish to restart the experiment.
   5. Repeat steps 1-4 with 0.13% of CO_2.

Light Intensity Markings	*Rate of Photosynthesis at 0.03% of CO_2. (No. of Bubbles given off per minute)*	*Rate of Photosynthesis at 0.13% of CO_2. (No. of Bubbles given off per minute)*
1 (no light)	0	0
2	19	20
3	35	40
4	45	55
5	47	56
6	48	56
7 (max. light intensity)	48	56

Questions:

1. What are the variables in this experiment?
   Intensity of light, percentage of CO_2 and time given before recording, number of elodea plant, amount of dilut sodium hydrogen carbonate solution used.
2. Why is the plant submerged in dilute sodium hydrogen carbonate solution?
   Dilute hydrogen carbonate solution does not contain any air or bubbles to be mistaken.

3. How is the number of bubbles emitted by the water plant per minute related to the rate of photosynthesis in the water plant? During photosynthesis, oxygen is given out. Underwater, the oxygen is given out as bubbles.So as the rate of photosynthesis quickens, the more bubbles are given out quicker.
4. Based on the values obtained for 0.03% of $CO_2$and 0.13% of CO_2, sketch a graph to represent the results that you have obtained. Remember to label the axes of the graphs and the graphs for 0.03% of $CO_2$and 0.13% of CO_2 Create the graph using Microsoft Excel and save a copy in your personal folder.

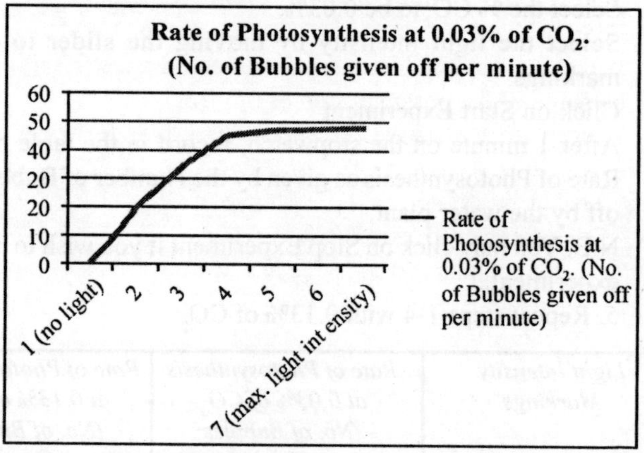

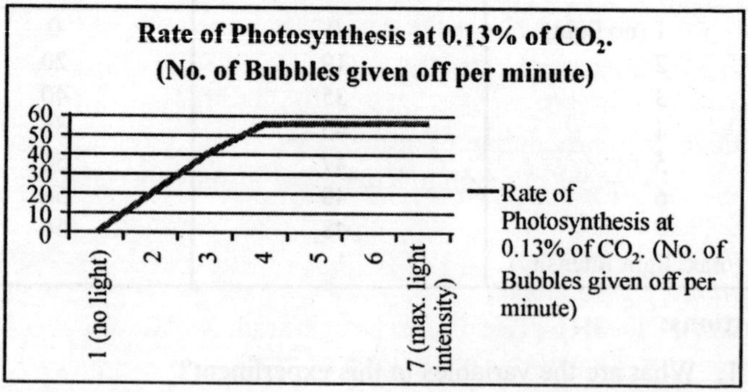

What can you conclude about the relationship between light intensity and the rate of photosynthesis? The higher the intensity of light, the higher the rate of photosynthesis.

5. What is the effect on the Rate of Photosynthesis when the percentage of CO_2 was increased?
The rate of photosynthesis is higher.

6. What is a *limiting factor*?
   It is a factor that stops something from going any higher.
7. With reference to the experiment for 0.03% CO_2, what is the limiting factor? 48
   Explain, using the graphs that you have sketched, how this limiting factor affects the rate of photosynthesis.
   The rate of photosynthesis will stop getting higher even as the light
   Intensity goes higher than the sixth marking as the limiting factor stops it from getting higher.
8. State another limiting factor of photosynthesis.
   Food produced
9. If you were to conduct this experiment in a laboratory, what can be some of the possible sources of error?
   I may miscalculate the percentage of carbon dioxide as it is very exact.

Subject: Science (Express/NA)
Level: Secondary 2
Topic: Osmosis
Purpose: Pupils will observe and describe osmosis as a process that involves the movement of water molecules when two solutions of unequal concentration are separated by a partially permeable membrane.
Description: Pupils will observe and analyse the movement of molecules, with the aid of an online resource and a structured worksheet, to learn about the concept of osmosis.
Background Knowledge: Pupils are able to observe and infer that diffusion is the movement of molecules from a region of higher concentration to a region of lower concentration
Pre-lesson Activity: Nil
Duration: 60 min
ICT Skills: SH1 – Use of search engines and keywords independently

Activities	*Duration*	*Resources*
1. Pupils recapitulate the concept of diffusion through an online resource. Volunteers will be asked to cite the key principles of diffusion. Some guiding questions may include: Can you describe the movement of molecules? Where are they moving from/to? Can diffusion take place between Matter of the same/different states? If so, can you provide some examples?	15 min	*Applet* Diffusion of perfume molecules (http://www.biosci.ohiou.edu/introbioslab/Bios170/diffusion/Diffusion.html)
2. Pupils will learn the concept of osmosis through an online resource, with the aid of a worksheet (Questions 1-4). *Note*: Teacher may need to provide further explanation on the concept of 'concentration' (i.e. number of molecules per unit volume).	30 min	*Applet* Osmosis Animation (http://www.stolaf.edu/people/giannini/flashanimat/transport/osmosis.swf) *Worksheet* Worksheet – S2 Osmosis.doc
3. Based on the observations made, pupils will be led to state the definition of osmosis (Worksheet, Question 5). *Extension Activity*: Pupils could research on the concept of "reversed osmosis" and state its uses with respect to water technology (i.e. in the production of NEWater).	15 min	

Maris Stella High School
Science Department
Lesson Evaluation

We are very interested in your thoughts and experiences in this lesson. Your ideas and suggestions are important. Please think about your course and answer the following questions based on your experiences. Thank you!

Put a tick in the box indicating SA, A, D, or SD to indicate your degree of agreement with each statement:

SA = I Strongly agree; A = I Agree; D = I Disagree; SD = I Strongly Disagree

S. No.	*Questions*	*Indication*			
		SA	*A*	*D*	*SD*
1.	In this class I have gained a deeper understanding of what we know about diffusion and osmosis.				
2.	For me, trying to answer biology questions in more than one way helps develop my reasoning skills.				
3.	I will be able to learn more about diffusion and osmosis on my own because of skills gained in this course.				
4.	I can see relationships between this material and some of the other material provided by my teacher.				
5.	Most of the time I am lost in this course.				
6.	I like this subject more because of attending this lesson.				
7.	The online resource helped me to understand the lecture material.				
8.	The knowledge learned in this course is very useful.				
9.	I learned more because I participated in class discussions.				
10.	The material (online resource) used in this lesson IS NOT very interesting.				
11.	I look forward to coming to such lessons.				
12.	The presentation of the material in this lesson is clear and systematic				
13.	I will be able to apply the information I learned in this lesson.				
14.	I DO NOT want to learn more about this subject because of my experience in this course.				
15.	Overall, I think this is an interesting lesson.				

Survey Results

S. No.	*Questions*	*Maris Stella Students (% Agree & Strongly Agree)*
1.	In this class I have gained a deeper understanding of what we know about diffusion and osmosis.	88.4
2.	For me, trying to answer biology questions in more than one way helps develop my reasoning skills.	75.1
3.	I will be able to learn more about diffusion and osmosis on my own because of skills gained in this course.	89.1
4.	I can see relationships between this material and some of the other material provided by my teacher.	77.9
5.	Most of the time I am lost in this course.	25.4
6.	I like this subject more because of attending this lesson.	79.1
7.	The online resource helped me to understand the lecture material.	85.7
8.	The knowledge learned in this course is very useful.	87.6
9.	I learned more because I participated in class discussions.	75.4
10.	The material (online resource) used in this lesson IS NOT very interesting.	29.5
11.	I look forward to coming to such lessons.	79.1
12.	The presentation of the material in this lesson is clear and systematic	84.3
13.	I will be able to apply the information I learned in this lesson.	87.2
14.	I DO NOT want to learn more about this subject because of my experience in this course.	18.7
15.	Overall, I think this is an interesting lesson.	89.4

APPENDIX-2

Lesson Plan S2 Osmosis

Subject:	Science (Express/NA)
Level:	Secondary 2
Topic:	Osmosis
Purpose:	Pupils will observe and describe osmosis as a process that involves the movement of water molecules when two solutions of unequal concentration are separated by a partially permeable membrane.
Description:	Pupils will observe and analyse the movement of molecules, with the aid of an online resource and a structured worksheet, to learn about the concept of osmosis.
Background Knowledge:	Pupils are able to observe and infer that diffusion is the movement of molecules from a region of higher concentration to a region of lower concentration.
Pre-lesson Activity:	Nil
Duration:	60 min
ICT Skills:	SH1 – Use of search engines and keywords independently

Activities	*Duration*	*Resources*
1. Pupils recapitulate the concept of diffusion through an online resource. Volunteers will be asked to cite the key principles of diffusion. Some guiding questions may include: Can you describe the movement of molecules? Where are they moving from/to? Can diffusion take place between Matter of the same/different states? If so, can you provide some examples?	15 min	*Applet* Diffusion of perfume molecules (http://www.biosci.ohiou.edu/introbioslab/Bios170/diffusion/Diffusion.html)
2. Pupils will learn the concept of osmosis through an online resource, with the aid of a worksheet (Questions 1-4). *Note*: Teacher may need to provide further explanation on the concept of 'concentration' (i.e. number of molecules per unit volume).	30 min	*Applet* Osmosis Animation (http://www.stolaf.edu/people/giannini/flashanimat/transport/osmosis.swf) *Worksheet* Worksheet – S2 Osmosis.doc

3.	Based on the observations made, pupils will be led to state the definition of osmosis (Worksheet, Question 5). *Extension Activity*: Pupils could research on the concept of "reversed osmosis" and state its uses with respect to water technology (i.e. in the production of NEWater).	15 min

APPENDIX-3

Maris Stella High School

Science Department

Lesson Evaluation

We are very interested in your thoughts and experiences in this lesson. Your ideas and suggestions are important. Please think about your course and answer the following questions based on your experiences. Thank you!

Put a tick in the box indicating SA, A, D, or SD to indicate your degree of agreement with each statement:

SA = I Strongly agree; A = I Agree; D = I Disagree; SD = I Strongly Disagree

S. No.	*Questions*	*Indication*			
		SA	*A*	*D*	*SD*
1.	In this class I have gained a deeper understanding of what we know about diffusion and osmosis.				
2.	For me, trying to answer biology questions in more than one way helps develop my reasoning skills.				
3.	I will be able to learn more about diffusion and osmosis on my own because of skills gained in this course.				
4.	I can see relationships between this material and some of the other material provided by my teacher.				
5.	Most of the time I am lost in this course.				
6.	I like this subject more because of attending this lesson.				
7.	The online resource helped me to understand the lecture material.				

8.	The knowledge learned in this course is very useful.				
9.	I learned more because I participated in class discussions.				
10.	The material (online resource) used in this lesson IS NOT very interesting.				
11.	I look forward to coming to such lessons.				
12.	The presentation of the material in this lesson is clear and systematic				
13.	I will be able to apply the information I learned in this lesson.				
14.	I DO NOT want to learn more about this subject because of my experience in this course.				
15.	Overall, I think this is an interesting lesson.				

Survey Results

S. No.	*Questions*	*Maris Stella Students (% Agree & Strongly Agree)*
1.	In this class I have gained a deeper understanding of what we know about diffusion and osmosis.	88.4
2.	For me, trying to answer biology questions in more than one way helps develop my reasoning skills.	75.1
3.	I will be able to learn more about diffusion and osmosis on my own because of skills gained in this course.	89.1
4.	I can see relationships between this material and some of the other material provided by my teacher.	77.9
5.	Most of the time I am lost in this course.	25.4
6.	I like this subject more because of attending this lesson.	79.1
7.	The online resource helped me to understand the lecture material.	85.7
8.	The knowledge learned in this course is very useful.	87.6

9.	I learned more because I participated in class discussions.	75.4
10.	The material (online resource) used in this lesson IS NOT very interesting.	29.5
11.	I look forward to coming to such lessons.	79.1
12.	The presentation of the material in this lesson is clear and systematic	84.3
13.	I will be able to apply the information I learned in this lesson.	87.2
14.	I DO NOT want to learn more about this subject because of my experience in this course.	18.7
15.	Overall, I think this is an interesting lesson.	89.4

5.

Pedagogical Framework for On-line Learning

Shyamal Majumdar

The educational arena of on-line learning is still in its infancy. While there are many institutions, offering on-line courses, an in-depth understanding of the pedagogical issues related to on-line education still remains an unexplored frontier. Literature provides some evidence of the effectiveness of using on-line education, little is known about which learning strategies should be used for education and training. How to construct these electronic teaching and learning environments so that they are based on specific epistemologies or knowledge bases? What is an appropriate pedagogical framework for on-line learning? This chapter discusses the characteristics of on-line education from epistemological and pedagogical perspective and suggests a conceptual framework for on-line learning based on co-operative/ collaborative learning strategies. It also discusses innovative ways to design on-line courses to enhance creativity and critical thinking processes. The author argues that where learning through facts, drill and practices, rules and procedures was more adaptive in earlier days, now learning through projects and problems, inquiry and design, discovery and invention, creativity and diversity, action and reflection is more fitting in the present times. So there is need of an urgent pedagogical shift from instructive to constructivist, behavioral to cognitive, didactic to facilitative, controlled to autonomous, fixed to open, interactive to collaborative, rigid to flexible, passive to active, surface to deep, learner centered to learning team centered approach to meet the demand of the on-line millennium learner.

The development of new broadband communication services, convergence of telecommunication with computers, recent developments in the field of communication protocol have fostered numerous proposals for the uses of these tools to aid the teaching and learning environment. The integration of computers and communications offers unprecedented opportunities to the education system with its capacity to integrate and interact with each other over a wide geographic distance in a meaningful way to achieve the instructional objectives. The growth of these communication and computer systems, their ease of use, the power and diversity of information transfer allow teachers and students to have access to a world beyond the classroom. It has the potential to transform the nature and process of the learning environment (Majumdar, 1997). Recent advances in technology from distributed to interactive and finally to collaborative technology through the Internet and www connectivity, encourage the development of a new teaching environment, and a paradigm shift in the learning process.

The link between distance learning and telecommunications is becoming even stronger, yielding new solutions to old problems, innovative educational resources and new teaching/learning models. One of the most innovative and promising outcomes of this relationship is on-line education. It is a process whereby teachers and learners are linked up in a computer network, to create a full-fledged learning community, in which all individuals take an active part and make a valuable contribution to the group.

The educational arena of on-line learning is still in its infancy. While there are many institutions that are offering on-line courses, an in-depth understanding of the pedagogical issues related to on-line education remains an unexplored frontier. Many on-line courses are nothing but web pages combined with e-mail and chat rooms without any pedagogical foundation. Most of the current use of on-line education transfers traditional classroom instructions to on-line setting, recasting reading materials to web based materials, which rely on information acquisition and rote learning. Both reflect low level learning experiences.

While literature provides some evidence of the effectiveness of using on-line education (Kearsley, et. al., 1995), little is known about which learning strategies should be used for education and training. How to construct these electronic teaching and learning environments so that they are based on specific epistemologies or knowledge bases? What is an appropriate pedagogical framework for on-line learning?

This chapter discusses the characteristics of on-line education from epistemological and pedagogical perspective and suggests a conceptual framework for on-line learning based on co-operative/ collaborative learning strategies. It also discusses innovative ways to design on-line courses to enhance creativity and critical thinking processes.

Distance Education and Online Learning

Over the past century, the steady evolution in communication technology has considerably influenced the parallel development of Distance Education (DE) system. The first generation distance education largely consisted of correspondence courses based on printed material where interaction between the teacher and the learner was few and far between. Distribution technology was the foundation of this generation, which supported the instruction-centered approach along with the information transfer learning objectives. The underlying pedagogical assumption was to transfer information, rather than to interpret or change it. The second generation DE system incorporated various media such as television, audio recording and, in some cases, courseware delivered in floppy. Teacher and learner interaction remained virtually unaltered from the first generation even if supported by telephone, fax, and the like. Interactive technology was the foundation of this generation that allows the learner to progress at his or her own pace towards the goal of skill acquisition. The underlying pedagogical assumptions were learner-centered approach, to interpret information, and not merely receive it. Thus first generation and second generation of DE systems were based primarily on production and distribution of learning materials. Communication between learners was virtually non-existent and DE seemed merely to be conceived to bridge the geographical distance. Hence, education was no longer seen as a social activity centered on learner-to-learner interaction, but rather as an almost totally individual pursuit (Trentin, 1997). There was hardly anything that would differentiate DE from self-study.

The driving force beyond the development of third generation DE systems is the re-definition of learning as a social activity involving extensive use of the computer network. In DE terminology, the third generation system is also known as on-line education or network based education. In this environment all the actors in the learning process – learners, tutors and experts are connected via computer network to overcome isolation, enhance group interactivity and promote collective development. Collaborative technology is the foundation of this generation, which supports the learning objectives of mental model change in conjunction with learning team-centered education. The learning team centered approach creates an environment in which knowledge emerges and is shared through the collaboration of individuals within learning teams.

Kaufman characterizes the three generations as a progressive increase in learner control, opportunities for dialogue and emphasis on thinking skills rather than mere comprehension (Kaufman, 1989). More significantly it is leading to new types of educational organizations. The forthcoming Fig. 5.1 has been illustrated in the light of generations of distance education (White Paper on *Distributed learning: approaches, technologies and solution*, 1996)

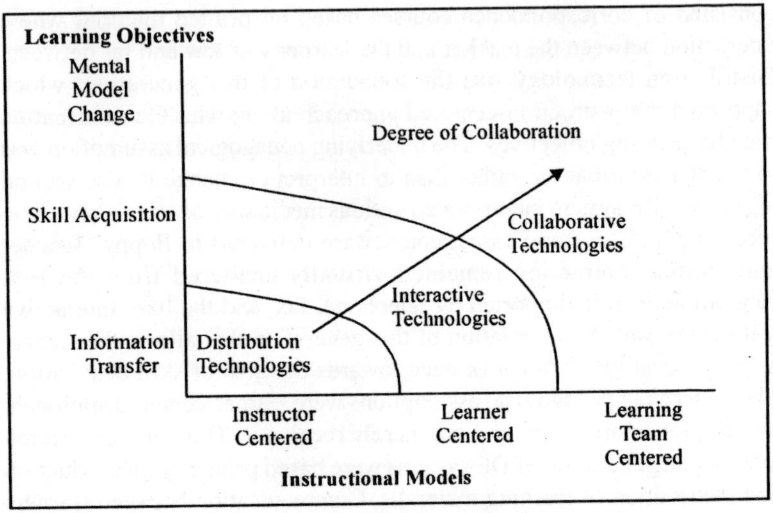

Fig. 5.1. Technology, learning objectives and instructional models in three generations of distance education

Pedagogical Framework: Objectivism, Constructivism and Eclectic Model

On-line educational environment can be developed based on two main schools of thought, the objectivist/objectivism versus constructivist/constructivism learning theories. Based on these approaches two types of learning on-line educational environments can be created.

a) On-line learning based on objectivism: In these learning environments, the student(s) by way of computer-mediated communication individually, learn by interacting with web based instructional materials stored at remote locations having minimum interaction with instructors/teachers and peers. As shown in the figure 5.2, 'student-A' and 'student-B' that are at distant places using their own computers interacts with the web based instructional material stored and delivered by the instructor from a remote place in an on-line learning environment.

This type of on-line learning environment is based on behavioral psychology, where a student is presented information, which they repeat back to the teacher (reproduction). It is based on learner's behavior on a particular kind of stimulus that can be modified by rewards and punishments (Inglis, 1996). The design is aimed at developing an on-line learning environment that is planned, structured, guided but often-rigorous study course(s) and tasks for individual reflection and problem solving. These planned courses have learning objectives, methods, materials and

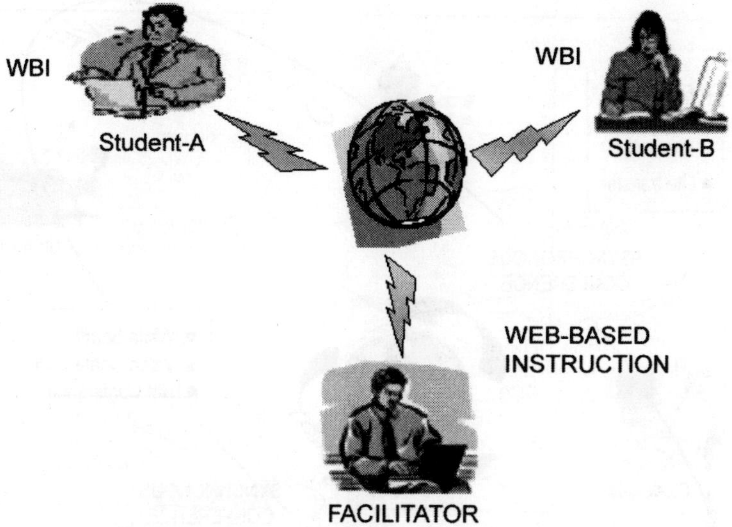

Fig. 5.2. On-line learning based on objectivism

evaluation scheme defined by the tutor himself. As far as the nature and authority of knowledge of learner is concerned, the learner individually undertakes and completes the task. This learning is based on the individual construction of knowledge and reproduction rather than on the social processes. It holds the idea that there is a body of objective knowledge that can be delivered to learners through presentation and explanation. Today's, online learning is dominated by the behaviorists school of thought and the use/role of technology is as a substitute for teacher for delivering instruction. Most current use of on-line learning environment transfers traditional classroom instruction to on-line setting, recasting reading into web based materials, lectures into on-line lecture notes or video clips and discussion into on-line conferencing (Bourne, et. al., 1997). Which is basically nothing but Internet based correspondence courses, which rely on information acquisition and reflect low-level learning.

The on-line learning environment based on objectivism suffers from a number of drawbacks, limitations and shortcomings (Mangal, 1990), as it does not encourage learner in their development of higher order complex skills like creative skill, problem solving, designing and decision-making abilities and construction of knowledge through social interaction. For this reason it has been subject to criticism, modification and refinement in a number of ways by the contemporary psychologists such as constructivists.

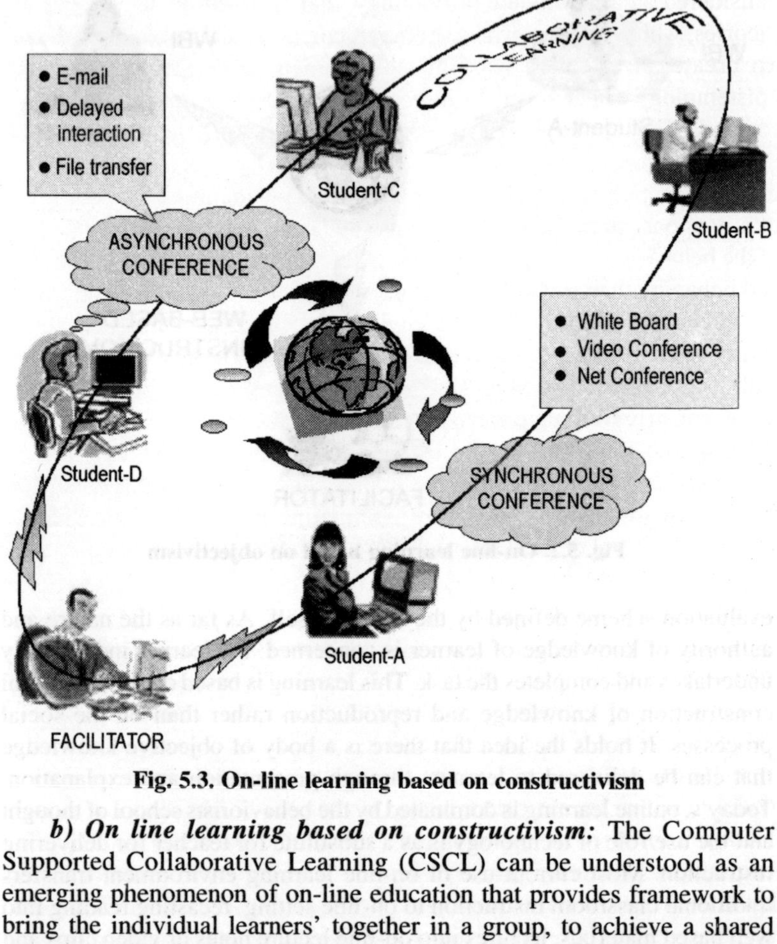

Fig. 5.3. On-line learning based on constructivism

b) On line learning based on constructivism: The Computer Supported Collaborative Learning (CSCL) can be understood as an emerging phenomenon of on-line education that provides framework to bring the individual learners' together in a group, to achieve a shared learning goal by way of managing their learning process. The constructivism school of thought is considered as the base of CSCL environment. A CSCL environment can be shown as in figure 5.3, where 'student-A; 'student-B', student-C' and 'student-D' who are situated at geographically distant places, collaborate, analyze, synthesize in a group with asynchronous and synchronous communication tools. They are based on a web-based curricula and works at a shared learning space to achieve a shared learning goal using their own computers. Learner works together to construct knowledge with peers.

Such collaborative learning environment develops complex skills like creative skill, problem solving, designing and decision-making abilities in the learner (Mc. Donald & Gibson, 1998). Constructivism can be considered as a worldview or ontology, that is based on set of learning theories, which fall somewhere between cognitive and humanistic views. To create an effective learning environment from this ontology an epistemology can be formed which can help to explain how knowledge is formed. The constructivist theory holds that knowledge has to be discovered constructed, practiced, and validated by each learner, learning involves 'active struggling by the learner'. The cognitive psychologists totally oppose to the stimulus-response and reward-punishment approach of the behaviorists. They maintain that there is something more to learning and behaving than just single responses to stimuli. The human mind does not accept information from its environment in exactly the same form and style as it is conveyed to him but he explores, interacts and reflects with it, to construct knowledge from experiences. Pedagogical methods using constructivist approach, includes collaborative learning, create learning situations that enable learners to engage in active exploration and social collaboration. Passive approaches to learning assume that students 'learn' by receiving and assimilating knowledge individually, independent from others (Johnson, 1979). In contrast, active approaches present learning as a social process, which takes place through communication with others. The learners actively construct knowledge by formulating ideas into words, and these ideas are built upon through reactions and responses of others. Collaborative learning refers to instructional methods that seek to encourage learners to work together on a given academic task. Collaborative learning is fundamentally different from traditional 'direct transfer' or one-way knowledge transmission model in which the instructor is the only source of knowledge and skill (Harasim, 1980). The conversation (verbalizing) multiple perspectives (cognitive restructuring) and arguments (conceptual conflicts resolutions) that arise in co-operative groups may explain why collaborative groups facilitate greater cognitive development than the same individuals achieve when working alone (Sharon, 1980 and Webb, 1989).

It is believed that constructing knowledge requires teaching and learning strategies and an environment, which present learners with knowledge building structures. There are three distinct viewpoints of the constructivist epistemology: a personality view, the social point of view and academic modes of knowing (Joyce and Weil, 1996). Each of these views provides important frameworks for the design and development of on-line courses. The personality view focuses on the students and their interaction. It focuses on the individual personality within the context and assist individuals with understanding themselves and their relationship to the world. The social point of view centers on the students constructing knowledge together. This framework establishes that knowledge building is based on the social processes provided by the context. The academic modes of knowing, also known as the academic inquiry view, centers on the academic disciplines. This view poses that the function of schooling is to provide students with the academic tool set to assist them with constructing knowledge. Information processing theory (Lange, 1965) provided a good framework for the use of academic tool set. In constructivism, learning is seen as a constructive process in which learners have an active role and learning is based on their cognitive functioning. The learners obtain new knowledge by constructing it on the basis of their earlier knowledge, upon their active functioning in continues interaction with the surrounding reality, and from other learners.

Based on the constructivist theories of learning, the online education environment can be designed assuming that learners themselves are an active agent of learning and they use social skills in undertaking and completing the group tasks. One of the limitations of these environment is "It does not always produce predictable learning outcomes". The facilitators should foster the constructive process of the learner and not attempt to closely control the process or result. The process of instruction and role of instructor should be as a guide to discovered knowledge', providing expert feedback during construction of knowledge through structured collaborative learning tasks. The learner themselves will have the thread of learning process. As far as the nature and authority of knowledge of learner is concerned, the learners in groups using their social skills and team skills based on his experiences undertake and complete the task.

c) On-line learning based on eclectic pedagogical approach: To ensure a uniform and predictable learning outcome in the CSCL environment based on constructive pedagogy, an eclectic andragogic/ pedagogic approach has been suggested. In these model most appropriate aspects of both constructivist and behaviorists perspectives has been used in the learning context. This type of learning based on eclectic andragogic/ pedagogic approach postulated from the two approaches will minimize the transactional distance as propagated by Moore, accommodating learner having multiple learning styles and learner who are not at a state of readiness for fully self-directed learning (Moore and Kearsley, 1996). This approach assumes that learners will learn fifty per cent by themselves and other fifty per cent by collaboration with others. The collaborative learning includes both synchronous and asynchronous learning component. However much emphasis will be on asynchronous component due to its inherent strengths of any time and anywhere learning. Synchronous interactions happen in real time, when learner and instructor are on-line at the same time having direct contact. In contrast, asynchronous interactions take place at the learners and teachers convenience. The key feature of an asynchronous learning is anytime anywhere learning utilizing the conferencing facilities of web. It may result in both immediate and delayed feedback. Immediate feedback happens when the program automatically links documents. Delayed interaction occurs due to the time required for the other learner to respond to list servers, forum and e-mail messages. Synchronous interactions require a set of tools that enable learner to see, hear, share, applications across the Internet. Complex topics can be explained directly using tools such as white boards, Internet relay chat, audio and video conferencing.

The figure 5.4 below illustrates the approach.

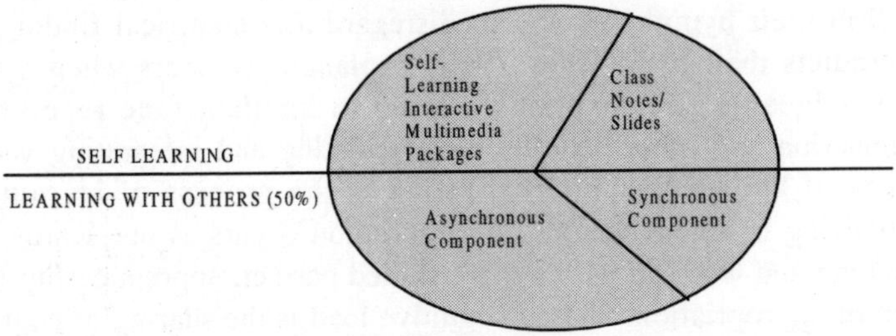

Fig. 5.4. Learning Components Based on Proposed Eclectic Model Coll

Collaborative Learning and On-line Education

Various theorists from socio-cultural to situated learning have stressed the importance of social interactions. It has been observed that "the student do not like to work alone, they like to share ideas with each other" (Chu, et. al., 1999). This strength of social interaction (learning) in form of collaborative learning and on-line learning being two different traditions of education had been difficult to be incorporated into on-line learning program for the learners at geographically distant places. But today, the collaborative/group ware tools can be used for social negotiation and group learning, enabling learner in groups learning, enabling learner in groups to interacts with more capable peers. Learning is distributed in an environment and among the learner. Knowledge comes out from community of learners who interact together. Students actively learning in cooperative groups have demonstrated an ability to generate higher-level reasoning strategies, greater diversity of ideas, more critical thinking, and increased creative responses as compared to those learning individually or competitively (Schlechter, 1990).

A variety of social-psychological mechanisms make collaborative learning effective (Dillenberg and Schneider, 1995), which includes:

a) Conflict or disagreement
b) The alternative proposal
c) (Self) explanation
d) Internalization
e) Appropriation
f) Shared cognitive load
g) Mutual regulation
h) Social grounding.

The conflict between learners postulates that when disagreement occurs between peers, social factors prevent learners to ignore conflict and force them to find out a solution. The alternative proposal referred to as the 'confirmation biases' subject tends to design only experiments that confirm their hypotheses and to disregard any empirical finding that contradicts their hypotheses. (Self) explanation occurs when a more knowledgeable peer explains a topic to another. One receives an explanation and other benefits by articulating and integrating various pieces of knowledge. Internalization is the process of learning by verbalizing in a conversation. Appropriation occurs as one learns from watching and working with a more skilled partner, apprenticeship is the form of appropriation. Shared cognitive load is the sharing of cognitive burden between learners implied by the task. Mutual regulation is the way of regulating partner's activities. Social grounding is the mechanism by which an individual attempts to maintain the belief that his partner has understood what he meant, at least to an extent, which is sufficient to carry out the task at hand. Group composition, task features and communication media plays an important role in implementing collaborative learning effectively.

It has been argued that the collaborative potential of computer conferencing enables learners to engage actively in their own knowledge building or knowledge creation, in three ways: idea generation, idea linking, and idea structuring (Harasim, 1980).

The four fundamental features of collaborative learning are:

- Learning being centered on student activities rather than teacher focused.
- An emphasis on students assisting each other to find answers to areas of common inquiry.
- Learning being based on the solving of problems by analysis and discussion by learner groups.
- An emphasis to promote creative and critical thinking.

But the question is, do we follow the above framework of collaborative dimension, while we design web courses? Are our strategies in web enhancing learner creative processes, critical thinking and problem solving skill? Do we exploit all the inherent capacity of conferencing facilities that is offered by web? But simply making an on-line conferencing available and asking learner to use it is not collaborative learning.

Developing an on-line course material for enhancing creativity require more than an understanding of hard technology i.e. bit & bytes, electronics & satellite, CGI, search engine or HTML. What we need to understand is the soft aspect of the technology that provides a framework to develop courses in Web to enhance creativity in collaborative environment.

A framework for pedagogical technique for computer-mediated communication has been organized into four communication paradigms. The paradigms are information retrieval, electronic mail, bulletin boards and computer conferencing. They have been further classified into four classes of techniques as characterized below (Paulsen, 1995).

- One alone technique: The on-line resources paradigm—on-line database, on-line journals, on-line libraries, and on-line application.
- One to one techniques: The e-mail paradigm—learning contracts, apprenticeships, internships, and correspondence studies.
- One to many techniques: The bulletin board paradigm-lectures, symposiums, and skits.
- Many to many techniques: The conferencing paradigm- debates, role-plays, discussion groups, brainstorming, forums, transcript-based assignments etc.

Most of the on-line courses utilize the first three classes of techniques, ignoring the many to many techniques, which is the core of collaborative learning environment. Some of the key co-operative learning techniques include (Paulsen, 1995, Harasim, et. al., 1995):

- Partner Activities and round robin Table: Sharing and summarizing deas through e-mail.
- Asynchronous Conferencing: Discussion & reflection through bulletin board.
- Synchronous Conferencing: Real time conferencing through relay chat, net meeting & video conferencing tools.
- Group Investigation: Selecting topic in a group, exploring individually and then compiling collectively.
- Project based Learning: Learning through project planning and development in a team.
- Other Activities: Panel discussion, symposia, debates, role-plays, discussion groups, brain storming and team competition in a group etc.

Creative Thinking on the Web

Researchers such as Davis, Perkins and de Bono have championed instructional techniques that address student's divergent or creative thinking (Davis, 1992, Perkins, 1986 and de Bono). On-line environment has provided a large array of tools and environment to implement instructional techniques that address the student's divergent or creative thinking. Web browsing software now exists to explore and search, find pattern and relationship, rank ideas, view results and send findings to peers and instructor. Apparently, the Web is an ideal tool to nurture the students willingness to take risks, commitment to task, curiosity, openness to experience, broad interest, originality, imaginative play, intuition, attraction to novelty, artistic ability, metaphorical thinking, problem finding, elaboration of ideas and breaking away from the norm, all of which are attributes of creative people (Davis, 1992, Starko, 1995 and Young). The anonymity of pen names and pseudo roles during electronic discussions encourages student idea experimentation and risk taking disclosure (Harasim, 1995). Some of the suggested techniques for Web to enhance creativity in electronic environment are:

- Brain storming and reverse brainstorming: Focus on Idea generation.
- Assigning thinking roles: Anyone in the roundtable is assigned a role.
- Creative writings: One starts writing, another expands the idea.
- Just Suppose: Just suppose you are education minister—what will be your priority?
- Idea-spurring questions: Suggestions to modify and improve.
- Semantic webbing: Give a word in the middle of semantic map; suggest attributes related to the concept.
- Simulation and Role-play: Role-playing in simulated environment.

It has been observed that discussion and interaction under asynchronous conferencing in different time and different place tend to be more extended and engaging for the learners than traditional environment. Learners can reflect their opinion in much relaxed way and their own convenient time, which creates a congenial environment for creative reflection.

Critical Thinking on the Web

Critical thinking is reasonable, reflective thinking that focuses on deciding what to believe or do. Learners learn to look at a concept or phenomena aware of their own biases and approach the situation objectively and logically. Creative thinking on the other hand is the ability to form new combination of ideas to fulfill a need or to understand a specific natural occurrence. Despite extensive divergent thinking avenues, enhancing critical thinking pathways may be an equally strong dimension of the Web. Some of the emergent ideas on critical thinking in Web are:

- Graphic Organizer: Emphasizing on spatial representation like model, Venn diagram etc. It facilitates critical thinking by helping learner to sort out the hierarchy and logical flow of ideas.
- Ranking Methods: To rank and categorize brainstorming ideas in web.
- Reflection: Writing, to think, activities for reflection and critical evaluation.
- Mock trail and debate: Encourage to come-up with arguments.
- Case-based Reasoning: Case study and comments.

Any activity which encompasses search for cause and effect, find pattern and relationships, rank ideas, develop timeliness, build taxonomies is a worthwhile exercise of critical thought (Bonk and Reynolds). In web, there are plenty of opportunities to enhance cause and affect relationship by using simulation and animation program in Web/CBT packages.

Guiding Principles

There are several guiding principles for designing effective on-line learning. These include:

- Present problem based learning environment
- Present authentic and realistic task
- Focus on construction of knowledge
- Promote active learning
- Use multimedia effectively
- Mix appropriate instructional strategies
- Design appropriate structured discussions
- Present contextual learning environment
- Focus on learning in groups

The role of a student in an on-line environment is that of a learner, and as well as a collaborator and a team member. There is a paradigm shift in educational practice of teaching and learning in network environment and knowledge explosion (Majumdar, 1999). Where learning through facts, drill and practices, rules and procedures was more adaptive in earlier days, now learning through projects and problems, inquiry and design, discovery and invention, creativity and diversity, action and reflection is more fitting for the present times. So there is a need to develop a conceptual framework on the pedagogical dimensions of on-line learning based on collaborative learning strategies. For this purpose, desirable shift required in each of the pedagogical dimensions of on-line learning are presented below:

Dimensions	*Undesirable*	*Desirable*
Pedagogical Base	Instructive Model	Eclectic Model based on Constructivism
Learning Focus	Content	Learning to Learn
Learning Strategies	Solely Interactive	Collaborative & Interactive
Learning Goal	External Controlled	Autonomous
Learning Theory	Behavioral	Cognitive
Teacher Role	Didactic	Facilitative
Delivery Modes	Fixed	Open
Learning Approaches	Surface	Deep
Learning Structures	Rigid	Flexible/ Modular
Instructional Models	Instructor Centered	Learning Team Centered
Learning Objectives	Information Transfer	Mental Model Change
Learning Methods	Passive	Active

Implications and Future Works

The way a learner learns in on-line setting has not been extensively studied. Designing and developing effective on-line courses require a new approach to various pedagogical dimensions of on-line environment. It requires knowledge of the new media from communication research, pedagogical perspective from educational research and group interaction from social psychological research. Each of these can be adapted, applied and integrated to help to explain what happen and why in on-line classes (Coppala, et. al., 1999). An instructional designer using on-line collaborative learning must integrate increased group work; work based learning and problem solving to encourage higher order thinking. Given the endless possibilities for higher order thinking and teamwork there is perhaps no debate that the world wide web has the power to generate novel learning strategies which will eventually be embedded in cognitive, social and cultural context (Majumdar, 2000). If on-line courses are designed incorporating the desired changes in pedagogical dimensions, the difference between teaching and training on the web and traditional methods can be profound.

REFERENCES

Bonk, J.C., Reynolds, H.T. "Learner-centered web instruction for higher-order thinking, teamwork and apprenticeship" Web based instruction, Ed B.H. Khan, *Educational Technology Publications* Englewood cliff, New Jersey. pp. 167-178.

Bourne, J.R., McMaster, E., Rieger, J., Campbell, J.O. "Paradigms for on-line learning: A case study in the design and implementation of an asynchronous learning networks course" *Journal of Asynchronous Learning Networks,* Volume-1 Issue2, August 1997.

Chu, K.C., Urbanik K.N., Yip S.K. & Cheung T.W. "The benefits of virtual teaching to engineering education." *The International Journal of Engineering Education,* Volume 15, Number 5, 1999, pp. 334-338.

Coppala N., Hiltz, S.R., and Rotter N. "Becoming a virtual professor: Pedagogical changes and ALN" *Fifth International Conference on ALN, University of Maryland, October,1999.*

Davis, G.A. (1992). *Creativity is forever* (3rd ed.). Dubuque, IA: Kendall/Hunt Publishing.

de Bono, E. *De Bono's thinking course: Revised edition* (3rd ed.). New York: Facts on File.

Dillenberg, P., Schneider, D. (1995). "Collaborative learning in the Internet" Proceedings, Fourth International Conference on CAI, Taiwan, S10-6 to S10-13.

Harasim, L. *Online Education: Perspective on a New Environment*, New York: Praeger/ Greenwood.

Harasim, L., Hiltz, S. R., Teles, L., Turoff, M. (1995). *Learning Networks: A field guide to teaching and learning online,* Cambridge, MA; MIT Press

Inglis, A. (1996). "Theories of learning in educational development: Relocating the paradigmatic divide" *Open Learning,* 11(2), pp. 28-37.

Johnson, D.W. (1979). "Conflict in a classroom: Controversy and learning", *Educational Research,* Vol. 49, pp. 51-70.

Joyce B and Weil M. (1996). *Models of Teaching*. Needham Heights, Mass Allyn & Bacon.

Kaufman, D. in Sweet, R. (Ed) (1989). *Post secondary distance education in Canada: Policies, practices & priorities*, Athabasca University/ Canadian Society for Studies in Education.

Kearsley, G., Lynch, W. & Wizer, D. (1995). "The effectiveness and impact of online learning in graduate education" *Educational Technology*, Nov-Dec, 35(6), pp. 37-42.

Majumdar, S. (2000). "Designing web based instruction to enhance creativity" accepted for publication and presentation in the *International Conference on Technological Creativity Development (ICICD)* to be held in Taipei, Taiwan, April 20-23.

Majumdar, S. (1999). "On-line Collaborative Learning" *Proceedings of the Fifth UNESCO – ACEID International Conference on reforming learning curriculum and pedagogy: Innovative vision for the new century.* Bangkok, Thailand, December 13-16, Vol. 1 pp. 72-73.

Majumdar, S. (1997). "Network based flexible learning: Prospects and challenges in the 21st Century: *Invited keynote address at the International Conference of Vocational Education and Training (IVETA '97)*, Helsinki, Finland, Aug 24-28, pp. 347–352.

Mangal S.K., (1990). "General Psychology", Sterling Publishers Private Ltd.

McDonald J. & Gibson, C.C. (1998). "Interpersonal dynamics and group development in computer conferencing" *The American Journal of Distance Education,* 12(1), pp. 6-21.

Moore, M.G & Kearsley G. (1996). "Distance Education Theory: A System View." *Belmont CA: Wadsworth.*

Paulsen, M.F. (Ed.) (1995). "The on-line report on pedagogical techniques for Computer-Mediated Communication," Oslo, Norway, August, *http://www.nki.no/~morten/*

Perkins, D.N. (1986). *Knowledge as Design*. Hillsdale, NJ: Lawrence Erlbaum Associates.

Schlechter, T.M. (1990). "The relative instructional efficiency of small group computer based training." *Journal of Educational Computing Research*, Volume 6(3), pp. 329- 341.

Sharon, S. (1980). "Co-operative learning in small groups: Recent methods and effects on achievement, attitudes and ethnic relations", *Review of Educational Research*, Vol. 50(2), pp. 241-247.

Starko, A.J. (1995). *Creativity in the Classroom: Schools of Curious Delight.* New York, Longman.

Trentin, A. (1997). "Telematics and on-line teacher training the POLARIES project" *Journal of Computer Assisted Learning*, Vol. 13, pp. 261-270.

Webb, N. (1989). "Peer interaction and learning in small groups", *International Journal of Educational Research*, 13(1) pp. 21-29.

White Paper on *Distributed learning: approaches, technologies and solution*: Lotus Development Corporation, August 1996.

6.

Educational Technology: What is It? Why It is?

Rajarshi Roy and Anjana Paira

In the present day of science and technology, whether we like it or not, but are unable to avoid the impact of science and technology over our lifestyle in the changing society. Irrespective of having a lower GDP in Indian economic scenario, mobile phone is a basic device for the common people now a days. It is one of the examples of impact of technology over human culture. Technology, in its crude sense, 'penetrated' in almost each and every walk of our life and culture. Whether impact of technology over human life is fair or foul, is a different issue of debate; however, it is difficult to ignore the impact of technology over human life.

Likewise, educational science is also not free from the influence of technology. Today it is a fact of life. Now-a-days, LCD projectors and other devices of the kind are of massive use in the field of education. These devices are assisting us to process information, as also for storage, preservation and transmission thereof. Infact these devices are helping to achieve the 'aim of education'. Educational technology evolved out of the fact to explore the scope of utilizing technological devices to achieve the aims of education.

Situationally, this concept of educational technology resulting confusions among the teachers, students and general public at large, which is experienced in the general forum of intellectual discourse in several occasions. The underlining reason of such confusion is mostly due to lack of knowledge base of 'Education' and ignorance of 'constructivism' supplemented with ultra modernism on part of a group of 'academicians', much keen to use each and every kind of technological gadgets in the process of teaching learning, without bothering the impact of such usage. The present chapter attempts to remove the confusions about 'Educational Technology'.

Educational Technology -What is it?

Educational technology emerged in Indian context since last around four decades. Emergence of educational technology is a resultant of use of various technical and technological devices and gadgets in the arena of pedagogical setup. As such, it is perceived by a section of people that educational technology is mere the application of technology in teaching learning situation. The trend of conceptualizing 'educational technology' provokes a section of educationist to comment that educational technology is the mechanization of educational process. Use of mechine in the process of education mostly takes place in three forms.

- Videotape, tape recorder, compact diskette, films and the devises of the kind are used *to preserve the existing knowledge.*
- Radio, television and projectors of various kinds are used *to transmit the knowledge* among the students and masses.
- Software packages and computers are in use for ease of research in education, leading to *advancement of knowledge.*

In nutshell, technology-based gadgets and devices of varied kinds help in the process of preservation, transmission and development of knowledge. Hence the use of such devises appears as 'educational technology' to a group of people, associated in academia. To them, educational technology is mere use of technology in education. These mechanical devices, which are based on technology, are termed as 'hardware'. So, to some, just use of hardware part in education appears as 'educational technology'.

However the contemporary educational psychologists, irrespective of schools, accept 'teaching' as 'art' and 'science' simultaneously. It is a fact that mere availability of technological devices and use thereof may not help in the process of learning without the basic knowledge of learning, i.e., knowing *how students learn.* In such scenario, learning will not be effective. Therefore teacher is aught to know how students learn. Effectiveness of technological gadgets depends upon the knowledge of the teacher about their uses. Modern educational technology aught to emphasis over these very dimensions of learning. These 'techniques of teaching', 'methodology, following which teaching takes place', and 'the task of teaching' together forming the bases of learning. These come under the purview of *learning technology*. Therefore all these techniques, methods and teaching are aught to come under the purview of 'educational technology'. These are technology of education, commonly termed as software. Hence, software dimension of education is believed by a section, to be educational technology.

From the forgoing discussion, two different concept of educational technology may evolve, which are presented schematically as follows:

Education → Technology IN Education → Hardware approach
Education → Technology OF Education → Software approach

However one is to keep in mind that availability and proper use of devices together should form the educational technology. As such, neither the hardware approach, nor software approach alone can be treated as 'educational technology' and should be considered complimentary to each other to perceive the real essence of educational technology.

In this backdrop, educational technology aught to be viewed as a synthesis of both hardware and software approachs to reach the goal of education.

Various educational practitioners are having different perceptions about educational technology. Citing a few of the definition will help deduce the concept of educational technology.

Professor E.E. Haddan, a professor of psychology, in his pioneering work, 'Evolution of Instruction' commented that 'Educational Technology is that branch of educational theory and practice, where it is concerned primarily with the design and use of message which control the learning processes. According to Hadden, educational technology possesses two dimensions. One is the theoretical dimension and the other is the practical aspect. The purpose of both the dimensions is to contribute for transmission of knowledge in the pedagogical setup.

In his work, 'The condition of learning', Professor Robert M. Gagne perceptualized educational technology as '...the development of a set of systematic techniques and accompanying practical knowledge for designing, testing and operating schools as educational systems'. He perceived it as a system. To him, educational technology is such a science, which will develop various techniques for the sake of proper planning and evaluate results thereof.

On the other hand, Psychologist Professor W.K. Richmond opines that educational technology is concerned to provide appropriately designing learning situations which holding in view the objectives of the teaching or training, bring to bear the best means of instruction'.

It is apparent from the above definitions that these psychologists emphasized over differing dimensions of educational technology, which includes 'educational theory and practices', 'concerned primarily with the design and use of message which control the learning process', 'to contribute for transmission of knowledge in the pedagogical setup', 'to develop set of systematic techniques and accompanying practical knowledge for designing, testing and operating schools as educational systems', and finally 'to provide appropriately designing learning situations for bring to bear the best means of instruction'.

At the present juncture of time, recognizing the need for emergence of educational technology, good many scholars from varied fields of knowledge, including educationists, psychologists and technocrats across glob are coming together and contributing towards the field. They formed several societies across globe and tried to define educational technology from differing viewpoints.

One such pioneering association is 'Association for Educational Communications and Technology', USA, abbreviated as AECT. AECT perceives, 'Educational Technology is a complex integrated process involving people, procedures, ideas, devices and organizations for analyzing problems and devising, implementing, evaluating, and managing solutions to those problems, involved in as aspects of learning'. Definitely, the definition is quite exhaustive and includes a wider range of dimensions.

Council of Educational Technology of UK defined educational technology in somewhat different way. To them, 'Educational technology is the development application and evaluation of system, techniques and aids to improve the process of human learning'.

The societies, councils and associations of educational technology across globe tried to encompass the dimensions of educational technology in varied ways. However the definitions in general failed to encompass the basic objectives of educational technology.

Hence it is desirable to emphasis over the objectives of educational technology. The ultimate aim of using any aids, technology or gadgets, in the sphere of education is to achieve the 'objectives of instruction'. Therefore, educational technology is aught to be the sciences of techniques and methods, by which the educational objectives can be achieved. We expect educational technology to contribute formulating objectives of instruction, plan and implement instruction successfully and help evaluate instruction.

The Issues

In this section an attempt has been made to identify and eradicate the general misconceptions about educational technology.

It is often observed that general hardcore engineering and technology is equated with educational technology by a group of 'scholars', belonging mostly from other disciplines, and not from education. However the two are not the same. General engineering and technology may help the process of teaching-learning activities. But it is not educational technology. The scope of general engineering and technology is restricted only within manufacturing of different teaching aids. General engineering and technology helps in the process of teaching by contributing gadgets, compact diskettes, audiovisual aids or the kind of teaching aids, and to its maximum extent, developing programmes for simulation, even being ignorant about the abcs of instruction. Therefore this contribution is 'indirect contribution' and supplementary by nature. Whereas, educational technology includes the following three basic components:

- Planning of teaching
- Organization of subject matters
- Planning and designing evaluation techniques for the students.

Educational technology thereby encompasses the entire process of teaching-learning, starting from *pre-active* phase through *interactive* till *post-active* phase. General engineering and technology may help only in the narrower phase, in restricted sphere of interactive phase only, mostly by contributing gadgets.

- A misconception prevails till date in Indian scenario to equate the use of teaching aids as 'educational technology'. In educational scenario, teaching aids are used to attain the objectives of instruction and to supplement learning. On the other hand, educational technology deals with framing content and curricula, content delivery strategies, each and any aspect of content delivery phase till evaluation phase. Therefore use of teaching aids, including electronic gadgets and audio-visual aids forms just a 'narrower part' of educational technology. These are mere supplementary by nature.
- Educational technology evolved in consonance with introduction of the concept of programmed instruction. Therefore some people think that use of programmed learning, teaching machines, programmed texts may be the educational technology. Here one is to consider that auto-instructional techniques are mere an insignificant part of educational technology. Here also technology is applied only to supplement the pedagogy. Whereas educational technology is applicable in the broader gamut of education.
- Since technology helps human to solve a great deal of problems, therefore a group feels that educational technology will solve all the problems of education. However it is not a fact. Its basic function is to help educationists in the process of teaching. Educational technology may solve a great deal of problems associated with education but unable to solve 'all the problems'.
- There is a misconception among the common people or those not much acquainted with education. They often feel that educational technology may reduce the importance of teacher in the teaching-learning scenario. These sorts of misconceptions are detrimental for the growth of educational technology. One should consider that qualitative excellence of product is dependent upon the input feeded in the system. Similarly quality of education is a dependent factor, which depends over the independent factor, 'quality of

information'. It is also impossible to 'produce' the content with the help of machines. Rather the teacher is to prepare the same. Therefore educational technology didn't curbed down the role of teacher in the educational scenario; rather the role of teacher got boosted. Educational technology may help teacher to perform his responsibilities.

Basic Objectives of Educational Technology

Educational technology is an important arena of academic discourse within the discipline: Education. In this age of specialization (rather super-specialization), it is considered as an independent area of knowledge. Though the area possesses the feature of dynamism and also application oriented, the experts are aught to carry on their studies with specified objectives. These objectives are quite broader and may be treated as objectives of educational technology. It is worthnoting that all these objectives are interrelated with the objectives of teaching-learning. Should we have a clear idea of objectives of educational technology, it would be easier to comprehend the concept of educational technology. Some such are as follows.

1. Determining behavioural objectives: It is essential to determine the behavioural objectives with a view to achieve the ultimate aim of education; this transformation is much required so that those behavioural objectives can be easily measurable. It is expected that educational technology will help us to analyze the philosophical aims of Education and to determine the behavioural values over the units. These will be treated as behavioural objectives of education.

2. Analyzing students' behaviour: One of the important roles of educational technology is to analyze and thereby to identify the students' behaviour in the learning situation. It is essential to reliably explore the student to plane the future teaching learning activities. Planning effective instruction is only possible, should the teacher is aware about the students' psyche. Therefore, one of the important objectives of educational technology is to explore the student in terms of its behaviour.

3. Content analysis: Another major important objective of educational technology is to analyze and organize the content to be delivered to the students. Teaching become effective, should the subject contents are organized keeping parity with the psychopedagogical maturity of the learner. Educational technology is expected to perform the role and thereby help in the process of instruction.

4. Determining motivational techniques: It is difficult to carryon the instruction in the absence of motivated learner. Educational technology is expected to contribute in this context in the form of exploring and determining the appropriate motivational techniques.

5. Determining techniques and methods: Educational technology aught to perform the activity to determine appropriate learning techniques, method of teaching as also to select appropriate instructional material. Appropriate techniques and methods are expected to make learning an easy task for the students as also an easy task for teacher to deliver the content, in tune with learning style of the learner.

6. Evaluation: Educational technology is also supposed to perform the task of evaluating the teacher, the student, the content, and overall, the entire pedagogical setup. These evaluation is prerequisite to explore the remedial steps and thereby to accord feedback to the system.

A glance perusal of the above stated objectives of educational technology categorically reveals that educational technology aims to improve the entire educational system and structure. Different fields of education perform similar roles. The basic difference stands with the other fields of education and educational technology is in terms of their perceptual differences. Varying aspects of educational technology and its subject matter will help explore the differences.

Aspects of Educational Technology

Educational technology is a complex connotation. Knowledge of technology is applied in various dimensions of Education. To comprehend the concept of educational technology, it is essential to explore the aspects of educational technology. As per psychologists, educational technology is comprised of three components.

The learner use to join the system with their entry-behaviour. After attending the instruction, they use to acquire some new behaviour in tune with specified instructional objectives. Educational technology takes care the each steps starting from entry behaviour to the end output as passouts with terminal behaviour in the system. Starting from entry-behaviour to terminal behaviour, educational technology encompass the following three stages:

Input (Entry Behaviour)	**Process** Teaching Learning Process	**Output** Behavioural changes in learners

As like in any mechanical system, we may have the three components; the same is inducted to elaborate the concept of educational technology too.

Here, entry behaviour refers to the maturity level of the student in terms of command over the content at the outset, prior to deliver the content A teacher aught to know the level of the student, prior s/he proceed for extending instruction to the student. The process refers to the teaching-learning process and output refers to the end product or the passouts of the system.

Entry-behaviour of the student is determined on the basis of the following five factors:

1. Past experience, abilities and level of the motivation.
2. Level of comprehension.
3. Effectiveness of prior teaching methods over the student.
4. Effectiveness of teaching methods.
5. Effectiveness of teaching aids.

In the interactive phase, i.e., the teaching-learning phase, the following issues are taken into consideration:

1. Preparation of an environment, conducive to present the content.
2. Identification and application of teaching style and methods.
3. Identification and application of appropriate teaching aids in tune with achieving the instructional objectives.
4. Identification and application of appropriate communication techniques in tune with achieving the instructional objectives.
5. Reinforcement for enhancing student's participation in teaching.
6. Teacher-pupil rapport.
7. Inter-pupil rapport.

The terminal behaviour generally refers to the output of instruction. The factors considered under this stage are as follows:

1. Analysis of content.
2. Determining the appropriateness of educational objectives.
3. Effectiveness of methods and techniques applied.
4. Evaluation of pupils' behaviour.

Educational technology aught to consider all the above stated factors to make teaching effective.

Educational Technology: Its Steps

Educational technology may be compared with a complex system. Effectiveness of educational technology enhances the effectiveness of its components and the synergic output of the gestalt system can be achieved. This approach of educational technology is deduced from the systems approach. Here comes the question, 'what a system is?'

A system refers to an assemblage of some interconnected and interacting components. The parts of the system are termed as elements. Every system is operational within a boundary, may be imaginative. The part falling beyond the boundary is termed as system-environment or the environment of the system. The system, which possesses no impact from the system-environment, is termed as closed system. On the other hand, a system, which reciprocates with the system-environment, is termed as open system. Open system possesses the transformation function. A system may operate independently, or may be a combination of various sub-systems. A system, possessing characteristic feature of combination of various sub-systems is known as combined system. In a combined system, various sub-systems possess the feature of open system too some extent.

Any given system functions to achieve the system goals. A system use to receive the input from the system-environment, processes the input against the resistance within the system, and thereby produces output. Synchronization of the process may help curb-down the system resistance.

Educational technology use to consider 'education' as a system. As a system, education possesses three components, the input subsystem, the process subsystem and the output subsystem. This systems approach in education place much emphasis over the 'process' and 'output'. Principles of education also emphasize over the 'process' and 'output'. Principles of education deal with the do—how to improve the process of education through improvement of instruction. In this sense, educational technology helped education for its improvement in a scientific way, which ultimately focuses over minimization of input and maximization of output.

The steps involved in this process are as follows:

First step: In this step, prior learning of the learner are evaluated. For the purpose, appropriate devices are administered. In the cognition-learning phase, these devices are mostly 'tests', which generally measure the academic achievement of the learner. Basic purpose of administering these tests is to explore the entering behaviour, as also to identify the level of needs and demands of the learner from the system. As per terminology of Educational technology, this stage is termed as '*determining entry profile*' of the learner.

Second step: Subsequent to determining entry profile of the learner, *objectives of learning and teaching are to be determined.* Since educational technology is objective (and not subjective) by nature, hence, objectives are formed in such a way so that those are expressed in behavioural term and are measurable. Usually, these consist of five components, such as *performer, task, action, condition* and *criteria*. Evaluation strategies of achieved behavioural objectives are also determined in this step.

Third step: The step *determines the desirable changes in the behaviour of the learner,* in consonance with stated behavioural objectives. All the unit behavioural objectives are enlisted in this phase. In nutshell, the content is determined in this step, apart from analysis and organization of the same.

Fourth step: This step deals with *strategies of presentation of the content*. Teaching aids, teaching methods, teaching materials and teaching strategies are determined in this step.

Fifth step: It is already stated that teaching is not a mechanical process. As like hardware, software is also essential for effective teaching. To achieve maximum output, with comparatively minimum input, motivation is indispensable. The step deals with the *specifying possible motivational techniques to be adopted in the process of teaching.*

Sixth step: The step is dedicated for actual transaction of instruction through *active teaching*. In this phase the teacher will frequently shift his role from teacher to learning assistant; will modify his style of teaching in tune with the learning style of the learner and take care to ensure learning.

Seventh step: After the active teaching, the teaching needs to be evaluated. Hence the output of the system is subject to *evaluation*. These evaluations are based on the specified behavioural objectives. To carryon the same, testes are kept ready in hand. Now, on evaluation, if the result thereof appears positive, the same is carried on for future instruction.

Eighth step: In case the result of the evaluation appears negative, it is to be presumed that the system bears fault. Hence it is the phase to *diagnose the fault in the system*.

A teacher, who uses the steps, stated above and accordingly uses to extend the instruction to the learners, is using the educational technology for the betterment of instruction and thereby enhancing the efficacy and effectiveness of the system.

Application of Educational Technology

Educational psychologists introduced some new terminologies while contributing educational technology in the arena of education. Often such terminologies result in confusion to the general mass to comprehend the concept of educational technology. The major three components of educational technology are:

- Teaching technology,
- Instructional technology; and
- Behavioural technology.

These major three terminologies are often overlapping in terms of the steps they follow and sometimes integrated and interrelated.

Teaching Technology

Teaching is an individualized social activity, performed in restricted social system, possessing similarity in terms of social atoms and structure. As like learning, it is a process of development. Teaching is a system of activities, which together facilitates learning through interpersonal relationship. Teaching technology is an applied science. It is the systematic application of philosophical, scientific and sociological knowledge to teaching for achieving some learning objectives. Application of technology in the process of teaching is based on some established principles of education. These are:

1. Teaching is a scientific process, comprising two components, *content* and *communication.* In other words, teaching thrives to present the content through communication. A single concept can be presented at memory-level, or at comprehension level or even at higher reflective level, i.e., presentation of content is a complex task and the task may be made easy through application of scientific techniques. Apart, ensuring communication between teacher and the taught is an important task in teaching. Usually teacher use to present the content to the students through numerous verbal and non-verbal techniques. Here the teacher uses to communicate with the student, which can be improved upon.
2. Learning can be initiated through teaching environment. Learning may be controlled by creation of appropriate teaching environment and the same may boost the level of motivation among the learners.
3. The third principle of learning technology proposes that learning can be enhanced by modeling teaching in tune with the level of maturity of the learner.
4. Teaching can be improved through application of scientific and technological knowledge.
5. Technology may support and improve teaching skill.

Based on the above stated five principles, psychologists and educationists are tempted to use technology in the teaching-learning process. Application of educational technology may take place in the following four stages of education:

1. Planning of teaching: In this phase the content is analyzed and behavioural objectives are deduced scientifically in consonance with analyzed content.

2. Determining teaching methods and techniques: Appropriate teaching methods and techniques are determined to obtain the behavioural objectives. These teaching methods and techniques are used during teaching.

3. Motivation: Identification of appropriate motivational techniques and using those during teaching.

4. Evaluating teaching: Evaluation of teaching is carried out to observe to what extent behavioural objectives are achieved.

Psychologists opined that teaching technology helps improve the entire process of teaching-learning. This is possible through satisfying the objectives of instruction. Individualized learning can be improved upon by using learning technology. It also enhances the teaching skill of the teacher. Teacher may well perform the teachers' task like diagnostic function, prescription and evaluative function.

Instructional Technology

Instruction is the heart of teaching. Sequel of systematic actions, which include learning in individual, is known as instruction. Instructional technology is the combination of techniques, which helps to achieve the stated objectives of instruction. As such, application of various psychopedagogical principles to enhance the efficacy of instruction is known as instructional technology. Instructional technology evolved in the psychopedagogical-testing laboratory. Programmed learning is an area of application of instructional technology. Hence, instructional technology and programmed method of learning proceeds in consonance.

Instructional technology is based on some experimentally proved principles. These are as follows:

a. Learning-content can be splited into small slices and those can be separately presented through instruction.
b. Synthesizing the components of content can create favourable learning environment.
c. During extension of instruction in the learning phase, students can be motivated to learn effectively.
d. Learning (acquainting with the content) is an individualized phenomenon.
e. Learner learns in consonance with its felt need and capacity (to learn).
f. Learner can learn even without the presence of teacher.

Based on the above principles, content of instructional technology is formulated. Instructional technology mainly deals with programmed method and its associated concepts. Basic principles of programmed learning, principles of formulating programmes, application of technological devices in the programme are dealt in instructional technology. Instructional technology mainly helps to achieve the cognitive objectives of instruction. It mostly takes care of the individual learner in the process of ease-learning by enhancing comprehension. Apart, it helps develop learning theories too.

Behavioural Technology

Psychology is the science of behaviour. On the other hand, learning is the change of behaviour. Education aims to bring changes among the learners. However, Educational technology don't discuss directly about the behaviour of the learner. Technology that applied to bring changes in the learners' behaviour is restricted only within instructional technology and teaching technology. Behavioural technology deals only with teacher's behaviour. However in its true sense, it is not supposed to be restricted within teacher's behaviour. Behavioural technology is aught to encompass the behaviour of professionals irrespective of profession. However, behavioural technology applied to education may restrict only within the behaviour of the teacher. Therefore it may be opined that behavioural technology in education is the application of scientific knowledge in modification of teacher's behaviour. It is often treated as 'training technology' too.

Behavioural technology possesses certain basic principles. These are as follows:

1. Teacher's behaviour is observable in the classroom set-up.
2. Teachers' behavioural characteristics are measurable.
3. Teachers' behaviour possesses relative significance.
4. Teachers' behaviour possesses social and psychological significance.
5. Teachers' behaviour is modifiable/ can be changed.

Based on the principles of behavioural technology, educational technology contributed several devices to modify teachers' behaviour.

The content of behavioural technology deals with

1. Theories and principles of teacher's behaviour.
2. Methodology to study teacher's behavior in classroom setup.
3. Methodology to analyze and interpret teachers' behaviour.
4. Teachers' behaviour model in classroom.
5. Microteaching.
6. T-group teaching

The behavioural objectives of teaching can be fulfilled with the help of Behavioural technology. It also supplements to improve the teaching skill of the teacher.

Postscript

The ultimate aim of educational technology is to improve the pedagogical process. Within a narrower span of time, educational technology deduced a hermeneutic approach of development, often faced by counter questions from different schools of thoughts and disciplines. The field, irrespective of dimensions and schools of thought are engaged in developing the system of education and thereby for betterment of human society. Now a days many good instructional designs are in use in varying educational setups. These are the contribution of Educational technology. Training psychology, cybernetic psychology and system analysis are the few examples in this context. These dominos of knowledge are helping to control and evaluate teacher's behaviour. Also it contributes a unique concept 'teaching theory', in retrospect with learning theory. Teaching models are the outcomes of this teaching theory only.

PART B
EDUCATIONAL TECHNOLOGY AND TEACHER

7.

Technologically-minded Primary School Teacher
A CASE STUDY—LATVIA

Dzintra Iliško and Svetlana Ignatjeva

A younger generation of children is grown up in a multimedia environment. Young people are bombarded with immense amount of information. Many talented children are creating their ideas in multiple formats from text, audio recordings, video, and music to mixed media. The increasing availability of wireless and mobile technology opens possibiiities for new innovative pedagogies. As the technology increases, schools and teachers need to be open in restructuring themselves in ways to react to these changes. Therefore, this is essential to make a good use of technologies in the classroom and doing inquiry. The paper is aimed to examine primary school teachers' assumptions about the use of technology in teaching, conducting inquiry themselves and with the primary school children. Technology is neither good nor bad. The use of technologies in inquiry and teaching must be pedagogically sound. The use of technology in the classroom and research with children depends on evaluation of all weaknesses and strength in order to ensure the effective use of technology. This depends on teacher's style, knowledge, being comfortable with the use of technologies, inner persuasion, the mode of chosen inquiry, as well from the other factors. Teachers need to understand appropriate circumstances and conditions for the use of various technologies. The choice to use technologies should be derived from the needs of learners in the particular context in which learning takes place.

Participants and Methods of Study

The paper explores primary school teachers' perceptions of their role when teaching and doing inquiry with children with the use of technologies. A self-reported questionnaire was designed to study primary school teachers' attitude towards the use of technology for teaching and research. The authors are in agreement with the argument of Levin and Wadnany (2006) that this is complicated to make generalizations from teachers' beliefs with self-reported data alone, therefore the data is supported by semi-structured interviews conducted for the purpose of this study with six teachers. Questionnaire data was collected from 123 primary school teachers who were attending in-service courses. The participants geographically represented four regions of Latvia: Latgale, Zemgale, Vidzeme and Kurzeme. 63 per cent of all participants were holders of bachelor degree, 15 per cent of them had a Master degree in education. All respondents were graduates of higher education. The participants ranged in age from 21–66 years. The response rate of participants was 100 per cent (123) primary school teachers. According to teacher's experience of work in the educational settings, teachers were divided in the following groups: (1-5, 6-15, 16-25 years of work) (mean = 17.5). 93 (75.6%) of all teachers stated that they have had an experience of organizing research with primary school children. 75 per cent of teachers described themselves as competent to carry out research work with the primary school children. To determinate primary school teachers' technological competency, the authors have identified 24 indicators, such as 'I process information with the help of SPSS', 'I analyze information designed in graphs', ' I know how to find needed information in electronic sources', 'I participate in the discussion forms in the internet educational portals.' Each indicator was analyzed in five point scale: 5 – 'I can do it better than others', 4 – 'I can do this well', 3 – 'I can do it', 2 – 'I partly can do it', 1 – 'I cannot do without the help of IT teacher.' First, item discrimination indices were used to address the validity of the items on the scale, that is, the extent to which the items tap the attributes they were intended to assess. Second, varimax rotation was carried out to determine the validity for the subscales.

Defining Technologies

There are numerous kinds of modern technologies available in the market. Still, the printed textbooks occupy a dominant position in formal education. Teachers use printed textbooks; prepare handouts because this is more accessible and more portable means of teaching. In comparison to books, television produces 'passive, mindless un unimaginative' recipients (Greenfield, 1984). Books provide a foundation for a scientific thinking. In combination with the open and constructivist approaches toward teaching, printed materials are a good medium for a deep learning. Harasim (1995) offers a good description of knowledge construction process with the help of printed materials: deep learning 'grows out of interaction with information and ideas – reconstructing ideas, setting ideas within frameworks, viewing multiple perspectives on ideas and posing theories or hypotheses about ideas' (p. 98). One of the critiques of using technologies in education and research is a lack of communication with peers or colleagues. As Bates (2005) argues, good textbook or printed materials can cause high level of reflection in the learner; similarly, well designed computer programs can offer a variety of alternative responses and ways to evaluate between them, thus offering a rich range of feedback and interactivity for learners. Video-conferencing is also a good medium for interaction between teachers, though this means of communication is expensive and is time and place dependent. One of the mostly used technologies is a computer. One reason of a widespread use of Internet is that most students have access to the Internet and their own computer. Internet activities have been incorporated into inquiry, both in formal and informal modes of teaching. Many face-to-face teaching contexts in schools of Latvia are successfully replaced by technology, particularly in science subjects. Schools that participate in European sponsored projects, were equipped with the latest technologies for showing children simulated experiments digitally. The use of whiteboards becomes a regular practice in many schools as well. Every new technology develops certain mindset (Mishra, Spiro, Fedotovich, 1996). For example, invention of a movable print in the 15th century caused changes in all spheres of life in Europe. Print created texts that are mobile, presentable, led to fundamental changes in human cognition.

The Symbiosis of Technologies and the Practice of Teaching

In order to understand teachers' attitude in regards the use of technologies, one needs to understand the complex nature of all underlying factors that determine the use of technologies. As Harris, Mishra & Koehler (2009) suggest, the symbiotic interaction of technologies with the *content knowledge* and *pedagogical competency* determine the use of technologies. Pedagogical competency includes teachers' goal, purpose, values, and strategies used, as well as many other factors. The authors (Harris, Mishra & Koehler, 2009) introduce the term '*technological pedagogical knowledge*' that includes teachers' knowledge about pedagogical advantages and constraints of a range of technological tools and resources as they relate to appropriate pedagogical designs and strategies. Several studies have been carried out to examine the role of technologies in teaching and research (Agostino, 1999, Ferdig, 2006, Becker & Riel, 1999). As Ferdig (2006) argues, the value of use of technologies in teaching should be viewed in the context of purpose for which it was created. The use of technologies also depends upon the pedagogical categories such as pedagogical goals, the purpose of teaching, people, and the context. Technologies should offer interesting and challenging content; technologies should provide learners with a sense of ownership, and to create opportunities for students' active participation. As Ferding (2006) stresses, there is a symbiotic interaction between the technology and the established practice of teaching. Also, the use of technologies requires continual learning, adaptation, improvisation and instant decision-making (Becker & Riel, 1999). Several studies (Yuen & Ma Will, 2008; Rosenberg, 2001; Lawton & Gerschner, 1982; Askar & Umay, 2001; Elliott, 2001) indicate that successful use of technology depends on teacher's attitudes and the acceptance of technology. These are teachers' beliefs that guide and determine the use of the technologies in research and teaching (Cuban 2001; Fullan, 2003; Palak & Walls, 2009). According to Calderhead (1996), teachers' beliefs, as well as teacher's thinking comprise the broader concept of teacher cognition. Teachers' educational beliefs about technology enable them to translate those beliefs into classroom practice. Ertmer (2005) discusses that establishing a clear understanding of relationships among these concepts, will lead to improving teachers' practice related to teacher technology use. As Ertmer (2001) stresses, teachers' pedagogical beliefs go deeper than technological capability or accessibility; beliefs define how teachers teach and do research with and without technology. Marcinkiewicz (1993) argues that full integration of technologies in the classroom setting is a distant goal unless there is reconciliation between teachers and computers. This is an issue of values and teacher's beliefs, align with other financial, institutional and personal factors. Several studies (Knezek & Christensen, 2000) also emphasize that teacher advances in technology integration require changes in teachers' attitude rather than skills. A number of studies (Cuban, 2001; Judson, 2006; Windschitl & Sahl, 2002) indicate that the use of technologies support teachers' existing style of teaching and approach towards organizing research with children. Another significant factor that determines the use of technologies is teachers' familiarity and skills to work with technologies. The teacher will display a higher level of use of technologies, if the teacher perceives herself/himself as competent in use of technologies. If the teacher views him/herself as less competent in using technology, there will be more hesitation to use technologies in teaching and research. As Kurbanoglu, Akkoyunlu, and Umay, (2006) discuss, that teachers' technological literacy is a complex concept that incorporates evaluating, synthesizing, and 'using information appropriately, ethically and legally, once it is accessed from media, electronic or print sources' (p. 730).

Research Findings

Almost all teachers and students use technologies (computers, mobile phones, cameras) both, in varied and extensive ways. All teachers reported that their schools use some kinds of electronic learning devices. Teachers use technologies most frequently to get in touch with parents, to post grades, and to prepare materials for the classroom use. Still, face to face teaching still is one of the most required forms of teaching. Teachers tend to teach in the same way that they themselves were taught. They had received little exposure to technologies during their schooling. First, teachers need to be familiar with technologies before they use them in the classroom. While technologies are available in a great range of possibilities, great demands are also placed on the teacher. This observation holds true to the group of teachers who participated in the study. Teachers have not integrated technology in the elementary school curriculum yet. Most teacher respondents held favorable views regarding technologies, but 56 per cent had reservation about the use of technologies in the classroom and inquiry. In order to learn about teachers' technological competency the authors have identified 24 indicators. Factor analyses allowed to distinguished three groups of factors: IK1 – teachers' technological competency to use IT in their teaching in research, to gather, to process and to present information with the help of information technologies; IK2 – teachers' competency to teach and to carry out research by gathering, processing and presenting ir.formation without the help of informational technologies; IK3 – teachers' communicative competence with children and other teachers in virtual environment. Factor analysis leads to the following conclusions.

1) Teachers' age is one of the factors that determine teachers' ability to process the information. Teachers in the age group from 46-60 can gather and proceed information quite well but without the help of IT, while younger teachers (from 21-35) evaluate their skills to use IT quite high.

2) Teachers' experience of work is another factor that determines teachers' use of IT. Teachers whose experience in the education setting ranges from 25-40 can process information very well, though without the use of IT, while younger teachers (5 years of work experience) choose IT as a tool for teaching and processing and presenting information. Teachers with longer experience of work are also encouraging their children to use IT in presenting their project work though they do not feel comfortable in using IT themselves.

3) Geographical locations also are of the factors that point to differences in teachers' use of the IT in their teaching and research. In those regions of Latvia where more emphasis has been pain in training teachers' IT skills, teachers competency to use IT skills is much higher than in regions where less attention has been paid for developing teachers' technological literacy.

4) The fourth factor is teachers' education. Teachers with Master degree, who had sufficient time developing their IT competence in processing data with data processing computer programs, are more willing to use IT technologies in their teaching in doing research with their children. Also, teachers with master degree claim participating in communicative activities with other teachers in virtual learning environments (in educational forums).

Factor analysis points to the following regularities:

1) Correlation between teachers' competency to organize teaching and research (F2) and their competency in gathering and processing data with the help of IT (IK1); ($r1 = 0.219$; $p1 = 0.015$; $r2 = 0.215$; $p2 = 0.017$)

2) Teachers' methodological competency to organize learning process and research and teachers' competence to use IT ($r = 0.186$; $p = 0.04$). The correlation is direct and statistically significant.

Almost all teachers admit that one-way linear transmission model of teaching must be enriched with the more autonomous and self-directed and more individualized forms of teaching. They admit that the model of transmission of information from teacher to student practiced in the contemporary schools is no longer efficient in the society where knowledge is changing so rapidly. Children need to acquire new skills how to critically analyze the information and to participate actively in the society. All teachers inquired for the purpose of this study are familiar with the use of Internet. As the main functions of Internet used in teaching and inquiry is communication via e-mail, finding information for teaching and inquiry, and a video-chat with friends. Rapidly, Internet for them and for their children becomes two-way, asynchronous communication with their friends. Video-chat is used mainly for personal reasons and less for the educational purposes or work related activities. For the work reasons, teachers prefer to use face-to-face instruction with their children and colleagues at the workplace, though they claim having good skills of video-conferencing. Teachers pointed to another critical factor that determines their choice to use technologies in their teaching and inquiry. If technology breaks down, this can disrupt the learning process. Another issue to be discussed is teachers' knowledge about the latest technologies. As the study indicates, sometimes children exceed their teachers in the use of latest technologies. Teachers need to meet many challenges not to be outdated in use of technologies both in teaching and doing research with children. There is an evident gap between teachers and a new generation. Teachers have not learned how to use technologies in all its offered variety. As Luke (2003) states, the understanding of teachers' views in regards of use of technologies is necessary with regards to future developments of technology and research and teaching integration in light of constructivist and post-structualist call for the reconceptualization of concepts of teaching. The authors have evaluated teachers' attitude towards the use of technology in the context of a number of socio-cultural and historic perspectives in which teachers are located. Teachers' historical background was also considered as important factor that determined how teachers framed their work and choices. Teachers tend to incline to familiar and favorable teaching approaches on which they built their current practices. Almost all teachers viewed technology in a positive light. They use the following functions of technologies: (1) finding information; (2) designing worksheets; (3) communication with friends; (4) communicating in educational forums with other teachers. Teachers used technologies as a facilitator rather than a catalyst for change. As teachers reported, inquiry with the use of technologies offer transformative learning activities for both teachers and students by the use of web-based resources, computer-simulated discovery and exploration. Though, teachers often lack clear vision how and why technology can be used to support educational practice (Roblyer, 1993).

Conclusion

Technologies occupy modest but useful role in education. The technology provides the opportunity to teach differently by reaching the needs of younger generation and meeting the needs of many types of students. The need to reshape schools to support the use of technologies in both teaching and research is one of the challenges the school is facing today. Technology helps to teach in a wide variety of ways. Technologies need to be used not for their own sake but for the sake of advancing students' learning and understanding.

The use of technologies in inquiry with children opens the space for more autonomous and self-directed students who become 'meta-behaviorally active participants in their own learning processes involved in reorganizing and reconstructing their existing knowledge with new knowledge' (Zimmerman, 1989, p. 4). Technologies cannot occupy teachers' role, but rather can be used as a tool that can mediate interaction between pupils and between pupils and teachers. Technologies should become a context for social interaction.

When technologies are being used, both teachers and students need to take in new roles, different from the ones in the traditional classrooms.

The challenge is to train a generation of teachers to make a maximum use of the digital world around them. As the study indicates, teacher's role in digital learning environment is influenced by their beliefs and perceptions about teaching and research regardless technology. The use of technologies has to fit into the teachers' pedagogical view of teaching and research. When teachers decide to introduce technologies in their teaching, first, they need to ask the question why technologies should be used.

This is essential to build up teachers' confidence in using technology in general that would increase their willingness to use technologies in teaching and research. Developing teachers' positive attitude towards technologies should become a key factor for integrating technology in teaching. Teachers should be provided training opportunities before they are able to use them in the classroom.

The number of issues needs to be further explored. The authors open the ground for the debate whether the use of technology replaces traditional methods of teaching or offers a new approach toward teaching and doing inquiry with children. How teacher beliefs influence the use of technology in the educational setting? What are appropriate instruments for measuring teachers' beliefs? Which are contextual factors that determine teachers' use of technologies in their teaching and research? To what extend can we expect teachers to use technologies in their classrooms and research? Are teaching and research in classrooms with use of technologies differing from teaching in the environment in which no technologies are used.

REFERENCES

Agostino, A. (1999). The relevance of media as artifact: technology situated in context. *Educational Technology & Society*, 2, 4.

Askar, P. & Umay, A. (2001). Pre-service elementary mathematics teachers' computer self-efficacy, attitudes towards computers, and their perceptions of computer enriched learning environments. In Willis, D.A, Price, J.D. & Willis, J. (Eds.). *Technology and Teacher Education Annual*, AACE, Charlottesville, VA, 2262-3.

Bates, A.W. (2005). (2nd ed.). *Technology, E-learning and Distance Education.* Canada: Routledge Press.

Becker, H.J. & Riel, M.M. (1999). *Teacher Professionalism and the Emergence of Constructivist: Compatible Pedagogies.* Irvine, CA: Center for Research on Information Technology and Organization.

Calderhead, J. (1996). Teachers: Beliefs and knowledge. In Berliner, D. & Calfee, R. (Eds.). *Handbook of Educational Psychology*. New York: Macmillan Library Reference, 709-725.

Cuban, D. (2001). *Oversold and Underused Computers in the Classrooms.* Cambridge, MA: Harvard University Press.

Elliott, A. (2001). Student teacher's information technology experiences in schools. In Willis, D.A. Price, J.D. & Willis, J. (Eds). *Technology and Teacher Education Annual*, AACE Charlottesville, VA, 2309-13.

Ertmer, P.A. (2001). Comparing perceptions of exemplary technology use to best practice, *Journal of Research on Computing in Education*, 33, 5, 23-35.

——, (2005).Teacher pedagogical beliefs: The final frontier in quest for technology integration? *Educational Technology Research & Development*, 53, 4, 25-39

Ferdig, R.E. (2006). Assessing technologies for teaching and learning: understanding the importance of technological content knowledge. *British Journal of Educational Technology*, 37, 5, 749-760.

Greenfield, P. (1986). *Mind and Media*, Cambridge, MA: Harward University Press.

Harasim, L., Hiltz, S., Teles, L. & Turoff, M. (1995). *Learning Networks: A Field Guide to Teaching and Learning Online*. Cambridge, MA: MIT Press.

Harris, J., Mishra, P., Koehler, M. (2009). Teachers' technological pedagogical content knowledge and learning activity types: Curriculum-based technology integration reframed. *Journal of Research on Technology in Education*, 41, 4, 393-416

Judson, E. (2006). How teachers integrate technology and their beliefs about learning: Is there a connection? *Journal of Technology and Teacher Education*, 14, 3, 581-597.

Knezek, G. & Christensen, R. (2000) *Refining best teaching practices for technology integration*: KIDS project findings for 1999-2000. Denton, TX: University of North Texas.

Kurbanoglu, S.S., Akkoyunlu, B. & Umay, A. (2006). Developing the information literacy self-efficacy scale. *Journal of Documentation*, 62, 6, 730-739, also found on www.emeraldinsight.com/0022-0418.htm

Lawton, J., Gerschner, V.T. (1982). A Review of the literature on attitudes towards computers: Anxiety, confidence, liking and perception and usefulness. *Journal of Research in Computing in Education*, 22 , 2, 137-150.

Levin, T., Wadmany, R. (2006). Teachers' beliefs and practices in technology-based classrooms: A developmental view. *Journal of Research on Technology in Education*, 39, 2, 157-181.

Marcinkiewicz, H.R. (1993). Computers and teachers: Factors influencing computer use in the classroom. *Journal of Research on Computing in Education*, 26, 220-237.

Mishra, P., Spiro, R.J., Feltovich, P. (1996). Technology, representation and cognition. In Von Oostendrop, H. (Ed.). *Cognitive aspects of electronic text processing*. NJ: Ablex Publishing Corporation.

Luke, C. (2003). Pedagogy, connectivity, multimodality, and interdisciplinary. *Reading Research Quarterly*, 38, 3, 396-403.

Palak, D., Walls, R.T. (2009) Teachers' beliefs and technology practices: A mixed-methods approach. *Journal of Research on Technology in Education*, 41, 4, 417-441.

Roblyer, M.D. (1993).Why use technology in teaching? Making a case beyond research results. *Florida Technology in Education Quarterly*, 5, 4, 7-13.

Rosenberg, M.J. (2001). *E-learning: Strategies for delivering knowledge in the digital age*. New York: McGraw-Hill.

Windschitl, M. & Sahl, K. (2002). Tracing teachers' use of technology in a laptop computer school: The interplay of teachers' beliefs, social dynamics, and instructional culture. *American Educational Research Journal*, 39, 1, 165-205.

Withrow, F.B. (2004). *Literacy in the Digital Age*. Scarecrow Education. Lanham: Scarecrow Education Press.

Yuen, A.H.K., & Ma Will W.K. (2008). Exploring teacher acceptance of e-learning. *Asia-Pacific Journal of Teacher Education*, 36, 3, 229-243.

8.

Educational Technology, Teacher and the Emerging Indian Scenario

R.P. Singh

Teachers or Technicians?

For the first time ever the Indian classrooms are finding it difficult to resist change. The classical image of the teacher – ever so knowledgeable, is currently finding his authority being challenged – and that too in his own domain i.e. both in delivery of content and in the nature and quality of content. At times the teacher comes across a student who happens to be more knowledgeable than s/he. This awkward situation arises because the teacher alone is no longer the most knowledgeable of all beings. The quantum of knowledge is undergoing change and so are the sources of knowledge. The information that was once an exclusive preserve of the teacher is being made available by alternate sources – like the Internet or ready to use compact diskettes (CDs). In certain classrooms teachers feel insecure because of their ignorance or lacuna in their latest information repertoire. This is happening in a few Public Schools where children have better access to these facilities than their teachers. This is one reason why recently the corporate sector refused to accept B.Ed. degree holders being churned out of our woefully incompetent system, approved and promoted by the apex body (?) NCTE. In fact at one time the government itself was informed in the Parliament that its own elite schools were unwilling to accept the 'unemployable' B.Ed. degree holders.

It is no longer possible to prepare a perfect textbook or impart knowledge whose advanced form is not or cannot be made available in no time. Instead of learning in the classrooms where a single teacher could once answer all queries, the present times are witnessing a sudden change. The one's who do not teach anywhere and are in fact not even aware how teachers are prepared or selected have come to produce material that undermines the authority of the teacher. The newer concepts like e-learning; auto-teach/self-learning, virtual universities, countrywide classrooms, digital books and even virtual teachers etc are no longer unfamiliar terms or ideas. Every passing day we notice the authority of the teacher is being challenged in one form or the other – especially in his all too familiar role of instruction in the classroom. Education is no longer the monopoly of any system – certainly not of the teacher – because the entire game of teaching has undergone change.

In the name of quality assurance we wish to give identical information to all and since it is impossible to ask any one teacher to be available everywhere, the technology can easily chip in to substitute him/her in this regard. In that case it is not the classroom but a 'virtual' teacher/classroom that could make this possible.

The 'social' divide would continue to bother us in future. Even the advanced countries like the USA or EU have not succeeded in bridging the gap between those who have access to all the alternative sources to classroom teaching. A survey had revealed that in the USA everyone does not have access to telephone and therefore it is understandable that inequality is inherent in all societies. This should not prevent the Indian system to adopt the best and the most advanced technologies in education. In this connection there is no need to bring in unnecessary debate like the question of basic equality of all or access to education for all or the like.

Lakhs of Indian students go abroad every year for higher education. It is now being realized by all that our educational system is fundamentally flawed. *It is neither flexible nor forward looking*. Yet we continue saying that this system is producing men and women whose caliber is in no way inferior to anyone else. In this discourse what is being overlooked is the fact that these extraordinary boys and girls have to put in their own efforts into their success. A large number of these brilliant products seldom come from within the system. Either they are born extraordinary or their families have put in extra effort to nurture them. The indigenous educational system itself is not very supportive. Our few successes have to be analyzed threadbare to come to some kind of conclusion. Look at the success of Indians in the Silicon Valley but that should not mislead us to believe that the credit for all this goes to our ingenuity or our institutional support. It is largely due to the individual effort and also to the challenges Indians faced in a foreign land where there were not many choices except the one 'either do or die' In a desperate situation like this the success of the few should not make us accept an argument that our educational system has come of age or become competitive.

The pitiable condition in which our system is made to produce world-class material is simply laughable. Look at the government's own admission year after year that thousands of our schools have no buildings and millions no washrooms (toilets) and where a substantial percentage of teachers never go to their classes; and, additionally our higher education is marred by the politicization of both the educational content and behavior. Therefore for those who cannot afford to send their children abroad and still wish them to succeed or come up to the levels others reach because they are exposed to an academic climate that suits their talents are matters that need hardly to be overlooked. Analyze why our IITs are so successful and you will know immediately it is largely due to the competitive nature of their admission policies and the challenge their content poses. Additionally, the academic climate that these institutions offer makes for all the glory their products earn. Children from ordinary schools cannot even dream of entering these institutions. Success in this country is not dependent on any single factor – be that economic, political, social or the like.

Therefore it is imperative that problems need to be addressed with that of providing the best of education with lots of caution and well-planned design.

Let us start with an analysis of classroom instruction. A given class is definable in terms of its level, content, content-quality and its relevance for future use. But the most important part of any education is the delivery of the content and the way students learn. It is not possible to standardize learning but now a day it is possible to homogenize teaching techniques and the delivery of the content. Everybody is aware that changes occur frequently in the content because of the inherent nature of modern societies and the speed with which they are changing. The older societies were more or less static or they changed slowly. But this cannot be said of our present day societies any longer. Because our markets are dependent on our likes and dislikes and to suit our tastes and demands the supply system has also to change. This brings in the role and the speed of earnings; and, hence of the nature of consumer societies. While a few continue to redefine themselves because of the possibilities they are able to generate for more and quick earning; it is not possible for others to do so. In between the growth of our economies comes into play the major role of scientific and technological development with their impact on education. Society therefore offers education because it finds education to be a tool for survival and progress. Competing with others and being able to maintain its position in the world order could be an additional fall out. Individuals themselves start bringing in their own goals into this scheme of things. It is not necessary that these goals have universal approval.

The main players in the education system are: a) individual child, b) teacher; and, c) society through its approved curriculum besides the expert who divides the entire curriculum of a class into bits and pieces besides fixing the sequence of learning and teaching. The entire process looks simple but its complexity is also equally well-known. No system functions in isolation. Individual nations feel the heat of international competitiveness. This problem of competition brings in varying types of measures nations adopt to remain a step or two ahead of others.

Planners of India therefore must also adopt the best of the measures to remain in step with others; if not exactly ahead of all others.

India must look at the options it now has in the field of teaching and what is more it needs to do so because India have to remain in contention internationally.

The choice before us is the use of machines in teaching both for making the system efficient and economical.

Teaching Machines

It is the time to have a look at the history of the use machines in teaching. The main function of Teaching Machines or mechanical devices is to present systematically a programmed sequence of instruction to a student.

The first teaching machines were designed by the American psychologist Sidney Leavitt Pressey in the 1920s to provide immediate feedback for multiple-choice tests. Immediate correction of errors served a teaching function, enabling students to practice test-items until their answers were correct.

In 1954 the American behavioral psychologist B.F. Skinner popularized the potential of teaching machines for academic instruction. Skinner held that classroom teachers, responsible for heterogeneous groups of students, could not be expected to provide individualized instruction for each student without assistance from mechanical devices. Teaching machines containing well-programmed sequences could provide step-by-step progress towards carefully defined Instructional Objectives (IO), with each step depending on mastery of all the prerequisite steps. A good program in a teaching machine could thus make efficient use of the principle of active responding by providing students with immediate feedback on success or failure.

The early linear teaching machines could not judge the student's response nor, indeed, even determine that the student had responded; they simply presented the correct answer on demand, providing a chance for the student to inspect that feedback before proceeding. Branching teaching machines, using multiple-choice questions, sent students to different next frames, providing either remedial information and a chance to try again, or confirmation of success and the next step in the sequence. Both kinds of machines were so simple in design that they were replaceable by programmed textbooks offering almost the same control over learner progress.

The potential of the computer as a teaching machine promises increasing design sophistication. Computers can be programmed to judge student input and to tailor lessons to each individual's level of mastery. In a tutorial mode, computers can present instructional input and require mastery of each step in ways that were not possible in the early machines. The sensitivity of the instructional designer to alternative patterns of student learning is the necessary key to full use of this advance in machine capacity. Simulation – using the machine to model a real situation – enables even greater sophistication, allowing realistic reactions to student input. Well-designed intellectual games can provide patient environments in which to practice important problem-solving skills.

Tomorrow's teachers will have to compete with machines like computers and information-mongering Internet. Since the cost of these machines both for transmission of information and the speed for communicating knowledge is going down everyday, the option to classroom teaching is beginning to become a reality.

India too has made tremendous progress in this direction. It holds out a promise to offer instruction via machines and the internet and that too of international quality, the future teachers need to sit up and take notice of the challenges that are likely to come in.

Is this not the time when teachers' colleges start incorporating in their teaching methods suitable programs for imparting instruction in learning a proper use of these machines and the technologies that are readily available today? Time has come when teachers must define their roles and face the reality to admit whether they would like to remain masters of the emerging technologies or would they prefer to accept the humble role of technicians in the classrooms. The digitalized knowledge in the libraries and the convenience of learning at will and at leisure is soon going to pose a challenge, which may not be easy to fact.

Change being the only constant in the world; are Indian teachers not aware that a change is no longer in the offing; *it is already knocking at their door?*

Only those who hear the knock are likely to survive and the rest will have to wait until they are told finally of having become irrelevant.

What is presented here is addressed to those who are conscious of their obligations and are always wide-awake to learn. A teacher not only teaches but is always ready to learn. And we are sure that the learners far outnumber those that have to be made to learn.

The Strange Case of Digital Divide

Contemporary education is witness to far greater changes in both the curricula and methods of instruction in the past couple of decades as compared to the past couple of centuries put together. Not only we have larger numbers of peripatetic teachers, but also we have tremendous variety of institutional mobility. The tools of instruction also appear to have changed in very many ways. In a way all this constitutes globalization. Globalization *per se* as a concept and practice both are not new to an Indian. Indian literature both ancient and modern is replete with references declaring that the world is a single large unit and most of the time we also practice the idea literally, which holds that 'the entire human race is but one family'. What greater proof for this practice could one offer than to point out the presence of millions of Indians living abroad? Indian religions too have unhesitatingly been unanimous about endorsing this view. Since this concept is embedded naturally in the Indian psyche we seldom face problems on that score. We could easily cite numerous hymns and verses from Indian literature both ancient and modern to endorse the statements made here.

The theme implies that if material conditions remained unchanged the process of globalization, the world would continue to remain homogeneous and basically equal. The fact is that thus far we have neither the knowledge nor the experience of any society that could ever qualify to be called either equal or homogenous. To the author, it looks as though the Divine intention itself was not to create a world that would ever be so boring as to be either equal or homogenous. What perhaps is possible is to offer an infrastructure that makes equity an achievable object. There are several philosophical systems that decry equality but support equality of opportunity. In brief, they are all for equity. The tragedy with this almost universal desire is that it is a mere formulation of a concept and not a roadmap for an action plan.

It would be advisable not to overlook the fact that equality is an unachievable goal. In reality it is a virtual impossibility to succeed in this direction. It is both sensible and relevant to say that it is also an undesirable value because no society could ever function with that kind of an impossible reality. All of us are aware that there are two types of constructs—the real and the ideal. An Ideal is what inspires one to work hard and compete and the Real is wherein one shall always fall short of the Ideal. Life acquires meaning by our efforts to bridge the distance between the Real and the Ideal. What the ancient Indians were talking of '*vasudaiva kutumbkam*' will forever remain an 'ideal' construct even as our dream to have equity practiced in today's world becomes a 'virtual' reality. This diversion was intentional lest we overlooked the main issues involved here. The main issue for debate in the author's opinion is whether or not globalization is bound to lead to digital divide. Author's contention in this regard is that globalization will have its impact in several other ways rather than create inequality. No society was ever equal and neither it is likely to ever become so. Inequality is embedded in the nature of society itself.

The other points relate to poverty and co-existence of numerous hierarchical layers of social and economic existence and progress. At no point of time in Indian history have Indians been free from the misery of poverty. Indeed, the very progress of Indian society has been totally unrelated to the reality of prosperity. Certain classes or castes in India have traditionally been rich at the expense of others. One needs to consult the history of our society to get an idea why prosperity has been praised by so many. *Praise is invariably reserved for the rare and the exclusive.* Let it be taken for granted what is readily available. Riches or fortunes are destined to be in the hands of few. We must also acknowledge the reality that Indian society is inherently and basically unequal. It is not merely the caste that divides us all but the political system that has grown overtime too has acquired a vested interest in poverty. For instance, what would happen to the Left parties if for some reason India came out of its vice-like grip of poverty? Not only will they become irrelevant because they will then lose the constituency they have thus far cultivated, they will also be forced to look for some other ideology to survive. Without going into a diversionary mode let it be stated here that it is not true that Indians have waited for countless centuries to see that as a society India should get divided digitally, *India has always been a remorselessly divided society with or without any innovation or scientific advancement.* Therefore, what happens now will in no way be worse than what the existing reality is. In other words, what the author is saying is that the so-called digital-divide is likely to do Indians some good instead of something unimaginably worse.

Here the author refuses to mourn the absence of equality in Indian society. The gadgetry involved in modern-day information technology and its mastery and command by a few will have on those means of transmission compares well with the inventions of gunpowder or paper or the wheel etc. Every time something new comes it takes time to percolate down to deliver its benefits universally. The ones who are fortunate or intelligent enough to receive it first constitute the vanguard elements of prosperity. In the process they are likely to accumulate unprecedented power either of expertise or the riches. This is some kind of universal law. Nothing new is likely to happen even now. The very concept of 'digital' divide is contextually misplaced and ill conceived.

What we must note at this juncture are a few important facts about India's new class structures. We already know that India is caste-ridden and is afflicted with regional biases with plenty of tribal dominated areas. Still, in order to describe this social reality we might as well use the well-known terms Lord C.P. Snow used some five decades back to describe the British society. India lives on in numerous concentric circles of parallel societies with minimum number of communication channels open for any kind of dialogue. The English speaking/knowing urban elite knows nothing or very little about the majority of non-English speaking/knowing Indians. Thanks to oil boom the non-English knowing India's unskilled workers suddenly hit the jackpot. They built big mansions from their earnings abroad in remote villages and are even willing to invest in education for children. The classical example of this trend can be witnessed both in Kerala and Bihar. The results of their monetary investment have not been universally beneficial.

India's traditional urban elites continue to have a vested interest in the preservation of the once discredited 'British heritage.' Therefore, they read, speak and think in English and attend the same clubs as their erstwhile rulers did. They have their exclusive schools, which charge heavy fees just 'to maintain standards.' Their children go to Mission Colleges and join All-India services or the multinationals. They marry within their class and should the caste also match they then have the best of both the worlds.

India has accepted the West as a model for modernization. In the process, Indians have ceased to be prejudiced against the use of English language, which during India's struggle for freedom symbolized foreign domination. Indeed, after independence, the mastery of this language has been instrumental in creating a class of rulers who are imposing Western ideas and institutions on the non-English knowing people. If this has led to a social division of Indian people, it is helping a few to attain a good deal of prosperity at the cost of others. More so now that India has joined the WTO regime, the information technology has come to rule the roost. The implications are there for all to witness. There was a time when the Tatas and the Birlas were the richest Indian business families, but now scenario is changed.

The majority of the non-elites join government run/ grants-in-aid/ charity/ municipal schools. These schools may teach the same curricula as the elites do but here the teaching is carried on in Hindi or in some regional languages. And from then onwards starts the discriminatory process eventually leading these children to a future of becoming second-grade citizens. Couple of decades back there was always a possibility that few of the non-elites will crossover the dividing lines and join the mainstream elites. This is going to become unlikely now.

Educationally the great urban-rural divide has become glaring in most parts of the country. The villages do have their schools – a vast majority of them being single-teacher. The re-affirmation of faith in the *Sarva Shiksha Abhiyan* (Education for All) by the UPA notwithstanding the village school retains, by and large, its 'community center character' where all varieties of social functions including political meetings and *gram panchayat* sessions are held. During summer and winter breaks its buildings serves as a *barat ghar* (wedding-hall) or when the teacher is away which is fairly frequent the students indulge in free-for-all games. The seriousness with which the government issues fiats for running these schools is truly a mockery of commitment where even the barest minimum of facilities and climate for teaching happen to be non-existent. Expecting such schools to bring up rural/tribal children ready for a highly competitive world is surely a cruel joke on an unsuspecting crowd.

All Indian cities are facing an explosion in population, a large chunk of which consists of migrant, unskilled labor, adding a shanty township each month. Since they serve as vote-banks for the ruling party before every municipal or parliamentary election, they are regularized. The inhuman conditions in which these people live are seasonally improved and gradually municipal schools start appearing as pleasant surprises in an otherwise bleak surrounding. However, what is shocking is that villages are gradually becoming slums – where the landless laborer and the old cobbler or blacksmith finds it difficult to survive. With the arrival of agricultural technology in Indian farming and the formation of co-operatives in certain states like Maharashtra, Gujarat, *etc.* rural life has become quite comfortable for the landowners even when their landholdings are not very large. With television covering most of the country's population and pocket radios available almost universally the complexion of social life is gradually getting urbanized even in remote corners of the country. While the banking services have now become available in majority of rural pockets, hoards of urban entrepreneurs have landed up in rural areas in search of cheap labor and land for their industries. The mushroom growth of plantation societies has more or less established that Indians can smell economic benefits from miles away. What I am trying to say is that even without much effort Indians seem to be happy with their socially divided existence and highly discriminating school system. If one added the presence of antiquated religious schools to this list, the divisions already in existence are arguably not dependent on any digital phenomenon.

Human progress since primitive times could be defined in terms of its march towards providing basic necessities of life to all. This progress should be seen as an effort to be creating conditions under which one could claim to have some dignity attached to human life. Recent meet on global warming endorses this point. These efforts are definable in terms of one's ability to earn one's livelihood and to live in reasonable safety. One should also see that even this modest goal has remained elusive in majority of the cases. The enlightened people are interested to see that human past does not extend beyond the pages of history read in school days. Probably this seems to explain the choice of the present sub-theme.

Let me now take up seriatim the problems of globalization vis-à-vis India as they cover areas beyond the territorial boundaries defined in terms of nation states. However, most of the problems arise when one talks in terms of Nation-States. Several thinkers believe that since all humans belong to the same race the world must be treated as a common habitat. The political process that led to the formation of Nation-States has now to be put into the reverse gear. To that end several world organizations are trying to iron out the political and other varieties of rivalries. Besides, it makes economic sense to fight jointly when faced with a common yet strong enemy. Modern technology and innovations and research are an expensive business. The European Union (EU) experiment therefore should be seen against that background. This holds out a hope that something like this may have to be evolved in the Asian region too. The SAARC strikes immediately as our response to the EU model.

One can see that Europe has gradually overcome the concept of nation-states and is becoming socially and economically a cohesive, externally competitive society. Others who had thus far not refused to be part of it are queuing up to join in. A typically Christian Europe is being wooed by a dominant Islamic country like Turkey to become a part of it. The very concept of Europe trying to unite is the result of an American threat to dominate and weaken it. Besides being a question of survival and acquiring the ability to stand up to American challenges, the economic reasons have far out-weighed other considerations. Educational system is getting defined to become an instrument of the latest warfare. Research is getting due weightage and the mobility of scholars is being deliberately promoted and encouraged. Without going into details let us accept that EU is emerging as a model of future trans-border arrangement to meet challenges of WTO and the IPR or the like. The march of globalization is largely livelihood-driven.

The world has somehow been unsuccessful in retaining sacrosanct the existing political arrangement called the nation-states and its boundaries and even the national languages are gradually losing out to the dominant world language. We have today numerous world organizations promoting socio-economic unity and almost all governments are a party to their running. Even in India the dominant languages that help one to migrate from one state to another are either English or Hindi. Therefore, one must acknowledge the reality of local and regional languages losing out to politically dominant and economically helpful languages. DTH might prove to be a great help in retaining and even enriching regional and local languages. But one is unsure about their bright future.

India is unfortunately facing tremendous internal ethnic and religious problems. These biases and disagreements are preventing it to become a Nation. The tribes, castes and regions besides multiplicity of languages are preventing it to put up a combined fight on any front. Consequently, it is the 'minority groups' among Indians that are reaping all the benefits, but as a nation we are losing out on almost all fronts. We not only lack imaginative leadership but the irresponsible behavior of the majority of our legislators gives us no hope for a better future.

A Microsoft entry defines 'globalization as a concept that encapsulates the growth of connections between people on a planetary scale.' Globalization involves the reduction of barriers to trans-world contacts. Many believe that through it people become more able—physically, legally, culturally, and psychologically—to engage with each other in 'one world'.

The same write-up continues to say: 'Global connections take many forms. For instance, jet aeroplanes transport passengers and cargo across any distance on the planet within a day. Telephone and computer networks effect near-instantaneous interpersonal communication between points all over the Earth. Electronic mass media broadcast messages to world audiences. Countless goods and services (such as Nissan cars and Club Med holidays) are supplied to consumers in global markets. Moreover, some articles (including much clothing and electronics) are manufactured through trans-world processes, where different stages of production are located at widely dispersed locations on the Earth. The US dollar and the Euro are examples of currencies that have global circulation. In global finance, various types of savings and credits (for example, offshore bank deposits and Eurobonds) flow in the world as a single space. Many firms (for example, Exxon), voluntary associations (for instance, Amnesty International), and regulatory agencies (such as the World Trade Organization) operate across the globe. Climate change (so-called 'global warming') and stratospheric ozone depletion are instances of anthropogenic (that is, human-induced) ecological developments that unfold on a planetary scale. Finally, people experience global consciousness, in as much as we define the realm of our lives in trans-world, planetary terms.'

With globalization the world as a whole also becomes a social space in its own right. Thus global connections entail a different kind of geography. Whereas other social contexts are territorially delimited, global relations transcend territorial distances and territorial borders to unfold on planet Earth as a single social space. In this sense globalization might be characterized as the rise of 'supra-territoriality'. Whatever it may mean to others for an Indian it is not easy to eliminate the significance of localities, countries, and regions. Nor does the spread of trans-world connections abolish territorial governments or dissolve territorial identities. The *global* co-exists and inter-relates with the local, the national, the regional and other dimensions of geography.

Globalization has also not encompassed the entire humanity to the same extent. In terms of territorial location, for example, global networks have involved the populations of North America, Western Europe, and East Asia much more than other parts of the world. In terms of class, global finance has been a domain of the wealthy far more than those of the poor. In terms of gender, men have linked up to global computer networks. Needless to say, this unevenness of globalization has important implications for social power relations. One could easily witness the impact of power relations. People with connections to supra-territorial spaces have access to important resources and influence that are denied to those who are left outside. In this regard, some commentators have deplored 'global apartheid', as manifested in the so-called 'digital divide' and other inequalities. Others have objected to a 'cultural imperialism' of Hollywood and McDonald's in contemporary globalization. Since the mid-1990s such discontents have provoked a so-called 'anti-globalization movement' marked by regular mass protests against global companies, the International Monetary Fund, and other prominent agents of trans-world relations.

Conceptually globalization may be easy to define but its practices remain both gloomy and indistinct. Semantically or even contextually too it fails to be distinct. Perhaps it has its origins mainly in business and operationally it borrows its attributes and the definition of its characteristics from the models offered by the MNCs. Politically it has its bases in the power equations. Each country today is defined in terms of political power it has or does not have. It would appear that the USA has the monopoly of defining who will do what and how. Deviations from that definition are not permitted. Those that defy her authority to do so face armed intervention. When applied to education it would mean IPR and world rating of institutions. By implications it means that standards of educational degrees will have to be defined in the international context. The analogy is available in the world of patents of drugs or industrial products. The copyrights and patents give certain privileges to their original creators/ innovators and others. From now on, the formerly shared intellectual privileges would stand withdrawn from common use without meeting the conditions imposed by the bodies where they are either patented or given copyrights. As of today richer countries are educationally advanced as well. Globalization both as a concept and practice is intended to retain that monopoly. The G-8 countries can today decide about other non-G-8 countries. They have every power to dictate in other areas as well. The present day concept of globalization is but an extension of the same power configuration. Education is just one of the several areas that will get stifled by the few that have the power which unfortunately others do not have. And in this area India has much to worry about. With 3.5 crore remaining outside the schooling system we may have to think of some other plan than the present one in operation i.e. *Sarva Shiksha Abhiyan*.

'*Imagine, There's no Country*' by Dr. Surjit Bhalla is the title of a recently published book taken from John Lennon's song. The context is globalization. In the midst of all kinds of depressing debates about the impact of globalization on poorer countries his findings suggest that in the two decades from 1980 to 2000, the proportion of poor people in the world has fallen from 40 per cent to 13 per cent. In these two decades poorer countries have grown twice as fast as rich ones. The respective ratios are 3.1 per cent to 1.6 per cent. According to Dr. Bhalla one third of the global population resides in China and India. In the same two decades these two countries have witnessed record income growth. In a way, these figures persuade us to believe that globalization is not too bad after all. There are numerous other forms of globalization, just as there is a variety in the reactions to the hegemony of American power. If European Union has been formed to meet that kind of challenge, SAARC is the other alternative model on the anvil WTO and IPR are the byproducts of the same process. The eventual goal may remain full integration of all nations or may be total dissolution of the concept of division of people on any bases whatever but today we are nowhere near realizing this kind of goal.

I am not competent to discuss either the political or the economic impact of globalization. I could however go into its impact on Indian culture, languages and education. I share the commonly held view that an already fractured and divided society will get further sub-divided and the technological revolution may sound the death knell to many languages, multiple cultures and create unbridgeable gaps between the 'digital haves' and the 'non-haves'.

The premise on which I am discussing the question of 'digital divide' is that Indians are well past that stage when they were being consulted whether or not they have any wish to join the bandwagon. Today there are no choices. Either join the mainstream or become extinct like dinosaurs or dodo. Having joined willy-nilly the rat race, as it were, there is no point in looking back. Indians are in the center-stage. They must take stock of what lies ahead of them and whether or not there is any possibility that they might still retrieve part of the lost ground. Each of these points has to be considered separately and contextually. Indians could react euphorically and say that a fraction of their population has done well both here and abroad. Hence, they are not likely to suffer too much as compared to X or Y. They may also stand up to say that the present scenario is too grim to describe therefore all that lies ahead of them is a grim reality and the chances are that Indians may do very poorly. The author hold the view that neither of the two is a certainty provided Indians know what they want and are willing to act rationally and with good deal of determination and foresight. But first Indians should wake up to the impending reality.

The fact of the matter is that even in the USA the Government has come to realize that their society has been impacted very badly by the digital divide. In a paper written by Beverly P. Lynch titled *'The Digital Divide or the Digital Connection: A U.S. Perspective'*, the multi-dimensionality of the concept has been framed by Pippa Norris into three distinct aspects:

1. Global divide – divergence of Internet access between industrialized and developing countries;
2. Social divide – gap between information rich and information poor in each nation; and,
3. Democratic divide – difference between those who do and those who do not use the new technologies to further political participation.

The above-cited section of the paper emphasized the digital-divide in its social aspects in the U.S. and paid particular attention to the role of the library in furthering equity of access to information. How much of this discussion will be valid for us in India could be imagined by the simple fact that majority of even urban population in India has only limited access to the Internet and few schools have libraries and the books and journals that are not dated or tattered, if they have any. For the sake of discussion only, the author has cited some figures from the most powerful and perhaps the richest country in the world.

In 1994, as the U.S. policy makers measured telephone penetration in the country since they realized that telecommunications policy would be influenced by the growing importance of computer and modem availability in households they created database. In 1995 the first Report, on "Falling through the Net: A Survey of the 'Have-Nots' in Rural and Urban America" was issued. Following its earlier formats of gathering data by household, the survey gathered household data on the availability of computers and modems and analyzed data by income, race, age, educational attainment, and geographic region (rural, urban, central city). The report gave interesting data and provided benchmark-data, against which subsequent studies have been compared showing the phenomenal growth in computing availability and Internet access between 1994-2001. In 1997 the telephone penetration was 94 per cent. Computer penetration was 36.6 per cent and PC growth by household was up 42.1 per cent from 24.1 per cent in 1994. The assumption was that PC penetration would be less than urban areas. In 2000 the PC penetration had climbed to 51.1. During 2002 the results showed that two million new Internet users were added each month. Children and teen-agers use computers more than others. In the lowest income groups too the growth was around 25 per cent annually. The use of the Internet among the richest and the poorest was 77 per cent and 35 per cent respectively. Efforts are on to bridge the gap between those who have access to Internet and others who do not have such facility.

Compared with what obtains in the USA, now let us have figures given by Mumbai-based Strategic Foresight Group for India. *The Times of India,* 1 December 2002, reported these figures. The report had said; that, 'with different segments of the population and different regions of the country moving in various directions. India may formally remain united (note the word 'may'), but in every other respect, it will go to pieces within the lifetime of an Indian who has just stepped into adulthood'. The report asserts that the disparities engendered by India's current development model have given rise to three broad kinds of economies. The Business-class economy, which gives access to luxuries, constitutes a bare 2 per cent of the population. The Business-class is the one about which we talk the most. Then we have the Bike-economy comprising 13 per cent of the population—its consumption includes television, the telephone, the radio, the motorbike and gas and water connections. The remaining 85 per cent belong to the Bullock-cart economy. While 50 per cent of this class has access to the barest minimum consumer comfort, the rest however are just about surviving.

The figures in this regard appear to have slightly improved. With the coming in of the broadband and wireless telephony the above-cited figures are bound to undergo a sea change.

Now to think of being able to compete with nations like China or any other country in Asia, the report has its serious doubts. The report would like Indians to have proper policies if the nation has to survive let alone compete and compete successfully, failing which Indians are likely to break up. The minimum Indians could expect from the Government is to reduce corruption and increase governing efficiency. An ORG-Marg survey reports that Indians pay ₹26,728 crores in bribe in a single year (*Times of India*, 18 December 2002). In the year 2005 the data as reported in the *Times of India* (14 March 2005) endorses the statement made by an Indian Prime Minister almost a decade back that the subsidized foodgrain intended for the poor does not reach the target groups because of the immense corruption in the system. Surprising as it might appear, the teaching profession (something least expected) figures in one of the three top-most corrupt categories. This question needs to be addressed by the NCTE. Nearly all concerning education regulatory bodies have lost their sheen. In this regard teachers too have earned a bad name.

In a country like India governance is simply unknown and the rule of law is restricted to those that are poor and politically unconnected. Under the circumstances, I think *the idea of 'digital divide' is in reality no more than a mosquito bite or a minor irritant that will be taken care of in the process itself.* However, if we are of the worrying type then we shall have to think of millions that are likely to die of hunger, unemployment and a whole lot of diseases without any medical aid. Depending on the type of category one belongs to in 'the digital divide' one could have One's own meaning and perception. By itself this term defines an idea and ideas have unfortunately a tendency of being interpreted according to the interest groups.

Tech-savvy Teachers Enter 21st Century: Virtual Teacher Goes Online

You can now get in touch with teachers and students across the country to seek help in studies, compare notes and give pre-board examinations like test several times at leisure with a click of the mouse during preparation for the crucial X and XII grade CBSE examinations.

Some times back a team of entrepreneurs in Delhi launched a website service that is a cross between social service website and a handy tutorial for CBSE students and teachers. Named cbsetutor.com this website contains the entire NCERT curriculum in toto, the extensive CBSE prescribed reference material, specially designed notes, and loads of tests on each chapter covered by the syllabus.

'In the next three months, thousands of students will need value-added study material to prepare for the boards. They will need to know where they stand on an all India basis. And they need to distress themselves under pressure of examination. The website tries to cater to these needs'

'To begin with the company has a panel of experts who are professional tutors, former educationists or the like, who have designed the tests and the content. In the UK virtual leaning is mandatory but not so in India because here we have not been able to provide intrinsic value to students and teachers. The best part of the facility is that it is absolutely free. ...'

The Hindustan Times, 31 December 2007

Seen against the above backdrop is the remarkable fact of continuously reducing the eligibility qualifications for teaching B.Eds. in the institutional-mushrooming scenario the NCTE has created; and now in its reformist zeal it has further brought down the marks percentages of future teacher-trainers from earlier 48 per cent to 45 per cent. In the past one year or slightly more we have learnt the reactions of both the Government and also of the corporate sector that even the present day products are totally unacceptable (when being taught by M. Ed.s & Ph.Ds), then where does the NCTE think it would make these 'unemployables' acceptable? Is NCTE playing tricks with the gullible lot? Also, it remains to be seen what impact it would have on the university departments of education that produce 'meaningless' M.A./M.Ed.s and the Ph.D.s in Education.

There is a lot that has been happening in the field of education, especially in the classrooms but thus far I have not come across any serious academic paper on the direction in which we are moving. Despite the NCTE (or, may be because of it) we are nowhere near preparing 'effective' teachers who are knowledgeable as well as 'reasonably good' communicators. After all, the main function of a teachers' college is to produce teachers who know how to communicate and present the updated subject matter in a manner that is easy to understand. But are we preparing teachers with these twin ends in view? I doubt it.

In fact all the indications are that we have miserably failed on both counts. Communication is a skill and skills can be developed only with practice. One has to see the functioning of a present day teachers' college (even among the so-called best ones) and realize that there is nothing in the teacher education program that ensures this type of training. Apart from a meaningless debate on the theme whether or not practice teaching should be based on 'block' basis, there is no model available for us to fall back upon. We have yet to come across a single university department of education in India where this question has been taken up seriously and some empirical research finding is made available for guidance. This obviously implies that generally teachers' colleges are not serious about imparting this 'skill'. If they were serious the reality should not have belied the truth. The perfunctory and mechanical way teaching practice is conducted makes a mockery of the 'communication' skill. Remember we do not bother about this skill. At the time of selecting a candidate for teacher training marks in an academic examination are considered and they are based on testing one's memory. And with the so-called management quota in self-financed colleges all academic and professional considerations are thrown to the wind. Who will or who will not become a teacher is dependent on the fees one can afford.

There are essentially two problems with this ongoing callousness about the neglect of this basic skill. Those that know nothing about how to speak or communicate are not merely under-rating the value of this skill and additionally they are corrupting the youth from the homes where purity of language is still considered a value and that which needs to be taken care of and for all others the choice of words, the syntax and the correct pronunciation have lost meaning. We seem to have forgotten that in the oral tradition one does not have to remember only the text but also the proper pronunciation as well. In such a scenario the importance of this skill is not lost importance by any chance. A whole lot is dependent on the quality of spoken language. A single mispronunciation can spoil the meaning in a poem or impact adversely the good taste. A bad communicator is unlikely to be good teacher.

The other point that needs to be paid special attention is that developments in technology have brought us to a stage where it looks as though we do not need to train teachers at all. Even otherwise teacher education is no more than two hundred years old. It has no philosophy or psychology of its own. Indeed all that we teach at this stage is merely derivatives from the basic disciplines. Everything that we teach at the teachers' college is borrowed – the entire content and all the methods. Therefore to claim that teachers colleges teach something that they have themselves created or evolved would be unreal. Those that survive on borrowed knowledge cannot be called scholars or innovators. After all only very few teachers are either creative and teach what they have evolved themselves.

To recall Kendal *'things outside classrooms matter more than within the four walls of the classrooms'* has acquired new context and meaning. For example, teachers' colleges are supposed to help imbibing values but surprisingly they have not been able to evolve any tool to assess whether or not the training has been demonstrably successful. Linked with this failure are its other failures also. Read any national daily and find out how many teachers are found morally deficient and criminally inclined. I wonder whether any university department has ever tried to unravel the phenomenon and suggested corrective measures. These lacunae speak volumes for the failure of the system and suggest that the ones who should be responsible for guiding others are in fact basically unthinking and lack the 'Will' to resolve some of the basic problems this sort of training curricula faces. It is possible to argue that all management courses do not equip or ensure every manager of either success or honesty. Yet the fact is that the majority of the products do succeed and management skills can be easily showcased.

Teachers' colleges can be accused of being both unimaginative for the way they select prospective teachers for initial training and being totally irrelevant for the courses they offer. Regarding the first allegation one could easily state that no one has thus far done any empirical research to suggest that the method evolved for selecting candidates for initial training are either predictable or demonstrable. There is also no proof to show that the cut-offs adopted in one university match with the norms followed in the other; or, for that matter the quality is or can be homogenized. In fact, talking about the quality of the products this is one area where the quality of the products is so uncertain that nothing could be ensured. 'Quality assurance' is an unheard of requirement and few, if at all, could guarantee that their products have matured to some level of quality. One rarely comes across a teachers' college, which enjoys the reputation of producing consistently good teachers. In fact, both the corporate sector and the Government of India recently admitted that these products are not even employable.

After the arrival of the self-financed colleges on the scene the overpowering greed among both the managers and the Inspectors drawn from the universities and from amongst the teachers' colleges has more than established that teaching is no more corruption–free than the other government departments and the claim that teachers are above material considerations because of their high-ended values fails to describe the reality. Teacher trainers can be shown to be as susceptible to common weaknesses as anyone else. The fact of the matter is that even the universities are found to be guilty of money making via teacher training is now public knowledge. The twin universities of Annamalai and Rohtak have for the past several decades have gone on scandalously minting money from teacher education courses and financing their other faculties is equally known to both public and the regulatory body called the University Grants Commission. The NCTE is equally guilty of not adhering even to its own declared norms anywhere in the country and for creating confusion by leaving several important areas and terms undefined. It has failed miserably in assuring quality control and preventing the unscrupulous elements from entering this area.

The meaninglessness of the teachers' courses can be shown by pointing out that even the NCTE finds it hard to explain why tailors and panwallahs (also, non-existent colleges) have come to offer teachers' degrees or prevent the *absentee* candidates from getting university degrees. This is one single cause that devalues teachers' degree or diploma that qualifies one to teach. It would be interesting to collect data after undertaking a proper comprehensive survey of teachers' colleges to learn about the real face of the owners of these teaching 'shops' and if a test were conducted on the staffs of the these teachers' colleges and the university departments of education about the subjects they teach and the quantum of new knowledge they have acquired in the field, the appalling lacuna in their knowledge would be more than apparent. The most miserable part of the finding would be that we would know for once that the content they teach became obsolete ages ago. The 'airy nothings' they produce in the name of educational research are mostly woefully short of real relevance and utility. Because of the lack of seriousness attached to the areas of research and the way areas of research are identified makes it much easier to obtain a Ph.D. in education than to pass a high school examination.

One of the major functions of universities is to be repositories of wisdom and the centers for the creation of new ideas. The great universities of the world function as the vanguards of change through innovations and creations of 'new' knowledge. If nothing else they at least give us new interpretations to age-old ideas. One would like to inquire and collect data on these scores from Indian departments of education where its present day functionaries are generally known only for their networking and mutual back scratching — in brief, for everything except for their academic excellence.

The basic point is that these departments of education are not even thinking of the days ahead wherein the whole variety of knowledge will have become a marketable product. The day is already very near when 'packaged' knowledge would be made available on the supermarkets. Already numerous agencies have entered this area and their products are available in selected areas. This is a challenge for the survival of teachers' colleges. The 'old' horses will have to learn 'new' tricks to remain in business/competition. Some one should show concern about the challenges that modern technology is posing for teachers in the area of classroom instruction. Way back in the late 80's, the author had talked of *Future Classrooms in India*—a book brought by a Delhi based publisher. At that time no one had thought of a day when most of the tutorial functions of a classroom teacher could be transferred to a machine and it would be possible to teach inexpensively across the nation without much ado. That these machines/products would one day make revision of a lesson easy and at one's own pace was absolutely unimaginable.

One needs to think seriously about the future course of action vis-à-vis modern technology in terms of what we are currently teaching and what could be taught inexpensively with the aid of internet, virtual classrooms and with multi-media techniques.

This thinking will have several dimensions. For instance, the first dimension of the problem raises the question of relevance of the theory papers those are being taught. Additionally, the items under each course of study have to be seen against the backdrop of examination that the system wishes to conduct. It is necessary to identify not merely the subject matter but also the tools of testing for ensuring that the same have been learnt. And this could be done only after devising the appropriate methods and tools to examine the candidate against the backdrop of the aims that had originally thought of and devise ways to teach the same properly and scientifically. The main question is that teaching has a purpose. And the function of examination is to ensure that the efforts have yielded results. There is thus a direct linkage among the goals identified, subject or the content fixed according to the laws of the possible, and eventually the examination to ascertain that the goal has been achieved. This triad in teaching is well known. The author would like this to be specified for each course of study. If supposing one had aimed to teach a given candidate to be able to communicate or acquire some values or learn techniques and canons of logic then the examination should be able to demonstrate one's success or failure. Where does the system stand in this regard?

The B.Ed. program should cover comprehensive, systematic, scientific approaches of Health Education and Health-care and include points usually considered necessary the world over in the light of the work done by the WHO and the UNICEF.

The new curriculum should reflect disability component keeping in view the Human Rights perspective. The needs of Special Children as covered in the Comprehensive National Action Plan may be included at the appropriate place.

The problems and the issues concerning the Education of the minorities as recounted in the Sachar Committee Report have to be included in the Indian Education paper.

All discussions on institutional life have to be based on values and ideals enshrined in the Indian Constitution among all stakeholders.

Reconsider issues related to promoting ICT as an integral part of teacher education and improving the quality of teacher education by giving more time to practice teaching than currently being given.

Consider upgrading teacher education program suited for a Knowledge Society.

A plan of action involving CTEs, IASEs and DIETs in in-service education of the school teachers and the teacher educators is proposed. Environment education is part of school-teachers' curriculum. Specialization in this area is proposed at the M.Ed level. While theory is compulsory, the duration of practice teaching has to be prolonged so that a regular internship program could be developed and practiced.

Gender Issues

There are special teacher education institutions for women teacher trainees. Comparative study of effectiveness of training of these trainees in separate women institutions and in co-education institutions might be of help. Comparative studies on the effectiveness of female and male teacher educators are recommended. Comparison of facilities available in the co-ed and non-co-ed is also advised for policy making.

Liberal use of technology (ICT) is advised and all teacher trainees should know how to use Internet and all the associated activities and functions of a computer.

National Resource Centre for Teacher Education

There is an urgent need for starting a National Resource Center for Teacher Education, which should function as a lighthouse in the field. It is expected that this organization will inspire, guide and lead the entire system through funded research, developing quality assurance tools and drawing blueprints for future like the Americans and the British do.

In the alternative classroom instruction and packaged knowledge it is essential to see that the teachers are given training and before being brought into this skilled job.

Lastly all the schools should be instructed to essentially include training as a basic norm to promote the good teachers which include their participation in various international and national seminars, conferences and should have at least minimum one basic research input for better skill development.

Alternative Classroom Instruction and 'Packaged Knowledge'

India is already a leader in information communication technology. While its application part is well known in numerous areas like banking, industry, business etc very little is discussed when it comes to the revolution it has already brought about in classroom instruction. Of course what is happening in the metropolitan classrooms is not nationally possible. But we must not forget the goal has to be simply that.

We started with a quote from what is happening in Delhi. Similar stories are possible from elsewhere too. In fact numerous agencies have already entered the area. We have the technology to create virtual classrooms and also simultaneously take classes across the nation. We have learnt to store knowledge and package it for its possible it uses according to our convenience. Once this packaged knowledge starts getting into mass circulation it would not be possible for the mediocre to survive. Bereft of the knowledge to use modern day technology the present mass produced B.Eds will find it hard to survive as teachers. No good school will ever hire a newly taught teacher whose language and other skills are markedly poor.

For instance, look at the title of a news item, which says 'Digital classrooms make learning fun'. This news item goes into detail as to what is going to happen within two years or even less in India.. You enter a classroom and have a teacher explain on a plasma screen in an audio-visual format. As and when she asks a question, you do not rush for your pen and the class workbook. Instead you log in to your palm top computer and press the answer option. No baggage of homework books, as the assessment is derived on the basis of your homework has been replaced by what skills you have. All this may sound futuristic but companies are already working towards changing school learning in India in this direction. Educomp Solutions, a technology driven company that has also made forays in "education process outsourcing" and has launched its Millennium Learning System (MLS) – a combination of technology, training and new learning methods for schools.

The system includes a whole new set of pictorial books, digital content, plasma TVs for classrooms and 3D multimedia content, to be followed by classroom PCs which are on the way. The content is based on NCERT syllabus, which opens up the possibilities of addressing schools across the country that follows NCERT agenda on educational content. Educomp will enter into a revenue sharing arrangement with the schools involving aspects like designing the classrooms, furniture and teacher training in building a tech-centered learning program. The company has already invested ₹20 crores in research and development of this system adopting MLS will be known as Millennium schools.

DPS Ghaziabad and R.K. Puram branches in the NCR are already carrying out the pilot project in new instructional strategy. Yet another school named Sanskar also has a system that is probably better than the one in use in the DPS chain. Now a PC is available with education software for a mere ten thousand rupees using LINUS system. This kind of system is available for both the normal and the challenged children. For them very soon the Microsoft and DAIS (Digital Accessible Information System) are jointly going to come out with plug-in software which will help the visually challenged to read digitally prepared books that they could never ever had access to. And to think of the software being free is beyond belief. The National Association of the Blind, which is a member of the DAISY, has called it "giant step towards creating equal access to information". Things, companies, software and costs are all changing and changing fast. Under the circumstances: a Minister at the Centre had promised computers everywhere and those too for ₹1500 each. How then would these NCTE' approved B.Eds. with 40 per cent marks fit into the system let the reader try to answer the question.

Roles of Teachers and Adoption of Educational Technology in the Chinese Context

Chang Zhu

A number of factors influence the adoption of educational technology at teacher and institutional levels. The present chapter focuses on perceptions of Chinese teachers' roles and the impacts on the adoption of educational technology in schools. Five types of teacher-roles – expert, authority, model, facilitator and delegator are reflected. Next to teacher-roles, teacher's computer attitude and computer self-efficacy are also examined and related to their adoption of educational technology. The results show that teachers of facilitator/expert profile and facilitator/delegator profile are more inclined to adopt educational technology. Teachers with a more positive computer attitude and who believe to a larger extent about their abilities in using computers for teaching activities are more inclined to adopt educational technology. The current development of ICT use in teaching and challenges faced in the Chinese educational context are presented.

Development of Educational Technology in China

Educational technology is the practice of facilitating learning and improving performance by applying appropriate technological processes and resources (Richey, 2008). The development of educational technology has become an important task in the modernization of Chinese education. During the last 20 years, the Chinese government has paid much attention to educational technology. Before 1990s, Educational Technology was mainly referred to distance correspondence education via radio television and satellite net. With the spread of information and communication technology (ICT) and the development of Internet in 1990's, computer multimedia technology and network has been used in distance education and started to be integrated in teaching in classrooms. In recent years, computer and Internet based technologies have been more widely used for distance education and integrated use of ICT for teaching in classrooms.

Policy development is crucial to support the wide diffusion of technology. In 1999, the Chinese government promulgated the Decision on Strengthening Educational Reform and Boosting Education of Overall Qualification. It was emphasized 'Computer and information technology education should spread in senior secondary schools and some qualified junior secondary and primary schools. All the higher education institutions and key secondary vocational schools should establish the educational science and research net, and secondary and primary schools will establish it step by step.'

Facing the challenges of the information age, the Chinese government has taken various measures to modernize education, and using educational technology is one of the important tasks of the educational modernization. Since 2000, huge investment has been made for constructing infrastructure, developing e-resources and opening information technology-related curricula. Policy guidelines were also made to encourage teachers to apply ICT and to integrate educational technology into their teaching process. The aim of these policies is to gradually change the instructional and learning methods and the interaction methods between teachers and students. The integrated use of educational technology is also expected to develop students' capabilities such as creativity, problem solving and collaboration. According to the tenth-five-years plan (plan period 2001 to 2005) of the Chinese government, a goal was set up that in 2005, all schools should establish computer classroom and have access to Internet. In 2003, the government implemented a modern distance education project, for promoting instructional resources to be shared between the city and village schools and improving village's instructional quality and efficiency. In 2004, Ministry of Education promulgated The Plan of Revitalizing Education from 2003 to 2007, which clearly points out the aim of educational development in five years, and emphasized the main task of educational development, including enhancing basic ICT facilities, developing instructional information resources, training teachers, thus promoting educational modernization development.

Factors Influencing the Adoption of Educational Technology

Educational technology has the potential to improve teaching practices in education; however, the integrated use of technology in education is a complex system. In the last decade, educational technology has made only modest inroads into changing teaching in schools and universities (Moser, 2007). What are mechanisms that support or hamper teacher behavior regarding the adoption of educational technology? Studies have indicated that there exist numerous barriers against teachers adopting educational technology (Cuban, 2001; Ebersole & Vorndam, 2003; Reeves, 2003). Past studies have indicated three types of factors influencing the adoption of technology at schools: technical factors, individual factors, and organizational factors. Technical factors include variables like access to technology, technical support, etc. (Schifter, 2000). Individual factors include the available time that teacher can spend in learning how to use technology (competence development, time commitment), their beliefs in the effectiveness of technology in enhancing teaching and learning (Adams, 2003; Ebersole & Vorndam, 2003). Recent research has paid more and more attention to the perception of teacher-roles. Organizational factors, such as a technology strategic plan, administrative support, professional development, and an incentive policy could also influence the adoption of technology (Barone & Hagner, 2001). In this study, a focus will be given to the following two main factors.

Teachers' Roles

Teacher's perceptions of teaching and learning, especially teacher-roles also affect the way teachers teach and interact with their students. Teacher-roles are influenced by a particular pattern of needs, and mental, spiritual and physical behaviors that teachers display in the classroom (Eble, 1976, p. 8). The research of Grasha (1994) summarizes several patterns that describe the role differences in teachers. They include the teacher as: *expert* (transmitter of information); *formal authority* (sets standards and defines acceptable ways of doing things); *personal model* (teaches by illustration and direct example); *facilitator* (guides and directs by asking questions, exploring options, suggesting alternatives); and *delegator* (develops students' ability to function autonomously). The adoption of specific teacher roles in the instructional process may facilitate or hinder students' ability to acquire content and skills (Grasha, 1994). Teachers adopting the social constructivist approach would adapt to the role of a facilitator or delegator, and would less likely play the role of an authority, an expert or a model (Bauersfeld, 1995). Whereas a teacher 'gives' a didactic lecture covering the subject matter, a facilitator or delegator helps the learner to develop his or her own understanding of the learning content. In the latter scenario the focus turns away from the instructor and the content towards the learner and his/her learning process (Gamoran, Secada & Marrett, 1998). This particular shift in roles implies that a facilitator or a delegator needs to display a totally different set of skills than an information or knowledge transmitter (Brownstein, 2001).

It has to be noted that almost every teacher adopts each of the five teaching roles to varying degrees. In different cultural contexts, teachers' roles are viewed differently with an emphasis on some of these roles or other additional roles. Teacher-roles can be generally related to two conceptions of teaching and learning (Cortazzi, 1990). One perception views them as hierarchical, positioning the teacher as all knowing and his/her knowledge as being transmitted directly to learners. Another perception views the relationship between the teacher and students as more egalitarian. The first perception has been often associated with Asian or high-context cultures, such as the Chinese culture, in which teachers are *authoritarian* (Cortazzi, 1990 p. 58). The latter perception is often linked to Western or low-context cultures that emphasize individual development, innovation and an egalitarian ambiance (McClure, 2003). Cortazzi (1990) stresses that both perceptions 'are present in most cultures but receive very different emphasis, with the result that varied expectations come about, affecting presuppositions about learning and teaching'. The relationship between student and teacher seems to take on a different character in the Chinese culture. Chinese students are expected to 'respect the teacher's authority without preconditions' (Wang & Mao, 1996, p. 148). Besides their *expert* role, teachers are regarded by their students as their 'parents' (Wan, 2001). This parental role makes the teacher-student relationship not as cold or authoritarian as they at first appear (Cortazzi & Jin, 1996). Moreover, teachers are expected to act as *models*, and relate students' intellectual development to their moral and personal development (Gao & Watkins, 2002). In contrast to the Western context, Chinese student-teacher relationship seems to be not limited to the classroom and the academic work of that arena (Pratt et. al., 1999).

Teachers' Computer Attitude and Efficacy

The use of computers has become an integral aspect of modern society. The importance of preparing teachers for the use of educational technology has been recognized by many national governments. The Chinese government has issued a series of technology-related curriculum guidelines for schools since 2001. Many schools and universities have invested largely in hardware and software. A survey in 2007 by a Chinese university indicated that in urban areas about 85 per cent of teacher use computer every week. However, in rural areas, on an average only 30 per cent of teachers uses computers regularly. In addition, most of these teachers use computer for searching information on Internet and some of them use it for preparing power-point slides for lectures or other documents; very few of the teachers 'use computer to organize students for exploratory studies'. It is a challenge for education institutions nationwide to train teachers to meet the demand of preparing highly technology literate teachers to teach the next generation. According to Myers and Halpin

(2002), attitudes toward computers and confidence in the educational use of computers are two major predictors in teachers' technology use for teaching. Positive teacher-attitudes toward computers are widely recognized as a necessary condition for the adoption of educational technology (Huang & Liaw, 2005). Previous studies point out that computer self-efficacy has a significant positive effect on computer use (Compeau et. al., 1999).

Objectives: Based on the theoretical and conceptual background presented above, the research focuses on the following two research questions:

1. How do Chinese teacher perceive their teacher-roles?
2. Is there a relationship between teacher-profiles (perceptions of teacher roles), computer attitude and efficacy, and their adoption of educational technology?

Methods

A case study was carried out in 2009 to address the above research questions. Participants in the study consisted of 125 teachers from a comprehensive Chinese school (primary and secondary) in Beijing. Teachers were randomly selected, teaching five different subjects: Chinese language, Mathematics, English language, Science (including chemistry, physics and biology) and Politics, but an attempt was made to select a representative sample in terms of gender and age.

TABLE 9.1: Chinese teacher participants in this study

	Chinese Language	*Mathe-matics*	*English Language*	*Science*	*Politics*	*Total*
Male	15	12	8	15	14	64
Female	16	10	12	12	11	61
Average age	39	37	37	36	41	38

Measures

Teacher-role: The Teacher-Role Survey was administered based on the instrument developed by Grasha and Riechmann (1990) reflecting five scales that centre on specific teacher roles: *expert, authority, personal model, facilitator* and *delegator*. When filling out the instruments, teachers were asked to reply to the items by reflecting on their experiences with a particular teaching course. Questionnaire with 40 items required respondents to indicate on a five-point scale to what extent they agree or disagree with the items, given. The internal consistency for the five factors was acceptable (α from 0.72 to 0.79).

Computer-attitudes: Attitude can predict a person's behavior toward certain targets (Ajzen, 1988). Several studies have emphasized that computer-related attitudes are related to real computer use in education (Clark, 2001). Attitude towards computers influence not only teachers' acceptance of the usefulness of technology, but also influence whether teachers integrate ICT into their classroom (Myers & Halpin, 2002). Eight items on Attitudes toward Computers in Education (Van Braak, 2001) were used to measure teachers' attitudes. Questions are on a five-point scale and the internal consistency was satisfactory ($\alpha = 0.90$).

Computer-efficacy: Self-efficacy regarding computers refers to a person's perceptions of and capabilities to apply computers (Compeau & Higgins, 1995). Previous research states that computer self-efficacy is positively correlated with an individual's willingness to adopt educational technology (Ropp, 1999). Teachers with higher levels of self-efficacy about computers uses computer more often and experienced less computer-related anxiety. On the other hand, teachers with lower levels of self-efficacy about computer become more frustrated and more anxious to use computer when they encounter obstacles. Nine items on Computer Self-efficacy Scale was used to examine teachers' self-efficacy about computers. Questions are on a five-point scale and the internal consistency was satisfactory ($\alpha = 0.87$).

Willingness to adopt Educational Technology: Teacher's willingness to adopt educational technology was measured with five items (willingness to invest time; willingness to learn, willingness to use computer for teaching, willingness to adopt e-learning, willing to use other educational technologies). Questions are on a five-point scale and the internal consistency was sufficient ($\alpha = 0.85$).

Results

The mean scores of Chinese teachers' perceptions of the five teacher-roles are presented in Table 9.2. In general, most of the teachers seem to be more in favor of the teachers as *expert, authority* and *model* compared to the roles as *facilitator* and *delegator*. Some differences were detected between teachers who teach different subjects. Teachers who teach Mathematics, English Language and Science are more likely in favor of the facilitator and delegator roles compared to teachers who teach Chinese language and Politics ($p<.05$). Teachers who teach Politics are more likely in favor of expert and authority roles compared with other teachers ($p<.05$).

Cluster analyses were conducted to understand teacher-profiles based on their dominant perceptions of teacher-roles. The results reveal that 35 per cent of the teachers prefer the expert/authority profile; 24 per cent of them belong to the expert/authority/model profile; about 18 per cent of the teachers support the facilitator/delegator profile, and 23 per cent of the teachers support both the facilitator and expert roles.

TABLE 9.2: Perception of teacher roles in a Chinese school setting

Teacher roles	*Chinese Language* M (σ)	*Mathematics* M (σ)	*English Language* M (σ)	*Science* M (σ)	*Politics* M (σ)	*Total* M (σ)
Expert	4.05 (.60)	4.00 (.38)	3.97 (.52)	4.08 (.51)	4.20 (.39)	4.06 (.42)
Authority	4.10 (.51)	3.56 (.45)	3.95 (.44)	3.85 (.63)	4.18 (.48)	3.93 (.47)
Model	4.05 (.55)	3.81 (.46)	4.03 (.50)	4.00 (.52)	4.05 (.57)	3.99 (.55)
Facilitator	3.60 (.58)	4.03 (.65)	4.10 (.40)	4.06 (.41)	3.32 (.59)	3.82 (.51)
Delegator	3.51 (.43)	4.01 (.58)	4.09 (.47)	4.11 (.30)	3.25 (44)	3.79 (.45)

TABLE 9.3: Teacher profiles and their adoption of educational technology

Teacher profiles & characteristics	*Willingness to adopt educational technology*
Expert/Authority (35%)	
Expert/Authority/Model (24%)	
Facilitator/Expert (23%)	+
Facilitator/Delegator (18%)	+
Computer attitude	+
Computer efficacy	+

+ reprcsents a positive relationship between the factors.

No significant relationship was identified between the expert/authority profile teachers and their willingness to adopt educational technology. This style is normally more in line with the 'traditional' teaching style and it sends a message to students that *'I'm in charge here'* and tend to create a 'cool' emotional climate and certain 'distance' between teacher and student. In contrast, a positive relationship was found between the *facilitator/expert* and *facilitator/delegator* profile teachers and their willingness to adopt educational technology. These teachers are more likely to send a message to students that *'I'm here to support you and to act as a resource person'*. A warmer emotional climate is created and students and teachers can work together, share information, and the boundaries between teacher and student are not as formal as the first two clusters as presented in Table 9.3.

Mean scores of teacher's computer-attitude and efficacy, as also willingness to adopt educational technology were presented by teaching subject in Table 9.4. Teachers who had a more positive computer attitude and who were more confident about their abilities to use computer in classrooms were also more willing to adopt educational technology.

TABLE 9.4: Teacher's computer-attitude and efficacy, and willingness to adopt educational technology by teaching subject

	Chinese Language M (σ)	*Mathe-matics* M (σ)	*English Language* M (σ)	*Science* M (σ)	*Politics* M (σ)	*Total* M (σ)
Computer attitude	3.49 (.61)	3.90 (.48)	3.55 (.57)	3.81 (.59)	3.51 (.42)	3.65 (.54)
Computer efficacy	3.32 (.66)	3.58 (.51)	3.69 (.62)	3.60 (.45)	3.35 (.56)	3.51 (60)
Willingness to adopt edu. Tech.	3.90 (.49)	4.45 (.55)	3.95 (.60)	4.50 (.71)	3.83 (.52)	4.13 (.57)

Discussion

Challenges for Teachers

Educational technology can provide many advantages for instructional and learning innovations. However, educational transformation also sets up new requirements to teachers as to their teaching and learning concepts and the roles of teachers. In the new scenario, teachers cannot just stick to the traditional transmitting methods of teaching; instead teachers will play new roles as a guide or a facilitator for students. In this way, students' interest can be better stimulated, and students can take more initiatives to learn more actively and develop their independent thinking and abilities to do things and solve problems themselves. Therefore, teachers need to adapt their beliefs about teaching and learning, and be prepared for the new roles that are deemed helpful in promoting student-learning when using educational technologies. Secondly, teachers need to adapt their computer attitudes and develop their digital literacy in order to tackle the technology issues properly to support teaching and learning. Only so can they take full advantage of educational technology, the interactive and communication technologies to connect and interact with their students and the outside world in a constructive way.

Other Challenges Faced for Innovation in Education

Education in China has been influenced by behaviourist-approaches for quite a long span of time. In the last decade, reform and curricula-transformation has taken place to promote more student active, participatory approaches. However, at many schools and universities, the boundaries between old and new teaching approaches are ambiguous and intertwined, and in some cases no sustainable model is available. For example, traditional learning content is sometimes shovelled on to the Web (a static version as in the paper-books or print-outs). Although computer and Internet technologies are used, they closely model instructor-led teaching, focusing mostly on broadcasting video-based lectures or synchronous classes on the Web. This is not sustainable and cannot improve student-performance and learning outcomes.

Secondly, although huge progress has been made in ICT infrastructure construction, there is still a lack of fund for developing e-resources, online instructional content and teachers' training. Thirdly, it is important to nurture a new environment that supports the changing of educational structure, form a new type of teaching and learning mode, and meet the demands of educational objectives in the new era.

REFERENCES

Adams, N. (2003). Educational computing concerns of postsecondary faculty. *Journal of Research on Technology in Education*, 34(3), 285-303.

Ajzen, I. (1988). Attitude structure and behavior relations. In A. R. Partkanis, S. T. Berckler, & A.G. Greenwald (Eds.), *Attitude structure and function*. Hillsdale, NJ: Erlbaum.

Barone, C.A. & Hagner, P.R. (Eds.) (2001). *Technology-enhanced teaching and learning: Leading and supporting the transformation on our campus*. San Francisco: Jossey-Bass.

Bauersfeld, H. (1995). The Structuring of the Structures: Development and Function of Mathematizing as a Social Practice. In L.P. Steffe & J. Gale (Eds.), *Constructivism in Education*. Hillsdale, New Jersey: Lawrence Erlbaum Associates Publishers.

Clark, K.D. (2001). Urban middle school teachers' use of instructional technology. Journal of Research on Computing in Education, 33(2), 178–195.

Compeau, D., & Higgins, C. (1995). Computer self-efficacy: Development of a measure and initial test. *MIS Quarterly*, 19(2), 198–211.

Compeau, D., Higgins, C.A., & Huff, S. (1999). Social cognitive theory and individual reactions to computing technology: A longitudinal study. *MIS Quarterly*, 23(2), 145–158.

Cortazzi, M. (1990). Cultural and educational expectations in the language classroom. In B. Harrison (Ed.), *Culture and the language classroom* (pp. 54-65). Hong Kong: Modern English Publications and the British Council.

Cortazzi, M., & Jin, L. (1996). Cultures of learning: Language classrooms in China. In H. Coleman (Ed.), *Society and the language classroom* (pp. 169-206). Cambridge: Cambridge University Press.

Cuban, L. (2001). *Oversold and Underused: Computers in the Classroom*. Cambridge, MA: Harvard University Press.

Ebersole, S. & Vorndam, M. (2003). Adoption of computer-based instructional methodologies: A case study. *International Journal of E-Learning*, 2(2), 15-20.

Eble, K.E. (1976). *The Craft of Teaching*. San Francisco: Jossey-Bass.

Gamoran, A., Secada, W.G., & Marrett, C.B. (1998). *The organizational context of teaching and learning: Changing theoretical perspectives. Handbook of sociology of education.*

Gao, L., & Watkins, D.A. (2002). Conceptions of teaching held by school science teachers in P.R. China: Identification and cross-cultural comparisons. *International Journal of Science Education*, 24(1), 61-79.

Grasha, A.F. & Riechmann-Hruska, S. (1990). Teaching Style Survey, University of Cincinnati, Cincinnati, Oh 45221. Copyright 1976, 1987, 1990, 1996. Retrieved 3 January 2008 from http://longleaf.net/teachingstyle.html.

Grasha, A.F. (1994). A matter of style: The teacher as expert, formal authority, personal model, facilitator, and delegator. *College Teaching*, 42, 142-149.

Huang, H.M., & Liaw, S.S. (2005). Exploring users' attitudes and intentions toward the Web as a survey tool. *Computers in Human Behavior*, 21(5), 729-743.

McClure, J.W. (2003). The experiences of Chinese international postgraduates studying in Singapore. Unpublished thesis of Doctor of Education, Griffith University.

Moser, F.Z. (2007), *Educause Quarterly Magazine*, Volume 30, Number 1, 2007. Retrieved on 15 August 2009 from http://www.educause.edu/EDUCAUSE+Quarterly/EDUCAUSEQuarterlyMagazineVolum/FacultyAdoptionofEducationalTe/157436

Myers, J.M., & Halpin, R. (2002). Teachers' attitudes and use of multimedia technology in the classroom: Constructivist-based professional development training for school districts. *Journal of Computing in Teacher Education*, 18(4), 133-140.

Reeves, T.C. (2003). Storm clouds on the digital education horizon. *Journal of Computing in Higher Education*, 15(1), 3-26.

Richey, R.C. (2008). Reflections on the 2008 AECT Definitions of the Field. *TechTrends*. 52(1) 24-25.

Rogers, E. (2003). *Diffusion of innovations* (5th ed.). NY: Free Press.

Ropp, M. (1999). Exploring individual characteristics associated with learning to use computers in preservice teacher preparation. *Journal of Research on Computing in Education*, 31(4), 402-424.

Schifter, C. (2000). Faculty participation in asynchronous learning networks: A case study of motivating and inhibiting factors. *Journal of Asynchronous Learning Networks*, 4(1), 15-22.

Van Braak, J. (2001). Individual characteristics influencing teachers' class use of computers. *Journal of Educational Computing Research*, 25(2), 141-157.

Wan, G. (2001). The learning experience of Chinese students in American universities: A cross-cultural perspective. *College Student Journal*, 35(1), 28-44.

Wang, J., & Mao, S. (1996). *Culture and the kindergarten curriculum in the People's Republic of China. Early Child Development and Care*, 123, 143-156.

10.

Guiding Strategy for Technology Innovation

A CASE OF THE UNIVERSITY OF BOTSWANA

P. Y. Thomas

If you don't know where you are going, any place will do.
– Cheshire Cat in *Alice in Wonderland*

Prologue

The University of Botswana (UB) is in the process of developing an e-learning strategy that takes into account its Vision 'to be a leading academic centre of excellence in Africa and the world'. This chapter critically examines the global trends in higher education and UB's unique needs and priorities by referring to the literature and official documents such as *Botswana's Vision 2016*, *National e-learning Strategy*, UB's *Shaping our Future* and the *Learning and Teaching Policy* (LTP). In order to attain the educational goals and quality standards set in these documents, the chapter recommends a blended learning model with e-learning as a component in order to transform traditional instructional approaches more learner-centred; if appropriately blended, it will help to maximise the strengths and minimise the weaknesses of both components, and will make learning a continuous process extending it beyond time and place constraints of the physical classroom. Against this background, the chapter sets out guidelines for developing an e-learning strategy to guide through all aspects of e-learning planning, implementation, evaluation, and satisfaction. It is hoped that the strategy will help motivate and engage learners in collaborative social learning communities, disseminate good practice, promote research, foster partnerships and enhance social inclusion, thereby contributing towards UB's competitiveness locally and internationally, and thus achieving its envisaged vision. Though the discussion is surrounding the UB context, it can also be useful to other educational institutions of similar organisational cultures, working under similar contexts.

Overview

In any educational institution, there is a need to better identify and document a comprehensive learning strategy that focuses on the question, 'What should we do in order to support improved student learning and performance?' and that helps achieve its overall organizational goals and objectives. This is highly critical more than ever before because advances in information and communication technology (ICT) are rapidly changing the educational landscape. The application of new technology to improve quality and delivery of education represents one of the most dramatic innovations in education of the past century. Since the beginning of this millennium, University of Botswana (UB) has been investing significantly in technology infrastructure and other related resources in order to promote the use of new technology in enhancing teaching and learning because it believes that it can achieve its Vision and strategic goals by, besides other strategies, 'Developing a student-centred, ... technologically advanced teaching, learning ... environment' and 'extending access to higher education through the utilisation of ICTs, within the framework of life-long and open learning' (Shaping Our Future, UB's Strategic Plan, 2004).

Adoption of e-learning by an organisation is a shift towards a new learning culture. Obviously an existing culture cannot be changed so easily overnight. How long it takes for the change to happen depends on several factors. While it may be tempting to jump on the e-learning wagon, jumping too fast can lead to a risky fall. Critical requirements for successful e-learning implementation are an effective e-learning strategy and appropriate change management strategies for specific organisational context. The purpose of this paper is to develop an e-learning strategy for integrating e-learning effectively and innovatively with the conventional methods of teaching and learning at UB in order to enhance students' learning experience. The strategy will cover all aspects of e-learning planning, implementation, evaluation and satisfaction. A comprehensive e-learning strategy will help all those involved to stay focused on the implementation process.

Advances in E-learning Technologies

The landscape of digital technology has been fast advancing, from the mainframes in the 1960s to microcomputers in the 1980s, then to the Web 2.0 and Internet 2.0 of today. With such advances, e-learning has changed from computer-centred long sequences of 'page-turner' content, and drill-and-practice-based learning to a medium of communication, collaboration, research, information gathering, and a learning tool in formal and informal learning situations. Now the emphasis of e-learning is to support learning communities and make dynamic content available online.

Information and Communication Technologies can play the role of facilitating dialogue, open and critical discourse and collaborative work (Geelan & Taylor, 2001). It provides a means for teachers to support learners individually as well as collectively and facilitate personalized learning. Learning communities help to tap the power of collective intelligence and lead to active construction of knowledge through productive discourse and reflection. Research shows that a sense of community also promotes commitment to group goals, cooperation among members, and collaborative-constructivist approaches. The technology provides easy access to the required resources in an organised manner. One can easily see how the current view of e-learning is different from that of the first generation e-learning where the emphasis was simply on the "e" i.e. the electronic technology. Today, due to many affordances of technology to support learning, I want to shift the meaning of 'e' in e-learning from electronic technology to enhanced learning, and to argue that e-learning is no more an option in the higher education institutions that want to remain competitive for students in an increasingly global knowledge-based economy. E-learning is even becoming main stream due to dwindling resources and physical space constraints, and therefore, the challenge to educators is that they must be alert at all time for the rapid developments in technology in order to keep abreast with the changes in e-learning and education as a whole.

E-learning at University of Botswon

In order to open up an in-depth understanding of the potential of technology in education, e-learning at UB is defined as the appropriate use of ICTs for advancing student-oriented, active, open, collaborative and life-long teaching-learning processes.

UB launched an e-learning pilot project with seven courses delivered online using WebCT platform in August 2002. After the pilot, it went online with 21 courses in January 2003.

UB promotes e-learning for on-campus students as well as for its distance learners who are enrolled through its Centre for Continuing Education (CCE). These distance learners have very minimal face-to-face contact but are adequately supported with other modes of delivery such as print-based materials, e-learning, audio and videoconferencing. UB supports e-learning through:

- Infrastructure that includes a learning management system (LMS) – WebCT, Videoconferencing facilities, multimedia projectors, in what is termed the technology-enhanced classrooms, etc;
- Training through workshops, and other training programmes for lecturers and students aimed at developing their ICT skills;
- An *Advanced E-learning Certificate* workshop series which aim

to develop e-learning course development skills and to ensure sustainable development of e-learning approaches;
- Electronic journals, e-books, electronic databases, and an extensive list of e-learning books at the UB Library.

By May 2009, 375 courses were using WebCT; this is a little less than 25 per cent of a total of 1550 courses offered in the University. This is low for a period of seven years (from 2002).

At UB, e-learning is not a separate mode of delivery. It is simply an enabler of more effective and efficient learning by gaining synergies with conventional approaches by:

- Increasing flexibility of educational provision by extending it beyond time and place constraints of the physical classroom;
- Accommodating greater diversity of student needs, through tailor-made content and its presentation in multiple formats to suit the unique needs, preferences, and learning styles of different students, thus ensuring equity of participation and student success;
- Having greater interaction with other students, lecturers and other experts in the discipline;
- Being able to provide individualised support based on performance and identified needs;
- Promoting self-directed, lifelong learning;
- Harnessing the wealthy resources of the www and the Internet.

The Need for an E-learning Strategy

Engaging lecturers and students to use new technologies innovatively and effectively is a challenge because of several expected and unexpected barriers to technology integration. Some of the established barriers found in the literature (for example, Ertmer, 1999; Becker, 2000; Cuban, 2001; Pajo & Wallace, 2001; Snoeyink & Ertmer, 2002; Rogers, 2003; Bariso, 2003) and relevant to the UB context are: fear of innovation, negative attitudes towards the use of new technology in teaching, resistance to change, and lack of enough computers, time, adequate technical support, effective administrative support, computer skills, teacher confidence, training opportunities, conducive environment whereby lecturers are unsure as to how to effectively integrate technology, matching with students' and lecturers' expectations, incentives to those utilizing technology, and a common vision as to how to integrate. According Rogers (2003) people fear innovation, and resist it unless positive conditions occur. It is natural to assume that if these barriers were removed, the level of technology integration would be higher. Therefore, it is highly crucial to formulate a clear, concise, and measurable e-learning strategy in order to overcome these barriers, create environments with enabling conditions and evaluate processes so that it will help speed up technology adoption by mapping implementation issues to each component of the strategy and achieve its full value in the UB teaching and learning culture.

A strategic framework provides a roadmap that runs from the start to the goal stage of a transformation process. A learning strategy is deeply embedded in the organizational strategy, and it describes the input, output, and measures of the system, based on the needs and expectations of all its stakeholders. The e-learning strategy lives through the learning strategy, meaning that the e-learning goals are firmly linked with the organisational goals. This linkage is critical to ensure the ultimate success of the entire e-learning approach. The purposes of e-learning strategy, in general, are to:

- define the goals for the e-learning programme,
- logically put in place systems and processes to facilitate attaining the set goals, and
- explain how to prove that the goals have been achieved.

Every institution has varying needs and priorities with regard to e-learning solution and it is largely dependent on the culture and context of the institution. In the UB context, the e-learning strategy will provide details around the following:

- Defining the initiative and vision around the strategy linked to the UB LTP, which, in turn, is embedded in the UB vision and mission;
- Enabling the faculty to take the in developing and delivering e-learning;
- Providing appropriate resources to implement the Strategy;
- Planning, designing, developing, delivering, and evaluating online courses, and e-learning environments;
- Defining the needs and expectations of the leadership, stakeholders that include academics, students and the community;
- Professional training to academics in order to ensure that people have the necessary knowledge to perform at a level required for success;
- Change management;
- Disseminating good practice, facilitating collaboration, and promoting research;
- Providing a coordinated and coherent approach to developing and using e-learning across UB;
- Making learning more widely available, by extending reach and access;

- Enabling sharing of learning resources and services, for quality and efficiency;
- Devising a methodology for evaluation of implementation.

Guiding Principles

At UB, e-learning approach is used as an enabler for students to acquire the generic skills listed in the UB Learning and Teaching Policy (LTP) more effectively and efficiently, and to ameliorate higher education in Botswana to be internationally competitive. The all-embracing guiding principles of the e-learning strategy are derived from:

- The aim, objectives and the five policy areas of the UB LTP, and
- The definitions of e-learning and the blended learning approach promoted in UB context.

In this way, e-learning is used as conduits in the learning process towards achieving the UB Vision of academic excellence. Therefore, this proposed e-learning strategy becomes an integral part of the UB LTP, which is deeply embedded in the UB vision, mission and strategic goals.

In support of these principles, the e-learning strategy aims to:

- *Empower the student* with the aim of producing graduates who are independent, confident, self-directed, innovative, able to think critically, professionally competent, reflective practitioners, and socially responsible. This is the highest priority goal of our strategy;
- *Empower the educator* to adopt e-learning technologies to create rich, self-paced, interactive, collaborative, extended and most importantly, enticing pedagogically sound learning environments that accommodate varied learning styles and preferences. This empowerment is crucial to overcome resistance from them in the technology innovation;
- *Develop UB's capacity* to achieve excellence in research by sharing research outcomes and ideas from e-learning experiences, to disseminate good practices and to respond rapidly to new and changing opportunities in mixed-mode higher and further education, and administration;
- *Make available e-learning resources*—infrastructure and support services, and create a climate that is conducive to support flexible, multi-modal, and innovative teaching/learning strategies;
- *Continuously review the implementation process and refine it* in the context of the wider LTP and best practices in e-learning adoption.

Strategic Goals

We can harness the new technologies to our needs only if we develop clear goals and strategies on how best to use them to achieve the overall goals of the institution. We will review the success of our strategy in the context of our wider integrated learning and teaching strategy.

From the guiding principles, a number of goals can be identified and they all may be classified into three groups: pedagogical, technological and organisational-social goals.

a) Pedagogical Goals: Pedagogical goals include:

- Development of rich learning content in different media and presentation formats (visual, audio, video/graphics, text, etc.) that can accommodate students' different learning styles, preferences and special needs (e.g., speech recognition software); this may include customization, adaptation and reuse of already existing content locally or from various other sources such as the internet and SCORM.
- Move to a new level of efficiency, effectiveness and quality in our educational delivery through a blended approach by appropriately harnessing new technologies, in conjunction with existing practice. Blending online delivery with the traditional classroom approach employs the best characteristics of online education and the interactivity that typically characterises face-to-face classroom instruction (for example, intense behavioural modification, complex physical skills that might only be effectively possible only in face-to-face formats), and thereby, improves teaching and learning by maximising the strengths and minimising the weaknesses of each component. The blended model provides even greater opportunity for collaboration and interaction that goes beyond the physical classroom as it is also evident from the engagement theory (Shneiderman, 1994; 1998; Shneiderman et al, 1995; Kearsley, 1997; 1999) according to which students must be meaningfully engaged in learning activities through interaction with others and worthwhile tasks. Technology can provide an electronic learning environment (with provision for asynchronous as well as synchronous communication tools such as email, online discussion, chat, etc.) that fosters the kind of creativity and communication needed to nourish engagement in ways, which are difficult to achieve otherwise. In addition, the blended approach leads to a deeper level of learning, critical thinking, and shared understanding, and further provides opportunities for developing information literacy, social and communication skills to such an extent that is not

normally achievable through traditional classroom approaches but is essential to meet the needs of the digital age, globalisation, the new knowledge society, and the changing needs of the 21st century workforce. Therefore, this chapter recommends a workable and manageable blended learning approach for technology adoption to be successful.

Content, its development, storage and delivery are critical elements in quality teaching and it should not be a problem at UB as there are well-qualified and experienced lecturers, professors, online instructional designers, media developers and technical supporters. Storage of digital content currently leads to a beneficial concept of "learning objects" and it brings a major change in the way educational materials are designed, developed, and delivered, due to its potential for reusability, adaptability, and scalability (Hodgins, 2000). A learning object is defined here as any entity, digital or non-digital, which can be used, or re-used during technology-supported teaching and learning. The fundamental idea behind learning objects is that instructional designers can build small reusable chunks of instructional media (Reigeluth and Nelson, 1997) that can be reused a number of times in multiple learning contexts. Not only instructional benefits, learning objects may also provide financial benefits as they can potentially increase the speed and efficiency of instruction development.

b) Technological Goals: Technological goals focus on the technological standards in processes and structures that are required for the development and delivery of high quality education supported by active participation, communication and collaboration between its users.

The technological goals include:

- Availability of appropriate reliable, easily accessible, and scalable (i.e., able to handle growth in terms of increased number of users and a greater variety of more demanding applications) infrastructure to lecturers and students including those with any disabilities, and its optimal use in the most effective, efficient and sustainable manner;
- Provision for developing the skills and knowledge that lecturers should have in order to fully tap the potential of learning technologies, and to accommodate new developments in technology such as Free Open Source Software (FOSS), m-earning, Mobile context-aware techniques and systems, AI techniques in e-Learning, Data modelling for e-learning environments, etc.

UB uses WebCT 8 as the platform to provide e-learning. It has powerful tools to manage content, electronic submission of assignments, assessments, grading and grade recording, interaction and collaboration, grouping students into manageable sizes, team work, student progress tracking, student self-evaluation, individualised remedial support, online survey instruments for course evaluation, timed online quizzes, email, conferencing, chat, searchable and linkable glossary, integration of SCORM, etc.

c) Organisational-social Goals: Organisational-social goals include:

- Contribution to the outside community and other educational institutions in Botswana, the outputs of research, and expertise acquired in e-learning practices and encouraging collaborative work with them; this is very important as UB is the only tertiary institution for the nation. It should also provide leadership in this area particularly to its affiliated and associated institutions; a good example for such an initiative is the eChina programme which is a Sino-UK collaborative e-learning initiative.
- Integration of LMS with the student management system such as ITS for important services that include access to information on all educational activities, online application, course registration, e-assessments, assessment results, tracking student progress, retrieving student information, access to library resources, etc through a newly developed UB student portal in order to foster community involvement and enable the community to appreciate the benefits of new technology. All these are beneficial to current and prospective students.
- Supporting national plans such as the Botswana's Vision 2016 and the Maitlamo Project that aim at developing a culture of lifelong learning with a view to maximising the potential within all citizens and accelerating innovation to develop a knowledge-based society.

Implementation Strategy

UB needs a flexible and scalable approach to rolling out a blended strategy, one that allows a phased implementation, finds ways to apply change management strategies and meet the growing needs of lecturers and students for effective e-learning. EduTech/CAD[1] will co-ordinate these activities and provides leadership, with the overall objective of making the implementation successful. There are several tasks essential in forging a highly effective e-learning strategy. They comprise the following steps:

i) Determine the e-readiness of lecturers and students through SWOT analysis or a questionnaire survey for specific areas to focus on, such as their perceptions, concerns, background of e-learning and e-learning status quo at UB. This is critical to provide a baseline for measuring future progress and the impact of the strategy.

ii) Summarise the strengths, weaknesses and preferences. Prioritise the weaknesses and address them in the order of importance. For example, if lecturers and students do not have the necessary competencies, skills and confidence, or are reluctant to learn new skills, or are not confident with the e-learning tools due to unknown fear or may not know the benefits of blended learning, etc, they may be addressed in the order of importance or by grouping related issues together.

iii) Engage lecturers emotionally in the new technology-supported teaching and learning approach. Considering lecturers as learners, use a holistic approach integrating cognitive and affective characteristics such that they become motivated and emotionally engaged in the new approach. Freeman (1997) argues that teachers who have positive experiences with technology and have adequate support are more likely to integrate technology into their own teaching. "*There can be no knowledge without emotion. We may be aware of a truth, yet until we have felt its force, it is not ours*." (Arnold Bennett quotes, 1867-1931). Their emotional involvement is crucial in order to guard against Zuber-Skerritt's (1992) argument that even with incentives and a willingness to change, teachers often prefer to retain their status quo, which is more comfortable.

E-learning requires all the same skills as traditional teaching, plus certain additional skills such as how to develop online activities and to use the communications and the new forms assessment tools of the LMS to achieve pedagogical goals. They also need first-hand experience as online facilitators. Some lecturers need specialist training in the development and use of mathematical and scientific formulas and equations; information literacy: capability to evaluate material found on a website and to adapt them to their course needs; development of FAQs and how to facilitate discussion forums, group work and to evaluate student contributions; awareness and compliance of netiquettes and legal requirements such as privacy, plagiarism, and copyright issues, etc.

iv) Develop appropriate change management strategies that will help lecturers challenge existing practices and make them feel that innovation is imperative. In order to move an entire institution in a new direction, crucial requirement is a shared vision about why the change is needed and a strong, positive climate for innovation implementation. Hall and Hord (2001) argue that facilitating change is a team effort and in this line, they expand the idea of a single change facilitator to a 'Change Facilitator Team'. To become effective and efficient 'change facilitators', the EduTech staff should have an in-depth understanding of the change process itself- how innovations diffuse, are adopted, and integrated to a social system, and how people in a social system react to change. Also, knowing *how* to change is crucial. This is critical particularly in a research-intensive institution such as UB where e-learning initiative by academics is not linked to performance management and is unlikely to contribute significantly to their chances of career progression. Again, for people who have been in teaching for many years, the problem is not how to get new innovative thoughts in their mind, but how to get old ones out and go outside their comfort zones. Perhaps, that is why Bates and Poole (2003) argue, '*Professors are often late adopters of new technology*'.

v) Run a pilot to get feedback on what they liked and didn't like, to identify any issues that might arise and to ensure that learners can achieve the objectives of the course. Build on their strengths to make rapid and visible progress. Proactive steps must be taken to make the first experience with e-learning an exciting and inspiring one. A second chance hardly changes the first impression.

vi) Develop best-practices framework for the purpose of bench-marking and an implementation/Action plan of embedding e-learning into existing practices.

Best Practices Framework

Best practice is a pointer to the desired results (derived from the aspirations and goals) of a process that was designed well and implemented successfully. It is crucial to develop a best practices framework against which the progress can be benchmarked and to find out whether the goals have been achieved.

The UB LTPP, the *Seven Principles of Good Practice* formulated by Chickering and Gamson (1987) and the work entitled 'Implementing the Seven Principles: Technology as Lever' by Chickering and Ehrmann (1996) underpin this proposed best practices framework. Chickering and Ehrmann contend that newer technologies now have the capabilities to enrich and expand these opportunities, supporting the use of a blended learning model for enhanced teaching and practices.

A broad measure of e-learning adoption success in terms of overall efficiency, effectiveness, and quality, in a blended learning environment may be based on: 1) the success of the e-learning implementation, and 2) the value that e-learning integration has added to the traditional classroom approaches, and centred around the three aspects listed below:

i) Quality of content and its presentation;
ii) Usability of the LMS (WebCT) to structure and deliver the content (that focus on teaching/learning, flexibility, interactivity, assessment and convenience);
iii) Support services to lecturers as well as students;
iv) Quality of overall outcome.

Broad Measures of Success in the Adoption of E-learning

According to Winston Churchill (1874-1965), 'However beautiful the strategy, you should occasionally look at the results'. Assuming the LMS has a high level of usability, scalability, stability, and the capability to support content from different sources and major learning standards such as SCORM, e-learning implementation may be considered successful, if:

i) Students are provided with a clear and concise course introduction that communicates high expectations. An online introduction should include:
   (a) The course goals, learning objectives and pre-requisites,
   (b) Explicit guidelines to the type of assessments and their grading procedures.
   (c) Basic information that includes awareness and compliance of netiquettes, guidelines for participating in online discussions, as well as suggestions for using email, grading criteria for participation and assignments, copyright/academic honesty regulations, etc.
   (d) Information on the lecturer's 'virtual office' time when students can contact him/her online for assistance. It may also include an icebreaker activity for students who may be new to the online learning environment.
ii) Lecturers singly or jointly produce and make available relevant, accurate, current, logically sequenced, and well-illustrated high quality learning material that is directly related to the learning objectives, that takes into account students' backgrounds, ability levels, expectations and special needs, and that will help develop appropriate cognitive, affective, and psychomotor skills;
iii) Students can easily access a variety of content as easily manageable chunks in different interactive media / presentation formats such that they can pick the one that suits them best and learn in multiple ways;

iv) The course contains sufficient active learning techniques such as simulations, quizzes, reflective writing exercises with relevance to their daily lives, links to additional information, content summary and references that will motivate students to engage in the learning process more effectively and efficiently;

v) Students are encouraged and supported to use synchronous and asynchronous means of communication such as chat, email, discussion tools, etc in order to work collaboratively in groups, to have frequent contacts with the lecturer and to interact with experts in the discipline and to benefit from their experience and professional expertise;

vi) Lecturers provide prompt feedback through the use of online self assessments, quizzes and virtual office hours;

vii) Students get 'just in time' assistance e-learning related technical issues through campus-wide help desks;

viii) Students can regularly monitor their achievements and progress online, and are provided with additional 'personalised' learning materials based on their levels of achievement through the use of 'selective release' feature of the LMS; thus, students take control of their own learning with enhanced flexibility and more convenience than it is normally possible from single mode traditional classrooms;

ix) Lecturers get effective support in designing, developing and or adopting well structured learning material and related learning objects such as pre-tests, quizzes, post-tests, assignments, assessments, etc that are essential for enhancing learning and assessing student progress;

x) Continuing professional support (CPS) with emphasis on informal, personalised assistance is in place to develop lecturers' technology skills and make them stick to the new teaching paradigm and thus, sustain the technology integration process. Many projects have failed to reach wide acceptance because adequate post adoption support was not provided (Hansen, Deshpande, & Murugesan, 1999; Surry & Farquhar, 1997);

xi) E-learning courses may take more time to develop and deliver; lecturers' extra efforts in effectively using ICTs for pedagogical benefits are recognised in their roles and responsibilities and in their professional progression; this is critical to overcome the usual resistance to change;

xii) The IT department is able to immediately address technical issues and continuously support the infrastructure and resource needs;

xiii) All lecturers and students understand and comply with copyright regulations;

xiv) E-learning becomes part of the UB teaching and learning culture; by Rogers' estimate, 84 per cent of lecturers are receptive to adopting ICT tools to enhance students' classroom learning experience (The remaining 16 per cent lecturers, according to him, could be laggards!);

xv) UB graduates are capable to access, evaluate, and communicate information, to use technology effectively, and to work well with people from all cultures around the world;

xvi) Effective mechanisms are in place to evaluate the e-learning implementation process formatively and to disseminate good practices.

In order to determine whether the goals are being achieved, it is essential to conduct surveys among students and lecturers on factors listed above in addition to other factors related to the usability of LMS, course structure, quality and effectiveness of the teaching and learning process, flexibility, technical support and pedagogical usefulness of technology, and evaluate their feedback in conjunction with related information gathered from the change facilitators.

Implementation Plan

The implementation plan stipulates actions needed from an institutional perspective in order to achieve the envisaged goals. Successful delivery of these actions depends on faculty's capability as well as readiness to handle change, and on the availability of appropriate resources; that is, funding and staff time in order to provide secure, robust, anytime access by adequately maintaining and integrating e-learning fully into the budget process. Individual faculties have to prepare e-learning implementation plans with particular emphasis on embedding e-learning in teaching, learning and assessment. Each department has to appoint a Coordinator to be responsible for e-learning, to give advice in relation to staff development of academic, technical and support staff and to implement relevant e-learning policies at departmental level.

Based on the above discussions, the following guidelines are suggested for implementing the strategy and to help develop a tool to determine whether what is preached is in place or actually practised within the framework of this e-learning strategy.

Intentionally, a time frame for achieving the objectives are not included in this plan as this chapter is just for academic purposes.

1. Pedagogical Goals

Objectives (What must be done to achieve the goal?)	*Activities (How will it be done?)*
1.1 Develop rich learning content in different media and presentation forms (visual, audio, video/ graphics, text, etc).	• EduTech to train lecturers on the characteristics and benefits of e-learning , on why a change in paradigm is needed, and on how to develop and implement e-learning by effectively embedding it in the traditional classroom model; • Lecturers to state clearly the course goals / objectives and the assessment procedures / techniques at the beginning of the course; • Instructional Designer to support lecturers in designing the learning objects and media formats to suit the varied needs of students; • Lecturers to create and structure course content, logically sequenced in small chunks, and well illustrated and presented to accommodate the needs of students with different learning styles, preferences and special needs (e.g., speech recognition software); • Lecturers to be encouraged to adopt and share learning objects including online resources without infringing copyrights; • Lecturers to include pre-test and post-test activities/self-assessment items to enable students to evaluate their own learning progress; • Lecturers to communicate high expectations and associate each learning object/activity with specific learning objective to make students know why they are important to them. *(Adults normally learn something only when they know the purpose of learning it.)*; • Lecturers to be encouraged to do research in e-learning related areas and disseminate research outputs to facilitate curriculum design and development.
1.2 Encourage achieving a new level of efficiency, effectiveness and quality in educational delivery by using new technologies.	• Lecturers to use technology only where it is educationally appropriate, that is, only where it can really enhance and extend the traditional classroom model, not just for the sake of it; • EduTech to develop strategies for raising e-learning awareness and skills of lecturers and students, and provide them training in relevant areas with particular focus on teaching and

	learning in a blended learning context, e-learning tools, techniques and methodologies; A stimulating online module in conjunction with face to face hands-on material on how to plan and develop / adopt teaching materials and how to handle copyright and plagiarism issues will be an indicator of this. • Lecturers to be encouraged to share resources, strategies, and best practices among members as scholarly and rewarding activities; • Lecturers to utilise online assessment instruments that may include individual tests, participation in group discussions, portfolio development, etc. • Lectures to promote and utilise communication features of new technologies as learning is a social activity and communication is central to any successful teaching and learning strategy • EduTech to apply appropriate *change management strategies* to challenge as well as encourage lecturers to tap the potential of technology for pedagogical benefits and further to keep pace with the rapid advancements in technology in order to address the changing skills needed of our students– the most important pedagogical goal of preparing students for life.
1.3 Promote the use of e-learning to extend students' learning process beyond the classrooms.	• Lectures to provide FAQ section and virtual office hours for consultation after classes from anywhere the students are; • Lecturers to encourage students to utilise the online communication tools to actively engage in dialogue, open and critical discourse, and collaborative work with class members as well as to interact with experts in the discipline and to benefit from their experience and professional expertise; • Lecturers to empower students by encouraging them to manage their own learning and to sensitise them on the need for self-directed lifelong learning.
1.4 Encourage innovation and promote excellence in learning.	• EduTech/CAD to evaluate the design, development and implementation process of this strategy by using the proposed best practices framework and the associated measures of success as a benchmarking tool for quality assurance;

	• Also, CAD to integrate the quality assurance procedures for e-learning into the existing quality assurance procedures; • EducTech/CAD to identify champions in e-learning and harness their strengths as a source of UB-wide systemic change; • UB to encourage and recognise good practices in the use of e-learning through professional recognition.
2. Technological Goals	
2.1 Make available appropriate reliable, easily accessible, stable, and scalable infrastructure with the capability to support content from different sources and major learning standards such as SCORM to lecturers and students including those requiring any special needs (e.g., speech recognition software);	• WebCT 8 LMS is already up and running; and it is available on a 24x7 basis accessible from anywhere; • EduTech to explore and provide other appropriate latest media/ technologies for lecturers to use where appropriate; • IT department to provide appropriate add-ons to accommodate the needs of students with special needs; • EducTech to provide training on the use of LMS and other appropriate technologies; • IT to provide more computers and timely technical support, which can make e-learning widely available to staff and students. • To ensure that e-learning is accessible to all students whatever their individual circumstances through fair access to computers and technology for all students including those students with special needs assertive technologies and appropriate equipment (e.g. Braille computers) in accessible locations for students with special needs.
2.2 Make provision for developing appropriate skills and knowledge to accommodate new developments in technology.	• IT Dept to review their own strategy regularly to ensure that it meets the up-to-date infrastructure needs of the e-learning strategy in the context of rapid developments in technology. • EduTech staff to sharpen their skills to match the developments in technology and corresponding pedagogical innovations and to support the increasing needs of lecturers and students in the context of rapid developments in technology such as Free Open Source Software (FOSS), mlearning, Mobile context-aware techniques and systems, AI techniques in e-learning, Data modeling for e-learning environments, etc;

	• Lecturers to be encouraged to collaborate with colleagues in the spirit of lifelong learning to keep pace with new developments in technology.
2.3 Encourage optimal use of technology in the most effective and efficient manner that will be sustainable.	• IT Dept. to establish a well-rounded e-learning environment with enough computers with WebCT access without any need for students to queue for long; • IT Dept. to reserve some computers only for e-learning use; • UB Management to recognise lecturers' e-learning initiatives as a scholarly activity particularly as part of research with a view to encouraging them to use more of their time in developing innovative teaching approaches using new technologies; • UB Management to consider the need for a distinct workload policy governing e-learning as e-learning courses may take more time to develop and deliver; • EduTech to support lecturers in selecting technical solutions pertinent to their courses and to provide them training and specialised assistance in developing pedagogically sound e-learning strategies; • UB to enforce the delivery of some of the GEC courses especially GEC 121 and GEC 122 only by online; • IT Dept to develop and enforce a clear policy on on-campus ICT usage (For example, physical security, guide to access computers, unauthorized access to files that belong to others, use of infected disks, use of unlicensed programs on UB computers, accessing pornographic site, sending unacceptable emails, etc and the possible punishments stated in the ICT policy) and to make it known to the whole University community.

3. Organisational-Social Goals

3.1 Contribute to the outside community and other	• UB Management to recognise the champions in e-learning and support them through funded research in such areas as to explore ways to make e-learning a part of the UB teaching and learning culture, and to make available the outcome of research, and the expertise acquired, to the outside community and other institutions

	educational institutions in Botswana, the output of research, and expertise acquired in e-learning practices and encourages collaborative work with them.	in Botswana as UB is the only tertiary institution for the nation. • Deans and HoDs to visibly contribute to the change management strategies, and to take initiative to update and review the e-learning strategy regularly. • UB Management to recognise and encourage lecturers' e-learning practices within and outside UB.
3.2	Use the new technology to streamline academic administration.	• IT to make provision for a student portal in order to integrate WebCT with ITS (student management system) for important services that include online application, course registration, e-assessments, assessment results, tracking student progress, retrieving student information, access to library resources, etc to foster community involvement and enable the community to appreciate the benefits of new technology.
3.3	Support national development plans	• UB Management to utilise the expertise of its staff to contribute to the national developmental strategies/priorities such as the Vision 2016 and the Maitlamo Project that aim to develop a culture of lifelong learning with a view to maximising the potential within all citizens and accelerating innovation to develop a knowledge-based society.

Conclusion

Though e-learning has not yet lived up to its initial ambitious promises in terms of pedagogical innovations, it is growing at a rapid pace especially in higher education institutions across both the developed and developing worlds. A comprehensive e-learning strategy is critical for making best use of technology resources while positively impacting student performance and organizational competitiveness. It is also essential is provide a distinctive teaching and learning experience that is informed by the institution's research-intensive environment, and to develop and maintain regional, national and international co-operation and partnerships in order to share good practice and collaborate on research and development activities.

Chickering and Ehrmann's (1996) *Seven Principles for good practice in the context of technology*, Kearsley and Schneiderman's (1999) *Engagement theory* and the UB's proposed teaching & learning policy, form the conceptual framework for this e-learning strategy initiative which advocates a blended learning approach. Every institution has different needs and priorities with regard to e-learning solution and it is largely dependent on the culture and context of an institution. The blended approach proposed in this paper is for the University of Botswana, but it can be also useful to other educational institutions with similar organisational culture and working under similar contexts. It is hoped that the strategy will help facilitate collaboration, disseminate good practice, promote research, foster partnerships and enhance social inclusion, thereby contributing towards UB's competitiveness locally and internationally, and thus achieve its envisaged vision

NOTES

1. Educational Technology Unit of the Centre for Academic Development.

REFERENCES

Bariso, E.U. (2003). The computer revolution: Friend or foe to FE college staff. *British Journal of Educational Technology*, 34(1), 85-88.

Bates, A.W., & Poole, G. (2003). *Effective Teaching with Technology in Higher Education: Foundations for Success*. San Francisco: Jossey-Bass

Becker, H.J. (2000). Internet use by teachers. In *Technology and Learning* (pp. 80-111). San Francisco: Jossey-Bass.

Boettcher, J.V. & Kumar, M.S. (2000). The other infrastructure: Distance education's digital plant. *Syllabus,* 13(10).

Chickering, A.W. & S.C. Ehrmann. (1997). Implementing the Seven Principles: Technology as a lever. *American Association for Higher Education.* Retrieved 12 July 2006, from http://www.aahe.org/technology/ehrmann.htm

Chickering, A.W., & Z.F. Gamson. (1987). Seven principles of good practice in undergraduate education. *AAHE Bulletin*, 39, 3-7.

Davies, D. (2003). *Design content for blended learning solution*, E-Learning Conference, Manchester, 18–19 March.

e-learning Guild, The. Available: www.e-learningguild.com.

Ertmer, P.A. (1999). Addressing first- and second-order barriers to change: Strategies for technology integration. Educational Technology Research and Development, 47(4), pp. 47-61.

Freeman, M. (1997). Flexibility in access, interaction and assessment: the case for web-based teaching programs. *Australian Journal of Educational Technology*, 13(1), 23-39.

Geelan, D.R. & Taylor, P.C. (2001). Embodying Our Values in Our Teaching Practices: Building Open and Critical Discourse through computer Mediated Communication. *Journal of Interactive Learning Research*, 12(4): 375-401.

Hall, G.E. & Hord, S.M. (2001). *Implementing Change: Patterns, Principles, and Potholes.* Boston: Allyn and Bacon.

Hodgins, Wayne (2000). *Into the future* [On-line]. Retrieved July 23 2006 from http://www.learnativity.com/download/mp7.pdf

Hulm, C. (2003). Implementing a blended approach with your e-Learning, E-Learning Conference, Manchester, 18–19 March.

Kearsley, G. & Shneiderman, B. (1999). Engagement theory: A framework for technology-based teaching and learning. Retrieved Aug 26 2007 from http://home.sprynet.com/~gkearsley/engage.htm

Kearsley, G. (1997). The Virtual Professor: A Personal Case Study. Retrieved June 25, 2007, from [http://home.sprynet.com/~gkearsley/virtual.htm]

Laurillard, D. (1993). *Rethinking university teaching: A framework for the effective use of educational technology*. London: Routledge.

Mason R. 'Evaluation reports on courses over JANUS' - Volume 1 Delta deliverable for project 2003 JANUS.

Pajo, K. & Wallace, C. (2001). Barriers to the uptake of web-based technology by university teachers. *Journal of Distance Education*, 16(1). Retrieved June 22, 2003, from http://cade.athabascau.ca/vol16.1/pajoetal.html

Rosenberg, M.J. (2001). *e-Learning: Strategies for Delivering Knowledge in the Digital Age*. McGraw-Hill.

Shneiderman, B. (1994) Education by Engagement and Construction: Can Distance Education be Better than Face-to-Face? Retrieved June 10, 2006, from http://www.hitl.washington.edu/scivw/EVE/distance.html

Shneiderman, B. (1998), Relate-Create-Donate: An educational philosophy for the cyber-generation. Computers & Education.

Shneiderman, B., Alavi, M., Norman, K. & Borkowski, E. (Nov. 1995). Windows of opportunity in electronic classrooms, Communications of the ACM, 38(11), 19-24.

Singh, H. (2003). Building Effective Blended Learning Programs November-December 2003 Issue of *Educational Technology*, 43 (6), pp. 51-54.

Singh, H. & Reed, C. (2001). A white paper: Achieving success with blended learning. Los Angeles: Centra Software.

Snoeyink, R. & Ertmer, P. A. (2002). Thrust into technology: how veteran teachers respond. *Journal of Educational Technology Systems*, 30(1), 85-111.

Surry, D. & Farquhar, J. (1997). Diffusion Theory and Instructional Technology. *Journal of Instructional Science and Technology*, 2(1).

Thorne, K. (2003). *Blended Learning: How to Integrate Online and Traditional Learning*. London: Kogan Page.

University of Botswana. (2004). *Shaping Our Future, UB's Strategic Plan*. Gaborone: University of Botswana.

Young, J.R. (2002). "Hybrid" teaching seeks to end the divide between traditional and online instruction. The Chronicle of Higher Education. Retrieved Feb 2 2006, from http://chroicle.com/prm/weekly/v48/i28/28a03301.htm

Zuber-Skerritt, O. (1992). Action Research in Higher Education: Examples and Reflections. London: Kogan Page.

PART C
EDUCATIONAL TECHNOLOGY AND ITS USE IN ACADEMIA

11.

Education Technology, Teachers and Social Capital: A Crucial Combination

Phillip Hughes

Education is facing an unprecedented task. While schooling is always in search of improved performance a special urgency now arises from the necessity to achieve improved level of performance for all students. New information, new knowledge, new applications of knowledge and new societal demands pose an increasing challenge. Those who left school without an adequate basic education are poorly equipped either to take-up productive work or to manage their own lives.

Education has a long history of effort to improve its effectiveness. The additional need to provide education for all, rather than for a selected few, poses a special challenge. This something to which the United Nations has given its top priority, pointing out the urgency in its Millennium Development Goals, which it developed in cooperation with the World Bank and other major international agencies.

'Millennium Development Goals' abbreviated as MDG of UNESCO stresses on:

1. Eradicate extreme poverty and hunger.
2. Achieve Universal Primary Education.
3. Promote gender equality and empower women.
4. Reduce child mortality.
5. Improve maternal health.
6. Combat HIV/AIDS, malaria and other diseases.
7. Ensure environmental sustainability.
8. Develop a global partnership for development.'

UNESCO, 2008.

The MDG's are notable for the breadth as well as the specificity of the goals, representing as they do have the experience of 60 years of effort in international cooperation and recognising also the new issues to be faced.

An Idea with a History

Universal education is not a new idea. *Jan Amos Comenius* proclaimed this as a goal almost 500 years ago. *Comenius* was born in Moravia, now part of the Czech Republic, but spent much of his life moving from country to country, persecuted because of his ideas, including the 'heretical' belief that all people deserved and needed a good education. Paradoxically his ideas were spread more widely through Europe because of the strong campaign to silence him. Fleeing from the inquisition, he lived and worked in many European countries, including Germany, Poland, Sweden, England, Prussia, Hungary and finally Holland where he died in 1670. His ideas remained active even after his death.

> *'We must aim unreservedly to restore to the human race freedom of thought, religious freedom and civic freedom for freedom is the most human asset created along with man and inseparable from him.'*
>
> Comenius, in Kuras, 2007.

In all the places to which he fled he played an active role educationally, aided by the fact that, like all learned people of his day, he wrote in Latin, ensuring a continent-wide audience. Comenius is best known for his books, numbering over 200, including *The Great Didactic* (1628-1632; trans. 1896, 1931) and *Visible World in Pictures* (1658; trans. 1659). The latter is believed to be the first illustrated textbook for children and indicates his eagerness to find new means of communication.

It is ironic that an educator born in 1592 should have such a relevant message for us today. Comenius has been adopted by the United Nations Educational Scientific and Cultural Organisation, UNESCO, as the symbol of its current major priority, Education for All. The death of Comenius in 1670 seemed to end his campaign for universal education. On the contrary that campaign has extended and broadened. After being confined to lectures on the history of education in many education courses, those ideas have become part of the main thrust in current education, central to the major campaigns of the international organisations. A few industrialised countries adopted this aim of universal education during the 19th Century and it was adopted as a major goal for all countries when the UN defined its Charter in 1946. This was the key task specified for the UN's special agency for education, UNESCO.

The urgency of the task was initially seen as an issue for developing countries where millions of students were not in schools at all. UNESCO and other international organisations have worked together for more than 60 years to help in the massive task of providing universal primary schooling for many countries and now seek to achieve that aim fully by 2015. During this long effort the concept has developed significantly. It now involves much more than achieving universal attendance and includes the successful provision of what UNESCO calls 'basic education'.

> *Basic education denotes the minimum skills and knowledge needed in order to be able to make a full contribution to one's environment and to be in control of one's life. In an increasingly interdependent world, the contents, and therefore the very notion of the 'quality' of basic education are evolving. It can no longer be reduced to learning reading, writing and arithmetic. It must also teach individuals to be, to do, to learn and to live together.* Maatsuura, 2000.

This extension of the concept to Basic Education for All changed the nature of the challenge. It is now significant for all countries, not only for the developing world. The demands for high levels of achievement rise continually but also the penalties for low levels of achievement have become much more severe. Employment opportunities for unskilled work have reduced consistently. The double task of higher achievement for the best students, together with an effective education for all, is one that all nations are pursuing. Few manage to succeed at both levels. Finland, Hong Kong, Canada and Korea feature among the few who come close to achieving basic education for all their students. They perform at high levels in the OECD test programs and also have a relatively small group of students failing to reach acceptable levels of performance. (OECD, 2005b)

Most other countries do not manage to achieve this dual success. Many fall into the next category with the achievement of the best students being high but with a substantial group of students whose performance is at low levels. For this latter group the effects are drastic. Not only are their employment opportunities limited but their participation more generally in their society is also restricted. In Australia, for example, the Business Council of Australia calculates that 35,000 students each year leave school without an effective education. That group is deeply disadvantaged, not just briefly but over the long term. The effects are very widespread. The Director of the Australian Council for Educational Research, Professor Geoff Masters, pointed out some of the cumulative effects when inadequately prepared school leavers join an existing group in the community of those unable to find work.

> *It is also where we are failing more than 300,000 young people aged between 15 and 24 who are either unemployed or working part-time and not undertaking full-time education. Currently, the overall level of unemployment is 4.3 per cent; the unemployment rate for 15-to-24-year-olds is more than double that rate at 9.1 per cent. Australia must pursue policies that close and prevent gaps in educational*

> *quality, such as gaps between schools in different locations or between private and public schools. All students should receive a high-quality education no matter which school they attend.* Masters, 2007

Masters goes on to point out that while Australia's schools do produce high-quality results they compare badly with those countries which had a substantial proportion of high-quality student performances but also manage to achieve reasonable levels of success for almost all students. A second group of countries such as England and New Zealand show the same disparity as Australia. Most other countries show results that do not have such high level results and also have large groups of students leaving without adequate levels of success. All now seek urgently to develop patterns where effective levels of success are reached by all students. In spite of the major difficulties this presents, this task is now universally accepted.

In the past, three major avenues of improvement have had successes in achieving effective change in education. One is through the efforts of teachers in developing new approaches: a second is through the use of new technology: a third is through building better connections between school and community. All countries now seek to improve their education systems through various combinations of efforts in these three areas.

Current assessments show mixed results: none of the eight Millennium Development Goals seem likely to be achieved by the target date of 2015. The proportion of people living on less than a dollar per day fell from 23.4 per cent in 1999 to 19.8 per cent in 2007, broadly on target but with massive variations between countries. The eradication of hunger is still a long way from being achieved, with 46 per cent of the under-fives in Africa registered as underweight. Infant mortality is down by one-sixth, as against the target of 2/3 reduction. Although China and India and other parts of Asia have increased school attendance significantly, 12 per cent of children globally and 30 per cent in Sub-Saharan Africa were still out of school. Other MDG targets, particularly in Africa, displayed similarly concerning patterns. (UN, 2007).

UNESCO's 2009 Monitoring Report is pessimistic about the possibility of success as it considers the impact of the global financial crisis.

> *When financial systems fail, the consequences are highly visible and governments act. When education systems fail the consequences are less visible, but no less real. Unequal opportunities for education fuel poverty, hunger, and child mortality, and reduce prospects for economic growth. That is why governments must act with a greater sense of urgency.* UNESCO, 2009.

Can Educational Technology Redress the Imbalance?

One possibility of major improvements for education is through technology, which has revolutionised much of modern life. The relationship between education and technology has always been complex. The major source of new technology has been through ideas fostered by education. Yet education probably makes less effective use of technology than most areas of modern life. While many areas such as communication, economic production and entertainment have been transformed through technology, much of the process of schooling today would look familiar to teachers from the past. Books, pen and paper, the blackboard, a teacher in front of a group of students: all these still feature strongly as the key elements in most school classrooms. This continuity with the past is in contrast to most areas of life.

Successions of major technological developments which owe their source to education have been tried in schools. Radio, film, television: these successive developments which have revolutionized peoples' homes, their work and their social environment have all featured in substantial attempts to improve education. None of them has done so. In spite of significant efforts, substantial investment and considerable time, their measurable effect on the quality of education has been slight.

The most recent major initiative to support education is through computers. In this case the conclusions have still to be drawn. After a period where they seemed to have the same marginal impacts as other technological approaches there are strong indications of a possible major contribution through computers. A recent book uses the challenging phrase 'revolution' in its title: *The Interactive Whiteboard Revolution* (Lee and Betcher, 2009). This outlines a strong case that a new technology can deliver revolutionary changes. The book does not ignore the past and the high claims made by past reformers, claims full of hope at the beginning and rarely repented as they become unreal. It recognizes the problem and the difficulty of such a task but brings together the experiences of teachers in many countries to make a strong and persuasive case. Their case is that the development of educational technology designed specifically for schools, such as the Interactive Whiteboard, abbreviated as IWB, can be a powerful influence in the daily practice of teachers, an influence similar in its impact to that other revolutionary introduction, the blackboard, way back in 1801 AD.

Why are such claims worth considering when education has shown itself to be so resistant to revolutionary change? *Mal Lee* is an experienced educator with long experience and is careful in his estimation of change in education. He has been involved in another publication, one with a less dramatic title, The Use of Instructional Technology in Schools, written in partnership with Arthur Winzenried. (Lee and Winzenreid, 2008). That book, also published by ACER, surveys the broad field of instructional technology, its claims and its achievements. It leads through well-documented argument to identify the potential of the IWB. The subsequent book, written in partnership with Chris Betcher, jumps from that solid platform of research and observation to detail the experiences of teachers in many places and at many levels to show, not just what can be achieved, but what is being achieved in many diverse settings. Its identification of the reasons so few teachers have used these technologies is powerful. It recognizes the realities of the classroom and the reasons why the most commonly used classroom aids remain: the pen, paper and black board. Importantly it identifies the processes needed to get all teachers to use the appropriate instructional technology as a normal part of everyday teaching. It is demonstrated that student learning is enhanced by adopting these new technologies. The basis of this success is partly through the format of the new technology itself and partly that it because it achieves such wide acceptance by teachers.

The IWB is much more than an electronic blackboard as it delivers to classrooms a massively increased flexibility, both in links with the wider world and in providing teachers with immediately available resources. In assessing this diversity of experience that title of 'revolution' becomes more plausible. The implementation of the IWB in England, continental Europe and Australia shows uneven use: at its best, however, this technology, designed specifically for schools, can achieve significant effects on teaching and learning. The authors make a vital qualification to their case for this technology.

> *'the key to creating a truly successful technology integration program is not how clever the technologists can be, but rather how well the school manages the ongoing training and support needed to help every teacher move forward in their use of technology.'* (p. 128)
>
> (Lee and Betcher, 2009)

To reach every teacher is the demanding step. A continuing revolution will need to be more broadly based than any of the past reforms in education but it is clear that technology which is specially designed for the work of teachers offers much more promise than any of the past attempts at its use in education.

School and Community: A Vital Interaction

In a successful education the importance of home background has been well documented. David Berliner, in his Presidential Address to the American Association for Education Research, affirmed the link in a summary of recent research.

'Among the lowest social classes, environmental factors, particularly family and neighbourhood influences, not genetics, is strongly associated with academic performance.' Berliner, 2005.

A significant element in his findings was that the factors linked with poor performance are not fixed by genetics but are subject to change. David Hargreaves makes the same point in identifying where help may be offered.

'Community, not curriculum, is where many of our improvement efforts now need to be focused. One of the most common causes of secondary school dropout is pupils' feelings that there is not one adult who really knows or cares for them. England is trying to solve a massive block in performance as children move from primary school to secondary school, by making improvements to the curriculum. But the curriculum is not the main problem. Kathryn Riley and her colleagues' research shows that pupils who do badly in the early years of secondary school experience incredible fragmentation in their lives - between different parents and families, and constantly changing homes. They are denied what is called social capital.'

Hargreaves, 2005.

For disadvantaged students, the help will only come by dealing realistically with their circumstances. Barry McGaw, in an OECD publication stressed this point, identifying the major benefits of social capital to economic well-being. He distinguishes the particular impact of social capital, as well as human capital, on individual and social progress.

'The resources devoted to education are among the most important investments that countries and their people make. Modern knowledge economies require a highly skilled workforce, not just an elite, since economic growth is driven by a powerful interaction between increased human competence and the adoption of new technology. Individuals need high level skills as well, since, without them, they are at great risk of exclusion.

Building only human capital is insufficient. Social capital – networks together with shared norms, values and understandings that facilitate cooperation within or among groups – is also essential to the development and maintenance of cohesive societies.' McGaw, 2005.

Robert Putnam, in his powerful book, Bowling Alone, identifies the same phenomenon in US society.

'Social capital, the level of social trust, personal connectedness, is the single most powerful predictor of educational performance: race, poverty, parental education are only indirect.' Putnam, 2000.

Putnam identified a major decline in US social capital in the period 1960-2000 and showed the powerful impact of the decline on many features of US society because of the strong correlation between social capital and other social indicators. His research showed the following relationships: Children's Welfare-Social Capital: correlation +0.8; Educational performance- Social Capital +0.8; TV watching-Educational Performance in Grades 4 & 8 minus 0.8; Health-Social Capital +0.7.

The results and comments of Putnam are relevant well beyond the US as he identifies links with everyday life common to many societies. He emphasises the need for strong social support from outside the school and the need for schools to recognise the power of their social milieu on what they can achieve.

> *'One reason that students from minority and impoverished backgrounds are disadvantaged educationally is precisely because they lack access to productive social capital, both inside and outside the school. One strategy, therefore, for assisting under-performing schools has been to foster a more active community and to link parents and community members more immediately to schools. A complementary strategy that has been shown to be effective is the use of mentors (that is, part-time lay teachers from the community) who can bring skills, experience, energy, and caring from the community into the schools. For example, one successful program in the US called Experience Corps draws on specially trained retired adults (often themselves members of minority groups) to mentor disadvantaged young children in school on a regular basis.'*
>
> Putnam, 2004.

The Role of the Teacher

A factor which emerges strongly is the importance of the teacher in this complex interaction of influences. The research on technology in education stresses the importance of the teacher in making technology more accessible. The teacher becomes especially important when home background is unhelpful or when students are finding school unhelpful. A longitudinal study over 15 years, involving 20,000 students, clarifies the role of teachers (Abbott-Chapman and Hughes, 1990). The study confirms that the socio-economic status (SES) of students is strongly related to their school performance and that the strength of this relationship increases over the period of schooling. However, 16 per cent of that cohort succeeded despite adverse backgrounds and circumstances. For these students the influence of particular teachers proved to be very significant. This group of teachers effectively acted as 'circuit-breakers', breaking the cycle of social disadvantage/educational failure/ increased disadvantage. These teachers were quite varied, showing considerable individuality but did show two common factors: their conviction that all students could succeed and also their capacity to use a wide range of teaching approaches. These teachers could not be classified under any of the common classifications: progressive, constructivist, traditional, progressive or learner-centred. Rather, they had a great range of teaching approaches, covering all these different categories but with the capacity to adapt their approaches to different circumstances and individuals.

The overall conclusion from this project was that the special qualities and characteristics of effective teachers are related less to teaching styles and such dimensions as the Progressive-Traditionalist spectrum than to the nature of the teacher-student relationship. Mutual respect and rapport with the students were seen as pre-requisites of effective teaching. (Holloway and Abbott-Chapman, 1992)

A recent study sheds confirming light on the importance of the teacher. Yair (2009) identifies the idea of 'turning points' from his research in Britain. He identifies 'educational turning points' as being highly significant for many learners. He examined accounts of 'positive turning points' from 1100 respondents' reports of key educational experiences. Students accounts typically involved experiences of continued failure and subsequent feelings of hopelessness that were 'magically transformed' by a teacher. Such teachers were usually new to the student and were encountered at the beginning of the school year. The reports were characterised by the teachers' high expectations and the subsequent trust and acceptance by the student.

Conclusion

The important aim of an effective education for all students is still far from achievement in spite of substantial effort in almost all countries over the past 60 years. There are now many positive indications that it can be achieved. That achievement, however, depends on a more holistic approach than is common, an approach which uses the skills of teachers, the insights of technology and a constructive relationship between school and the home environment.

Bibliography

Abbott-Chapman and Hughes (1990). Identifying the Qualities and Characteristics of the 'Effective' Teacher. YES Centre, University of Tasmania.

ACER, (2003). Rothman and McMillan. Influences on Achievement in Literacy and Numeracy. ACER Report 36, 2003.

BCA, (2003). The Cost of Dropping Out. The Business Council of Australia, Sydney.

Berliner, (2005). Presidential Address to AERA, Montreal, Canada, 2005.
Comenius, J.A. (1628). *The Great Didactic* (1628-1632; trans. 1896, 1931).
Comenius, J.A. (1658). *Visible World in Pictures* (1658; trans. 1659),
Dakar, (2000). The Dakar Framework for Action. UNESCO, Paris.
Hargreaves, A. (2005). Teaching in the Knowledge Society. Buckingham: Open University Press and New York: Teachers College Press.
Holloway and Abbott-Chapman, (1992). Identifying the Qualities and Characteristics of the 'Effective' Teacher. Part 2. YES centre, University of Tasmania.
Kuras, Benjamin (2007). *Restoring Comenius.* Ideal Publishing House, Prague.
Lee and Betcher (2009). *The Interactive Whiteboard Revolution.* ACER Press, Hawthorn, Victoria.
Lee and Winzenried (2008). *The Use of Instructional Technology in Schools*, ACER Press, Hawthorn, Victoria.
Masters, G. (2005). 'Raising the question: are we world class?' In *Education Review*, February 2005.
Masters, G. (2007). Restoring our Edge in Education. Report to Business Council of Australia.
McGaw, Barry (2005). *Evidence or Ideology: Developing evidence-based policy in education.* OECD, Paris.
O'Brien and Rollefson (1995). Extracurricular Participation and Student Engagement. NCES, National Center for Education Statistics. NCES pp. 95-741
OECD, (2005a). *Work and Education*, 2005-2006. OECD, Paris.
OECD, (2005b). *First Results from PISA*, 2003.
Putnam, Robert D. (2000). *Bowling Alone*. Simon & Schuster, New York.
Putnam, (2004). *Education, Diversity, Social Cohesion and Social Capital.* OECD, Paris.
UNESCO, (2008). *Millennium Development Goals.* UNESCO, Paris.
UNESCO, (2009). *Global Monitoring Report.* UNESCO, Paris.
Yair, J. (2009). Educational Turning Points. *British Journal of Educational Research.*

12.

A Suggested Model of E-Twinning of Academic Institutions

Nilasco Arputharaj and *Shobana Nelasco*

Prologue

E-Twinning of Academic institutions is the process of linking various institutions or organizations for academic purposes with electronic communication system, so that the resources available in one place can be utilized by the teachers, researchers and learners in another area. This model is categorised into intra-country, intra-institute, inter-institute and inter-country program. Vertical and Horizontal e-Twinning are the two methods through which this model can be implemented. The major purpose of the chapter is to bring about a model of e-Twinning of academic institutions, and to explain as how to do, with whom to do, what are the possible areas of e-Twinning and the like. Various methods of E-Twinning such as sharing of infrastructure among institutions and countries, conferences, staff-exchange programmes, research networking, student-exchange program are also discussed. Videoconference, conference room conferencing, web-communication, web-conferencing, virtual-world and on-line collaborations are the medium of bringing the academic world together. The importance of e-Twinning is also emphasised. This chapter also studies the challenges facing the implementation of this model and the methodologies that can be adopted for overcoming this problem. More e-workshops, e-twinning of institutions, e-twinning of Workshops, inter-institute exchange programs, inter-country exchange programs etc. are suggested for promoting the adoption of e-learning and virtual learning across the world.

Introduction

E-Twinning of academic institutions is the process of linking various institutions or organizations for academic purposes with electronic communication system, so that the resources available in one place can be utilized by the teachers, researchers and learners in another area. This is a method, which will help the institutions to have a better coordination of the work done, better understanding of the problems, better utilization of the resources available and finally better administration of the work.

This chapter is a virgin contribution of the authors and hence not based on any earlier literature. The existing inequalities within countries and between countries have motivated the authors to present this study.

Every country has different demographic, socio, economic and political condition. Based on these inequalities, the educational growth and availability of educational infrastructure and resources are also different among themselves. Within the countries also, the level of academic development is different. Hence it is imperative for the academic institutions to share the available human, financial and physical resources and infrastructures, so that students from various parts of the country and from various countries will have access to a uniform learning ground. In most of the countries, both private and public academic institutions are available. Unlike in some of the countries, investment in education is very less. Hence, an academics e-Twinning of institutions will help the less fortunate public institutions to receive the benefits from private institutions.

Asia-pacific experience reveals that apart from exceptions, the academic institutions of metros are equipped with learned scholars, good laboratories, play-fields, costly software packages and other infrastructures, whereas the ones in the hilly, remote places and in rural area are not blessed with the same. Again, meritorious teachers are not ready to work in these remote villages. In such a situation, the electronic media comes forward to save the situation by e-Twinning.

The minimum requirement for this is a computer with a broadband Internet connection and if there is a possibility, they can acquire a projector. Audiovisual room and other modern electronic gadgets can also be added to the existing facilities.

When linked through this e-learning platform, the students in the remote area can have an access to the teaching of academically adventurous staff. They can also get access to the first hand experience of the experiments done in the laboratories, which is not available in their institutions. The possibility of attaining depends upon so many important factors.

This e-Twinning of academic institutions is supported by the European Union's e-learning programs. This enable the schools of European countries to use ICT (Information and Communication Technology) so as to set up partnerships with other institutions and to develop a program of exchange activities.

Two major types of E-Twinning

There are two major categories of e-Twinning. One is inter-country e-Twinning of academic institution's program and another one is inter-institute or intra-country e-Twinning of academic institution's program. These can be implemented by e-Merging of conferences, e-Merging of workshops, e-Twinning of institutions.

Who should do E-Twinning?

The foremost important question is 'Who should do E-Twinning?' This can be done among individual teachers who are likeminded to have exchange of lectures. A team of teachers who are in the same projects, same subjects and same departments can come forward for such networking programs. They could be from two or more different institutions. Staff, teaching the same subject from different departments may come together for some common research or for some common projects or experiments. Or, there is possibility of networking developmental activities of colleges, schools or societies. Even the administrative managers, principals and head of the institutions can come forward for some form of e-Twinning. Librarians of various colleges can think about library sharing. E-library sharing is the best method of sharing knowledge. Science and Computer Faculty can think about laboratory sharing and software laboratory sharing, respectively. IITs of India have good library sharing and laboratory sharing among all their institutions. Complete e-Twinning of institutions as in European countries will be a best solution for this concept. E-Twinning is possible horizontally as well as vertically.

Horizontal Networking: Different levels of educational institutions like schools, arts colleges, science colleges, technical institutions, medical institutions, management institutions etc. can network among themselves. Sharing of e-infrastructure among like-minded institutions and same levels of academic structures will help them to benefit mutually.

Vertical Networking: The vertical e-Twinning will be made possible, when the linkage is promoted in the order of working hierarchy or power hierarchy, then it can be called as vertical e-integration or e-Twinning. Inter-linking among governments, ministries, directorates, Universities, colleges or the schools will result in vertical e-Twinning.

Possible Areas of E-Twinning

It is also necessary to think, as what are the areas of application of e-Twinning. It could be as follows:

- Any topic or area of interest of students.
- Any topic or area of interest of staff/scholars

- Any topic or area of interest of society.
- By framing a common curricula
- Exposure on differently prepared curricula
- Cross curricular based themes and inter-disciplinary themes

Methods of E-Twinning

There are already many methods adopted by various institutes to work together with other institutes and other countries. They can be listed as follows:

***Sharing of Infrastructure among institutions and countries*:** Some countries and institutions are blessed with wealth and good infrastructure while others may not to that extent. More inter-country and inter-institute programmes can be organized to use the resources of the blessed countries and institutions optimally.

***Conferences*:** International conferences are a major source of bringing a network among countries. Exposure of research outcomes of various institutions and various countries will enhance the knowledge about other countries.

***Staff exchange programmes*:** Inter-country staff exchange programmes will help the academicians of various countries to get acquainted with the infrastructure usage and application of advanced technology of various countries.

***Research Network*:** Combined research work should be promoted. Two or more country researchers joining together for a project will help analyse that particular problem from different perspectives and from different directions.

***Student exchange programmes*:** Student exchange programs give access to education abroad for students from member and affiliate institutions through reciprocal exchanges. A University exchange can last anywhere from a single semester to an entire education. A long-term exchange is considered an exchange, which is designed to last for six to ten months or up to one full academic year. A short-term exchange usually may take place during the summer months.

The e-Twinning helps students in gaining independence, gaining a sense of responsibility and purpose, first hand knowledge of another culture, exploring differences between countries, understanding traditions and taboos, learning more about one's self, friends and family, a better understanding of homeland, building connections between countries, learning a foreign language, discovering abilities and limitations etc.

Medium of E-Twinning

Videoconferencing, conference-room-conferencing, web-communication, web-conferencing, tele-presence, virtual world and on-line collaborations are the major source of bringing the world together.

***Web communication/videoconferencing/video-teleconference*:** Web-based videoconference is a set of interactive telecommunication technologies, which allow two or more locations to interact via two-way video and audio transmissions simultaneously. Video conferencing is communication between two computers in different locations, either on or off a corporate network. Each computer has a web cam for video, and a microphone/speaker for audio. This middle-ware communicates back to a core/ host system that manages the voice/ video session. It has also been called visual-collaboration and is a type of groupware.

Multiple participants (more than two) can speak to and view each other, conduct chat sessions, upload and share documents, display their own computer's activity or take control of another user's computer.

***Web conferencing*:** Web conferencing is used to conduct live meetings or presentations over the Internet. In the early years of the Internet, the terms 'web conferencing' and 'computer conferencing' were often used to refer to group discussions conducted within a message board therefore not live. In a web conference, each participant sits at his or her own computer, and is connected to other participants via the internet. This can be either a downloaded application on each of the attendees' computers or a web-based application where the attendees will simply enter a URL or website meeting address to enter the live meeting or conference.

***Webinar*:** A webinar is a type of web-conference that tends to be mostly one-way, from the speaker to the audience with limited audience-interaction, such as in a webcast is transmission of information in one direction only, like watching a concert on the internet. A webinar however, can be very collaborative, and include polling and question-answer sessions to allow full participation between the audience and the presenter.

***Conference room conferencing*:** The communication is between two or more conference/ meeting rooms, typically employing higher-resolution videoconference cameras and higher-quality audio equipment.

In a two-way (also known as *point-to-point*) videoconference, the cameras communicate each other over a network. In a videoconference with three or more participating sites, a *Multipoint Control Unit* (MCU) or video 'bridge' is required. In 'voice switch' mode, an MCU determines who is the predominant speaker and automatically switches the video of that person to all the screens. In 'continuous presence' mode, it splits the screens and sends the video from each site to every screen. In 'chair mode', someone can manually control who is on screen at any given time.

Virtual Reality (VR) Sharing

Virtual Reality (VR) is a technology that allows the user to interact with the computer-simulated environment by actually being in it. Virtual-reality-labs can be established in two or more institutions and the software can be shred by e-Twinning of institutions. These laboratories will be involving in the modeling and animation of three-Dimensional inhabited virtual worlds. VR software includes MindRender VREK, PC Blox, Superscape VRT-5, 3-D Website Builder, Virtus WalkThrough Pro, Vista Pro and VR Creator. This VR interfaces can bring about a fully Immersive Virtual real systems or Non-immersive Virtual real Systems. The fully immersive virtual system enables the user to directly experience a simulated environment.

Importance of E-Twinning of Institutions

This international exchange has lot of positive impact on education. Videoconferencing provides students with the opportunity to learn by participating in a both-way communication platform. Furthermore, teachers and lecturers from all over the world can be brought to classes in remote or otherwise isolated places. Students from diverse communities and backgrounds can come together to learn about one another. Students will be able to explore, communicate, analyse and share information and ideas with one another. Through video conferencing, students can visit another part of the world to speak with others, visit a zoo, a museum and so on, to learn. These virtual field trips can bring opportunities to students, especially those in geographically isolated or the economically disadvantaged regions. Small institutions and less advantaged institutions can use this technology to pool resources and teach courses (such as foreign languages) which otherwise couldn't be offered.

Researchers of various institutes can work together to bring about a fruitful result. Faculty of other institutes and experts from other countries can contribute for standard researches.

Adventurous and efficient faculties can be absorbed in competitive salaried jobs and their brilliance will be recognised while the sharing process is going on.

- The infrastructures of many institutes are less, while few others are blessed and hence infrastructures can be shared.
- Brilliant and adventurous expert teachers are few. And they should be used optimally by making them share their technical and other expertise. Only when there is e-Twinning there is possibility for all students to access the expertise of best faculty.
- Often the capacity to shoulder the paid-programmes for majority of potential stakeholders is below the requisite cost as specified

by the institution. But those students cannot be left out without latest exposures. And in such a case e-Twinning come forward for the rescue operation.

- E-Twinning also helps in long-term educational partnerships. Because this saves time, money, human power and all other energy.
- Integration of all institutions will also help the students to access quality study materials.
- This e-Twinning also saves the students by the avoidance of human bias and partial treatments.
- There is also chance for the students to have a dust-free learning atmosphere.

Considering all these advantages, E-Twinning is an indispensable tool for educational advancement.

Challenges for E-Twinning of Education

- Innovations are many and they are protected and are patented for the sake of commercialization by the innovators.
- Less-fortunate developing countries, slow-growing institutions, less-brilliant staff and slow-learners has the fear of new technology.
- The unwillingness to learn new technology or new skill has become a major character of settled permanent salaried teachers.
- In developing countries even the so-called bigger institutes does not have the needed infrastructure.
- To work together and for E-Twinning, there is less scope for self-discipline and hard-work
- Competitiveness among institutions is another major challenge. The more fortunate institutes or countries are not ready to share their infrastructures with less fortunate countries.

These challenges can be overcome by serious and sincere efforts:

- The less fortunate institutions and countries should work in the direction of exploring researches done in Western countries.
- More fortunate institutions and more fortunate developed countries also should come forward to share their latest advancements with developing world.
- The Emulation and absorption of established institutions and countries will not only bring the latest innovations into the less fortunate institutions and countries, but also the attitude of sharing will bring about overall peace in the world.

Can this be made possible? Will the sophisticated institutions come forward to lend their infrastructure and expertise to those poor guys?

Now-a-days the education has become more commercialised and hence the schools, colleges and even universities are running like commercial organisations. Hence, there is necessity for government interference in this regard. The richer institutes should also come forward realising their social responsibility.

Conclusion

European countries do not find much ripple of unrest after the introduction of their regional co-operation. Co-operation on various directions like European Union, introduction of Euro, e-Twinning of academic institutions etc. have helped them to develop a good rapport. This model should be brought to the one-world so as to bring peace and harmony in the whole world. More e-Workshops, e-Twinning of institutions, e-Twinning of workshops, inter-institute exchange programs, inter-country exchange program etc. will help to promote the adoption of e-Learning and virtual learning in the whole world. One-world of e-learning will help us to see the one-world of peaceful living in future.

REFERENCES

Beteille, A. (2001). Equality and Universality. *Economic and Political Weekly* 36: 38; pp. 3619-25.

http://en.wikipedia.org/wiki/Computer_Supported_Collaborative_Learning

John Davitt (2004). Learning, a virtual reality, e-learning. Bett show, London Olympia The Guardian, Tuesday January 6, 2004.

Kevin Kruse. The Benefits and Drawbacks of e-Learning http:// www.e-learningguru.com /articles/art1_3.htm

Kingdon, G. (1996). Private Schooling in India: Size, Nature and Equity Effects. *Economic and Political Weekly*, 1996, 31: 51; pp. 3306-14.

Krishna Kumar. 'Quality of Education at the Beginning of the 21st Century-Lessons from India. Central Institute of Education, University of Delhi.

Lawrence Auld and Veronica S. (1999). The Virtual Reality and Education Laboratory at East Carolina University. Pantelidishttp://www.thejournal.com/articles/1442

Megha Banduni, (2005). The future of e-learning in India. www.express computeronline.com, 14-November 2005.

Robert J. Seidel and Paul R. Chatelier (Eds.). Virtual Reality Trainings future-Perspectives on Virtual Reality and related emerging technologies. *Defence Research Series*, Volume 6, Plenum Publishing Corporation, New York.

Zarrin T. Caldwell (2006). One World US, Making the Grade: Knowledge for a New Century. www.us.oneworld.net, page visited on Sept. 1, 2006.

13.

Internet Based Virtualization of Laboratory Experiments

A REALITY THROUGH EDUCATION TECHNOLOGY

Rajiv Tiwari

Prologue

A brief about the continuing education and development of education technology for the distance education in premium institutes of India is presented in the chapter. This covers activities involved in education technology centres in these Institutes to cope up the present need to improve the quality of engineering education in India through the information and communication technology (ICT). The main premise of the present chapter is to give a brief overview of the engineering education challenges especially related with the laboratories and as to how the ICT can help to overcome these challenges. Basic building blocks on which these virtual laboratories are being developed are briefed. Some of the real challenges to give feel of laboratories will be briefed and various options available at hand are explored. At the end conclusions and future challenges are presented.

Introduction

Under the auspices of Ministry of Human Recourse and Development (MHRD), Government of India, an ambitious National Mission of Education through ICT (Information and Communication Technology)[1] has been launched under the eleventh planning commission[2]. Among various programmes related to engineering educations the two major components are (i) *National Programme on Technology Enhanced Learning* (NPTEL)[3]: Under this programme development of the web and video based supplementary course materials are being developed to suit syllabi of most of the technical education in India as well as in the world. (ii) *Virtual Laboratory* (VL)[4]: Under this ambitious programme it is planned to develop internet based laboratories under three main themes. These are as follows:

(a) Numerical based experiments,

(b) Measurement data based experiments, and

(c) Remote triggered based experiments.

VL is the main theme of the present chapter and it will be covered in more details about the various themes, complexities and virtual tools available at hand in implementation of virtual experiments. Apart from these, other programmes on higher technical educations are on pedagogical methods, the standardization of quality assurance of contents and certification, the certification and testing modules for virtual institutions, open ware computing software, applications of robotics, haptic devices, etc. are being developed[1, 5].

No one can replace a real teacher and a real laboratory. However, due to lack of motivated teachers and the state-of-art laboratories, these have challenged our ever increasing engineering education system. The best part in India, unlike in the Western and European countries, is that we have large population of students who are keen to pursue engineering education and to match the demand we have ever increasing education Institutions. The fatal part is that most of the recent Institutions are private owned and these have not enough teachers and laboratories due to lack of fund allocation to justify and sustain the engineering education in the long run. The NPTEL and VL are two programmes, aimed at solution of these problems to the extent possible by providing supplementary course material and laboratories virtually through internet to remotest possible places and to multitude of learners.

A review of the continuing education in IITs and IISc, and an evolution of the education technology activities in these premium Institutes to cope up the present need to improve the engineering education in India is performed. The main aim of the present chapter is to provide information about the virtualization of experiments and challenges associated with it, to provide a learner a feel and a confidence of performing real experiments. Differences and similarity in the real and virtual laboratories, role of internet in VL, basic components of VL, basic themes of in virtualization of experiments, virtual tools and means available for virtualization of laboratories and experiments are dealt in detail.

A Brief Review on Continuing Education and Educational Technology in IITs and IISc

Continuing education programmes and subsequent development of the education technology in Indian Institutes of Technology (IITs) and Indian Institute of Science (IISc) for the distance education are related. Hence, the present section presents activities of the continuing education and subsequent development of the education technology for distance education in these premium Institutes. Continuing education programmes have been there in such premium Institutes in some form of other since 1960's. Training programmes were being offered by IIT/IISc faculty to people from other educational institutions and organizations in the country. These were conducted as part of Continuing Education Programme (CEP) or Quality Improvement Programme (QIP) at IITs/IISc to start with. Also, this category of activities includes special training programs being conducted by some Centers/Departments for specific groups of participants. Teachers in engineering institutions get an opportunity to study at IITs/IISc (apart from other Institutes of national importance) under the QIP.

One of the areas in which the IITs/IISc have been contributing significantly for national development is the Quality Improvement of Technical Teachers and Continuing Education of working professionals, which is assuming tremendous importance in shaping the human resource of the country. The Quality Improvement Programme has started in 1971 under the Ministry of Human Resource Development, Department of Education, New Delhi since its inception and has been endeavouring to improve the quality of technical education in the country with the help of the All India Council of Technical Education (AICTE – A Statutory Body of the Government of India). This programme has been constantly making efforts to upgrade the teaching curricula and enhance the knowledge of teachers of various engineering colleges/institutions. IITs and IISc are the major QIP Centres in the country; these centres have been pursuing all major objectives of QIP which include:

1) Degree Programmes (M.Tech. and Ph.D.),
2) Short Term Courses, and
3) Curriculum Development Cell Activities.

Apart from QIP, it would be worthwhile to review activities and development of the centres of the continuing education and the education technology in these Institutes individually, since they have some commonality and some differences.

In the IIT Madras, the Centre for Continuing Education (CCE) coordinates the continuing education programmes of the Institute. Among its activities, it helps in the organization of Continuing Education Programmes aimed at industry as well as short-term courses under QIP, meant for faculty in engineering institutions. Further, the Centre facilitates other programmes such as book writing scheme, continuing education modules for industry, etc. The Educational Technology Cell, established by MHRD under NPTEL for the purpose of creating educational web and videos of broadcast quality in Science and Technology using the expertise of the faculty and the facilities at the institute, is also associated with this Centre. The contents are based on the model curriculum suggested by All India Council for Technical Education (AICTE) and the syllabi of major affiliating Universities such as Anna University (Tamil Nadu), Jawaharlal Nehru Technological University (Andhra Pradesh) and Visvesvaraya Technological University (Karnataka). The program took off under the chairmanship of Prof. M.S. Anath, Director, IIT Madras in 2003 (Table 13.1). The Video courses are uploaded in the YouTube[3] and are also submitted for transmitting through DD GYANDARSHAN-III called the Eklavya channel[6]. The web courses and video courses are developed in order to provide students supplementary learning material over the net.

TABLE 13.1: The Continuing Education and Educational Technology Activities Centres in IITs and IISc

Sl. No.	*Name of the Institute*	*Continuing education*	*Educational Technology*	*Remarks*
1.	IIT Bombay	Continuing Education Programme (CEP)	Centre for Distance Engineering Education Programme (CDEEP)	Initiation live lectures to remote e-class room
2.	IIT Delhi	Continuing Education Programme (CEP)	Educational Technology Services Centre (1987)	Initiation of the telecast of pre-recorded video lectures through Eklavaya Channel
3.	IIT Guwahati	Centre for Educational Technology (CET)	Centre for Educational Technology (CET, 2003)	Activities started with NPTEL & QIP
4.	IIT Kanpur	Centre for Development of Technical Education (CDTE)	Distance Education Program (DEP), Media Technology Centre and Web Studio	Initiation live lectures to remote e-class rooms
5.	IIT Kharagpur	Continuing Education Programme (CEP)	Centre for Educational Technology (CET, 1987)	Initiation of the streaming of the video-on-demand
6.	IIT Madras	Centre for Continuing Education (CCE)	Education Technology Cell (ETC)	Initiation of the NPTEL took place

7. IIT Roorkee	Continuing Education Centre (CCE)	Educational Technology Cell (ETC)	One of the pioneering centre in the area of continuing education
8. IISc Bangalore	Centre for Continuing Education (CCE)	Digital Information Services Cell (DISC)	Initiation of Indo-French Cyber University project

In the paradigm of rapid technological advancement that is taking place around the globe, it is important for engineers and scientists to continue to learn new technologies, update and upgrade their knowledge, much after completing formal education in the college. IIT Kharagpur, the largest and the most diversified technical institute in the country, has been handling this responsibility almost from its inception in early 1950s through the continuing education programme (CEP). In the IIT Kharagpur, the Educational Technology was recognized as a formal activity in IIT Kharagpur in 1987. In 1995, the Institute decided to provide a significant boost to this activity by allocating additional space, manpower and budget. The Centre for Educational Technology (CET) moved to a new complex in the year 2002. The Continuing Education Programme (CEP) of IIT Kharagpur provided a great deal of assistance to CET during the first few years of its existence. The Centre has three especially designed multi-camera video studio-cum-lecture theatres which can record live classes of up to 106 students at a time in one studio and 50 students at a time in the other studios, using professional quality video equipments. The production control room, in addition to the usual audio-video switchers, SEGs, etc, also houses on-line and off-line editing equipment. Facilities for CD and DVD duplication are currently available in the centre. Nearly 40,000 hours of video-based instructional material are copied annually for dissemination to educational institutions, R&D organizations, industry, government and corporate sectors in India and abroad. CET has launched Master of Technology in Media and Sound Engineering from the Academic Year 2006-07. Virtual Classroom technology has been developed and successfully demonstrated within the campus. This can be extended to include remote users at an appropriate time. Given the authorization, any student can join a live class at IIT Kharagpur from anywhere (but this facility is now within the campus.), asking and answering questions through both-way audio and viewing the proceedings of the class through a one-way digital video link. All communications take place via computers. The faculty, at all times, can monitor and control access to the class, the timings and the extent of interaction. All students can see and hear the faculty, but can only hear the other students.

In pursuance of the national objectives of maintaining excellence in education and training of engineers, technologists and scientists (Statues, 1963) and (Review, 1970), the Indian Institute of Technology, Delhi established a Educational Technology Services Centre in 1987. It continues to offer guidance and assistance to faculty and curriculum designers across the country. Major activities of the Centre include providing support for enhancement of teaching-learning process; developing media-based instructional resources; conducting academic and applied research and undertaking consultancy and sponsored research projects. The Centre has a well-established programme for faculty development which is recognized and widely utilized by national and international sponsoring agencies. Over the years, the Centre has produced a large number of complete video courses, single concept video programmes and CAI packages with the help of the faculty members of the Institute covering a vast range of subjects from Computer Science and Engineering to textile Technology. Major activities focused are: (i) Design & Development of Instructional Resources, (ii) Dissemination of Instructional Resources and (iii) Telecasting of Video Courses.

The Quality Improvement Programme (QIP) Centre at Indian Institute of Technology Roorkee, Roorkee has started in 1971 and has been endeavouring to improve the quality of technical education in the country. From 1994, the Centre has been transferred under AICTE. Being one of the eight major QIP Centres in the country, the centre at Indian Institute of Technology Roorkee has been pursuing all major objectives of QIP. Continuing Education Centre looks after the continuing education programmes of the Institute and the Educational Technology Cell looks after the NPTEL and similar distance education activities.

In an electronic age that has seen the walls removed across states and countries, benefits of academic excellence at IIT Kanpur are disseminated globally. As part of a social responsibility to share the expertise with fellow academic institutions across the country and abroad, the IIT Kanpur moved towards this goal with the initiation of a Distance Education Program (DEP). The following initiatives have been taken under this scheme till now (i) Courses in the area of Engineering and Biological Sciences delivered to the students of the State of Chhattisgarh (India) using VSAT transmission. The project is an initiative by ChiPS agency of the state of Chhatisgarh. The State has signed a comprehensive MoU with IIT Kanpur for IT visioning of the State. IIT Kanpur is committed to deliver courses from IIT Kanpur to the students the of National Institute of Technology, Raipur and the Government Engineering College, Bilaspur (full course- 30/ 35 hours) and also deliver some short term courses for the faculty from the state of Chhattisgarh, (ii) Indo-French Cyber University in the areas of emerging technologies (University Pierre et Marie curie, Paris is the Partner University). In 2001 a virtual university was opened between IISc Bangalore and the University Paul Sabatier in Toulouse. It is currently in operation for courses in applied mathematics. The Council of Ficus met in Paris in January 2004 and proposed to extend the program in aerospace between IIT-Kanpur and a French University; the Universitė Pierre et Marie Curie (Paris VI) is candidate. It was decided to start with a series of seminars to be delivered by both the sides and with live interaction through the ERNET connectivity. The IIT Kanpur setup a Media Technology Center and a Web Studio to assist in development of courses for the NPTEL and other distance education program.

In IIT Guwahati, the Centre for Educational Technology (CET) is a central facility of the institute to assist Teaching Learning Process. The Centre is primarily concentrating on development of infrastructure for Technology Enhanced Learning. At present, the operational objective is to set-up studio/laboratories for video and web courses. The Centre has the state of art video recording and analysing equipments, and macro media software. The centre has also Video Conferencing System. CET has been involved in one of the National level major project along with other IITs and IISc under MHRD, Government of India namely National Programme on Technology Enhanced Learning (NPTEL). From the year 2003 the Quality Improvement Programme is being coordinated by the Institute.

With the rapid pace of growth in technological knowledge and frequent paradigm shifts in technology, Continuing Education of working professionals in industry is a vital need. The Continuing Education Programme at IIT Bombay has been set up to meet the manpower training and knowledge up gradation needs of the industry. The goal of Distance Education Programme (DEP) of IIT Bombay is to offer courses to a large number of participants across the country. Each course is offered through video broadcast lectures supported by course handbook. The broadcast is through satellite transmission to a large number of registered Remote Centres (RCs). Each RC projects the lectures on the screen, in a classroom for up to fifty participants guided by a local supervisor. Participants have the opportunity to ask questions during the lecture, which can be immediately answered by the distant instructor, as in a real classroom. The Centre for Distance Engineering Education Programme (CDEEP) was started by the IIT Bombay with the express aim of providing high quality distance education in engineering and science to a large number of participants throughout the country and abroad. The courses offered through distance education are the very same ones that are taken by IIT Bombay students. To reach as many learners as possible, CDEEP is using different mediums and various technologies.

The Indian Institute of Science (IISc) Bangalore had for a long time been concerned with ways to make its expertise and facilities available to qualified technical personnel in industries, universities and research establishments. On a small scale, the Institute's facilities were always being used through short-term/refresher courses, but these activities were not coordinated by a single entry. The Centre for Continuing Education was set up in 1975-76 to function as a focus for all such activities and to promote a variety of programmes relevant to specific target groups. NPTEL and related outreach activities are being implemented at Digital Information Services Cell (DISC) of IISc.

From the above survey it is very clear that these premium Institutes of India for last more than 50 years putting every effort towards continuing education and use of education technology towards the enhanced learning and the distance education. These efforts were mainly focused towards theory courses in the form of web and video. However, till recently activities in India towards virtual laboratory were very scanty and localised at individual level efforts. Now the remaining of the chapter is deal with mainly the future challenges of the virtual laboratory.

Real and Virtual Laboratories

Through ICT with the help of internet and access devices (like desktop, laptop, palmtop, mobiles, etc.) now we can perform day-to-day activities like booking of train/air tickets, paying various bills, reading and watching news and accessing other information, writing and sending letters, performing banking operations, etc. In these activities a User performs various operations through access devices without the involvement and intervention of human at other end. In these activities the User has no physical train/air ticket or billing counter, no news paper or TV or books, no physical paper for writing letters, no physical bank counter and staff to attend the banking operation, etc. These could be termed as virtualization of ticketing (i.e., electronic ticketing or in short e-ticketing), mailing (e-mailing), information (e-information), banking (e-banking), etc. Conventionally, to buy a train ticket one had to go to train ticket counter from the station from where one had to board the train during office hours only, stand in the queue for hours without the information of whether the reservation was available on the day he wanted to travel, etc. Because of e-ticketing now the younger generation may not know the concept of ticket counter; however, still now they perform ticketing virtually. There are virtual games that gives feel of playing games, virtual simulators are present to give training to airplane pilots, train drivers, maintenance engineers of airplanes, etc. and in these involvement of the user (player/trainee) is there by various control buttons.

Now question arises, as to how the real and virtual experiments are similar and they differ. The real laboratory (RL) must exist physically in some Institute whereas the virtual laboratory may or may not exist depending upon the basic theme of the virtual laboratory. In RL, generally a group of students perform a single experiment whereas in virtual laboratory in most of the case it is designed such that a single student can perform the experiment. In RL, the teachers and technical assistants are present to brief about the experiments and to help perform the experiment in case of difficulty at any stage whereas in the VL, it is designed so that the student learns himself/herself about the experiment and then perform the experiments in most of the cases without the help of any manual help/ interference. The RL can be performed during office hours in fixed slot assigned to student whereas in the VL, a student is free to choose the slot 24 × 7 to perform experiment except in some exceptional cases. In real experiments all the human sense (visual, odour, sound, tactile, taste, etc.) can be used to perform experiments whereas in VL, only the visual & sound and in a few cases limited tactile senses could be used to perform VL experiments. In real experiments, apart from the real experiment a student learns to operate equipment; on the other hand, in VL, this aspect is a real challenge. In RL, some specialized commercial software developed over the years are available, however, in the VL mostly the design of experiments are such that usage of only the open source software is encouraged. In the case of real experiments some non-trivial behaviour of experiments may arise and for interpretation of that an instructor is needed, however, in VL, in most of the case the experiments are designed very systematically so that student has no navigational problem during experiments. In RL the students have freedom to explore the phenomena with some modification in the experimental setup or range of parameters specified to perform experiments whereas in the VL, it is limited. Precautions are to be taken by a learner in RL; in VL the developer has to take care of it in design of experiments. The aim of brainstorming differences between the RL and VL is to put up challenges in front of VL developers to bridge the gap between the RL and VL, so that to make VL as a reality. With the present educational technology it is possible to fill the gap between the VL and the RL so that a remote student can benefit to the extent possible.

Motivations for Virtualization of Laboratories

The main motivation towards virtualization of laboratories is to make available the state-of-art experimental facilities exist in premium Institutes of the country to students of other Institutions where such facilities are not available. This will ensure equal exposure to all students of the country irrespective of the location or financial disadvantages of their Institutes. The premium Institutes of India have four fold responsibilities: (i) teaching (ii) research (iii) helping industries through consultancy and (iv) helping in the overall development (teaching and research) of other not so privileged Institutes. Recent escalation of engineering Institutions in India has posed a challenge to premium Institutes to focus more on the fourth responsibility and the virtualization of the laboratories is one of such mega effort. This effort would obviously give return to such premium Institutes in the form of better quality of students with better exposure in their graduate and research education programmes.

Role of Internet in Virtual Laboratory

Internet plays a vital role in VL since it is a constraint to the VL developer while it is a freedom to a learner. VL put constraints in the VL developers in the form of using open source software (or openware) so that a learner can acquire them free of cost if needed. In VL, the internet is a means of communication between the learner and virtual experiments. While designing the VL it should be kept in mind that all the input a learner gives to perform experiments and all outputs to the learner from the virtual experiments goes through internet only.

The VL through internet/intranet has several advantages in it; some such are: (i) access to multitude of learners located at physically distant places (ii) scope for scalability, (iii) availability of lab all the time, (iv) non-dependency and non-interference of human to conduct experiments, (v) breaking the boundaries within a countries and breaking frontiers among the countries, etc.

Virtualization of Laboratories

A laboratory is virtualized if a learner is able to access the laboratory and perform experiments remotely through intranet/internet. A VL developer has role of carefully designing experiments so that there is tradeoffs between the restrictions and the freedom a learner has while performing experiments. The VL website should have clear-cut descriptions of laboratory and the list of experiments with basic aims. A prerequisite for performing laboratories, supplementary material to give a revision of basic concepts, and a testing module before entering to perform experiments should be provided since an unknown learner may not be aware of the subject itself. Sufficient learning and testing modules at every stage of experiments should be provided especially for the case it involves certification of performing successful experiment by a learner.

Virtualization of laboratory is a challenging task unlike the development of the web and video based theory courses where the design of presentation of material is more or less standardized or fixed. The concept of virtualization of one laboratory may not work for the other laboratory at all. So the efforts and involvements in designing virtual experiment and its virtualization are very high as compared to the web and video theory courses. It involves proper choice of platform software to be used that should have capability to provide graphical user interface (GUI) to enhance interactiveness between the learner and VL. It should have in-built signal acquiring and analysis capabilities. For the real-time trigger/control of experiments and instruments the platform software should have provisions to perform such tasks through some actuators. The basic platform software should be able to work the same way as on the designer's desktop/ laboratory without the original software with freely downloadable run engines through internet after publishing the VL in the internet through a server.

Basic Components in a Virtual Laboratory

Depending upon various themes of VL and the level of automation required the VL developers could opt modules in the VL from the following: (i) Test bench and rig, (ii) Sensors and instrumentations, (iii) Data-acquisition system (iv) Signal processing, analysis and virtual instrument software, (v) Computer-aided instructional software, (vi) Computer-aided learning software, (vii) Computer-aided testing and certification software, and (viii) Computer-aided course management software.

Virtualization of Experiments

Now question comes how to virtualize an experiment, so that a learner can perform the experiments and learn the basic theories and concepts while performing the virtual experiments to correlate with the practice. There are differences in the examples given previously of the day-to-day activities (mainly the service orientated) and the laboratory experiments (mainly the learning and testing oriented). Let us have a glance perusal on the challenges in virtualization of experiments more elaborately in the form of following points:

i. In the former case the user has no knowledge as to how the particular activity has been performed at backend of the computer and his main concern is getting his/her service done. However, in the latter case the task is to give feel of sequence of operation performed during the real experiments through the virtualization.

ii. In the latter case learning components is the main focus rather than the service as in the former case.

iii. In the latter case testing of the learner is also important and that is also a part of the virtualization.

iv. In the latter case the certification is also a real challenge after the effective testing of the learner virtually.

v. For the 'see and feel' of experimental setups and instruments various computer-aided tools like animations of motions, three-dimensional solid objects with control to learner to see it from various angles, virtual reality videos through technology like stitching of high-resolution still images, etc. should be used.

vi. Videos with sound of experimental set up, practical application, detailed lecture of basic theory and how to perform experiments, demonstration of performing real experiments, webcam to demonstrate live video of experimental set up and demo of experiments should be available periodically. Control to webcams to the learner for focusing to see and feel various components and features of the experimental set up should be given.

vii. Provision for the remote triggering of some of experiments and instruments should be there. In all experiments it might not be possible to have complete control over the experimental setups; in that case intervention of human may be necessary.

viii. The attempt should be to demonstrate virtually by all possible means either numerically, measured data based, pure remote trigger based with automation of all activities during the experiments or with some intervention of human being, if necessary.

ix. Feel of experiments cannot be obtained fully by just visuals and sounds during performing virtual experiments. The virtual experiments should integrate 'touch and feel' by the help of haptic devices. The same could be extended for other human senses like smell, sound, feel of environment, etc.

In experiments a learner observes a physical phenomenon and validates the theory he/she studied in theory courses. During virtualization the following points to be covered carefully for effectiveness of virtualization of experiments:

i. Develop environment and basic background of a laboratory.

ii. Choices of experiments to be performed to be provided with clear cut definition of objectives.

iii. Basic theoretical concepts about the experiments to be briefed.

iv. Involvement of students in setting up and learning about the experimental rig, instruments, data-acquisition system and computer with relevant software.

v. Wherever possible provision for exploring learning materials by learners depending upon their capabilities and interest should be provided.

vi. The virtualization should accept experimental data from learners, if s/he has, for further analysis and interpretations.
vii. Method of performing experiments should be given so that learner knows the sequence of steps for performing real experiments.
viii. Feel of motion of experimental set up to the learner through internet using visuals, sounds, haptic devices, etc.
ix. Provide excellent navigation while performing virtual experiments.
x. A step-by-step methodology to perform the virtual experiments should be provided.
xi. Testing of learner at every stage to ensure his learning comprehension.
xii. Feedback from learner to be taken for every experiment and for the whole laboratory to improve upon the virtualization.

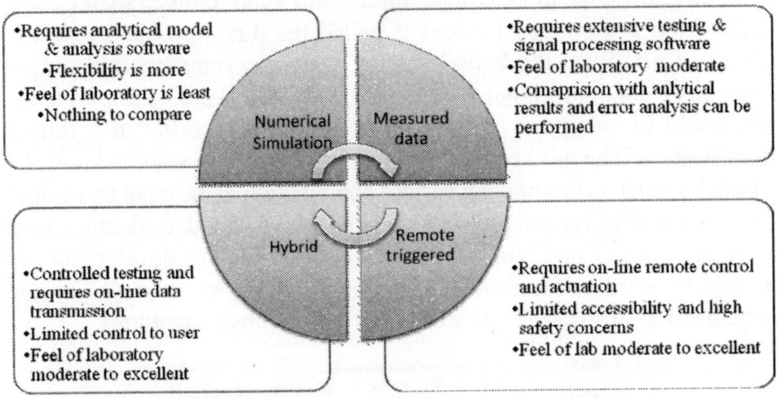

Fig. 13.1. Basic premise and features of a virtual laboratory

The main theme in accessing laboratory experiments is through internet. Learner could be able to perform experiments and get a feel of doing experiment through internet is a real challenge. While performing experiments the learner not only study about the basic theory about experiments but also get exposure of equipment functioning and its usage, how to arrange various components of experimental set up, sequence of operations to be performed to collect data, etc. The learner also has to perform various physical activities like lifting a weight, setting a sensor on a test set up, coordination activities with a group of students, fear of handling a new instrument, safety precautions to be taken for possible accidents/ short-circuit/ fire/ breakage/ dangerous smoke, etc. To create a real impact of these aspects in virtualization is not easy tasks. To some extent these activities can be included by haptic and other devices; however, these are not amenable to learner since these are costly and have to be procured by Institutes where the learner wants to perform virtual experiments remotely. Let the reader have a more detailed elaboration of the basic themes based on which virtualization of experiments could be realized (Fig. 13.1).

Virtualization Based on Numerical Simulation

The virtualization based on numerical simulation relies on fundamental governing equations derived from basic theories of the phenomena to be studied. Here three different categories of experiments could be designed. In any system, it can have three different components (Fig. 13.2), i.e. (i) the system parameters, (ii) input parameters to the system, and (iii) output from the system corresponding to the input. Depending upon out of these three components which two are known and which one is unknown, three different categories of experiments could be performed. With the knowledge of system parameter and input to the system getting output from governing equations is called the direct problem and it is easiest of all. With the knowledge of system parameters and output parameters obtaining input parameters is another kind of experiments that could be designed. This type of problem is called the source identification. The third type of problem is in which we want to know the system parameters by knowing various combination of the input and output information. This type of problem is called the system identification. Last two categories of problem are not so easy and require development of method to extract unknown information from known information and virtualization of experiments would fall in these two categories.

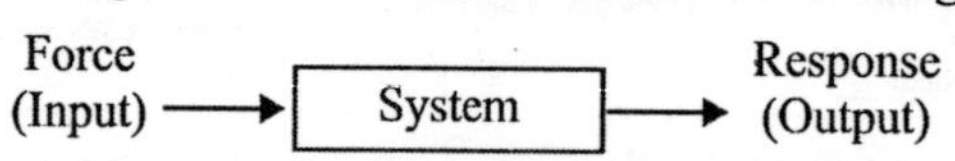

Fig. 13.2. A typical dynamic system with input and output

Virtualization Based on Measured Data

This concept is better than the numerical simulation in giving feel of doing experiments. It is easier and more versatile than the remote trigger because of the full automation is very difficult to achieve and also it has safety concerns as to how much control of equipment handling to be passed on to a learner. In measurement based virtualization the designer has to provide various options to cover different features of the experiments. All the required data are actually measured for set of pre-planned experiments to be virtualized. These data are used step-by-step in the virtualized experiments and it will be accessed by the learner (Fig. 13.3). While performing experiments a learner chooses a set of input parameters of his/her choice available to him/her and proceeds for conducting virtual experiments. These data are measured from real test rigs so there is little chance of getting infeasible results by the learner as it may be the case with the numerical simulation based in which a user can use infeasible inputs to get infeasible outputs.

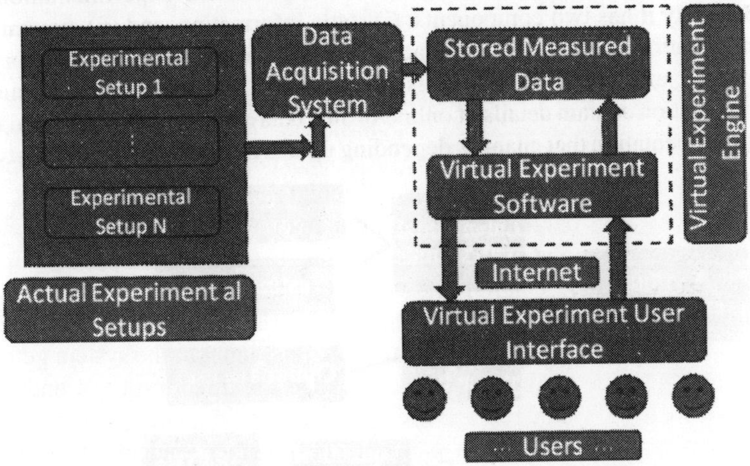

Fig. 13.3. Measurement based virtual experiments

The best part of such virtual experiment theme is that it can be available to learners 24 × 7. Once the virtualization is done there is no need of day-to-day maintaining and operating of the real laboratory, unless otherwise there is plan to have real experiments by group of net learners periodically during vacations of the developer Institute where this virtualization has been performed so that their academic activities do not suffer.

Virtualization Based on Remote Trigger/Control

This concept is very attractive and most difficult to implement. In this category depending upon experiments various classifications could also be made. For example, (i) live demonstration of experiments with no control to the user, however, s/he gets real-time data through internet of the experimentation, (ii) a real experiment triggered (however, as such no control of equipments) by a learner at a remote location and a learner collects data on-line instead of off-line as in the case of measurement based, and (iii) a remote learner has control over some of equipments through internet and s/he performs experiments based on his/her inputs and collects data on-line. The most common and easier to implement is the trigger type, in which user has limited control of one or two parameter of ready-to-use experiment set ups. A learner can see the experimental setup and instruments through webcam to observe on-line changes due to change in the parameters, s/he can even acquire the experimental data and analysis himself/herself or through data processing software available on-line.

An Overview of a Typical Virtual Experiment Website

Fig. 13.4 shows various components a virtual experiment website should have for an effective learning and for a proficient experimentation. Basically it has two components: (i) static information, and (ii) dynamic information. The static information contain details such as laboratory manual and associated visuals and sounds, whereas, the dynamic information contain details of online/offline data a learner gets from virtual experimentation that changes depending upon a learner's choice of inputs.

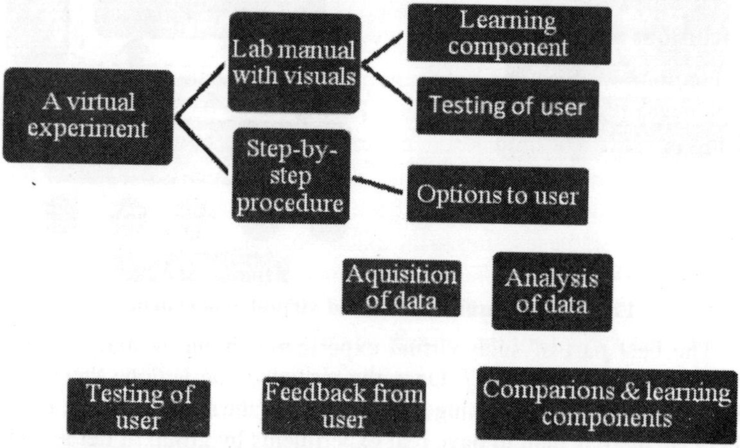

Fig. 13.4. A flowchart of a typical virtual experiment website

Feel of Experimentation

Various important aspects in all the themes discussed above on virtualization of experiments are: to impart feel and satisfaction of performing experiments, interactiveness, instructiveness, learning components, attractiveness, easy to navigate, self evaluation, etc. Now have a glance over various visual and sound aids that can help us in improving virtual experiments front-end software: (i) diagrams, (ii) graphs, (iii) photographs, (iv) animations of motions which are difficult to capture by video and to illustrate a particular phenomena, (v) off-line and on-line videos: Pre-recorded videos with audio about the laboratory, about experiments and its procedure would be helpful in enhancing the feel of laboratory. Pre-recorded video of some practical application of the experiments will help a learner to correlate the theory with practical aspect. Through several webcams the on-line transmission of video and audio will give better feel of laboratory and performing experiments. The webcam can have facility to give control to the use to move and focus the camera as per their wish through internet to explore the laboratory and equipments, and (vi) virtual reality (VR): Good for panoramic view of laboratory. It is very good tool by which a learner can have a virtual tour of the laboratory and according to user's wish can move around the laboratory virtually and could be able to zoom-in or zoon-out depending upon the inquest to see an experimental setup or an instrument. However, it is off-line virtual video and the user will see the same view all the time s/he visits. It is very effective for viewing monuments where you do not expect to see any change in due course by the visitors.

Conclusions and Future Challenges

The continuing education and the evolution of the education technology activities for distance education in IITs and IISc to deal with the present need to improve the engineering education in India have been reviewed. In the chapter, internet based virtual laboratory concept has been described. Various challenges involved has been brought out and VL developers could touch upon these issues to the extent possible to have more effective virtualization of laboratories. At present the main focus of the feel of experiments is through visuals and sounds, however, it should be extended to other sensory feels of human being like odour, taste, tactile, etc. Apart from enhancing the feel of laboratory, challenges are there to integrate learning components while performing virtual experiments along with testing the learner. Learners also have to break the barrier to experience virtual laboratory and gain as much as from the traditional laboratories. Hence, the challenges are there to both the developers and learners, and with several around of evolvement based on feedback from variety of learner the virtual laboratory will be a reality.

REFERENCES

1. *National Mission of Education through Information and Communication Technology*, (2009). Ministry of Human Resource and Development, Government of India. (http://www.ignouonline.ac.in/sakshat/)
2. *Eleventh Five Year Plan 2007-12*, (2007). Planning Commission, Government of India. (http://planningcommission.gov.in/plans/planrel/fiveyr/welcome.html)
3. *National Programme on Technology Enhanced Learning* (NPTEL), (2003). (http://nptel.iitm.ac.in/ and http://www.youtube.com/iit)
4. *Virtual Laboratory* (VL), (2009). (http://www.vlab.co.in/)
5. *Sakshat Portal*: (http://www.ignouonline.ac.in/sakshat/)
6. *Eklaya Techology Channel* (2003). (http://web.iitd.ac.in/eklavya/about/index.htm).

14.

Role of Information and Communication Technology (ICT) in Higher Education

D.N. Reddy and K. Lal Kishore

'...A major problem that we face is in the quality of higher education that our institutions impart. Unfortunately, most of them produce pass-outs who are nowhere near international standards. Even if we meet our targets of higher access and enrolment, even if we spend huge amounts on higher education and even if we open a large number of new institutions, this issue of quality will not get addressed by itself. In fact, one dimension of the quality deficit is the difficulty being faced in recruiting top class faculty for the new IIMs, IITs, Central Universities and other such institutions that the Government has decided to establish in the last five years'.

Dr. Manmohan Singh
In his convocation address
at Punjab University

Higher Education in India: An Introduction

India's higher education system has been the third largest in the world, after China and the United States. The main governing body at the tertiary level is the University Grants Commission (UGC), situated at New Delhi, which enforces its standards, advises the government, and helps coordinate between the centre and the state.

India has more than 120 million people in the 18-25 years age group. Only 10 per cent of these have access to higher education. For an economy that is growing over 8 per cent and projected to grow even more rapidly, and with an industrial growth of over 10.4 per cent, the need for skilled workforce and trained graduates is estimated at 750,000 annually. India is viewed as a young country with young population. This makes the policy makers more responsible to bring more population under literacy framework and ensure that the school dropouts are minimized.

Despite the high efficient delivery of public services, high levels of teacher absenteeism and non-teaching activity, many Indian students remain motivated to succeed on the college entrance exams.

The increased demand for higher education is not currently being met. India's large and young population requires access to affordable and credible higher education in order to raise equity and promote inclusive growth. It's emerging role in the global economy, as well as its declining age-dependency ration in an environment of dwindling workforce in developed countries, afford it a key role in international industrial service sectors. India also has the capacity to transform into global education service provider.

India and Washington Accord

One of the greatest milestones achieved by Indian technological education is that India has entered into the prestigious Washington Accord on 31st October 2007, which is an international agreement between registering bodies of member countries accrediting academic engineering programmes at the university level. The accord covers professional engineering undergraduate degrees. The Washington Accord will bring international recognition automatically to all engineering programmes accredited by the National Board of Accreditation (NBA)[2]. The accredited engineering degrees of India will be treated on a par with the U.S. degrees as well as other engineering degrees from the countries that are a party to the Washington Accord. The engineering programmes of the Indian Institutes of Technology (IITs) have already had international recognition.

Structure of Higher Education System in India

Depending on the academic, administrative and financial systems, Higher Education in India is of different types. Universities may be established by Central or State Governments. The central government may also recognize institutions as 'Deemed to be Universities' or set up 'Institutions of National Importance'. The institutions may be funded publicly, be aided by the government, or be funded privately. Foreign Universities or educational bodies offer different courses through twinning arrangements or programmed-based collaborations.

Scenario of Technical Education in India

1. Number-focus: Presently, higher education in India has become a number game focusing less on quality and employability. There is a visible need to improve upon the policies and procedures related to admission, teaching, Infrastructure and examination so that the large number of students admitted every year can be handled more efficiently and effectively. Proliferation of engineering colleges even in rural areas in different states of the country is a manifestation of focus of numbers rather than of quality.

2. Inadequate financial compensation to faculty: Many engineering colleges do not pay well to the faculty and this is one reason why competent members of faculty are not available in good numbers. The imbalances in the financial compensation of faculty in private and government engineering colleges are more visible across many cases.

3. Encouragement to Private participation: One can see enormous private participation and growth of engineering colleges in terms of number of colleges and students enrolled. Considering the requirements of the Indian economy to handle its knowledge economy, the number can be justified but if one sees the quality and general employability, the position is not encouraging. There has been in the erosion of quality of delivery of engineering education.

4. Focus on syllabus completion rather than skill-building: Considerable number of the qualified engineers lack experimental, analytical, communication, mathematical, problem solving skills and other soft skills. Consequently, the focus is more on syllabus completion rather than building the competencies to handle engineering functions such as R&D, design. Design-modification and technology-absorption.

Investments in Higher Education in India

The government investment in education in India is less than 3 per cent of GDP, including a share of higher education at 0.4 per cent, or around 12 per cent of the aggregate education budget. The central government spends slightly more than 25 per cent of total public expenditure and the state governments spend the remaining three-quarters. About 50 per cent of the central government's technical education budget went to the Indian Institutes of Technology (IITs) and Indian Institutes of Management (IIMs).

The national policy on Education 1986 has set a goal of 6 per cent of GDP as total expenditure on education. This would include 1.5 per cent for higher and technical education.

Expanding expenditure on higher education is a major challenge. The magnitude of the required expenditure will necessitate involvement of both public and private funds. Innovative mechanisms in user-based charges combined with systems of grants, aid, loans, other sources of funds, and encouraging private investment will need to be developed. But the public expenditure on education as a percentage of government expenditure across all sectors has been (as given the Fig. 14.1) as high as 14.6 per cent and averages 13.5 per cent over the past few years. On average, every household spends 41 per cent of its income on education towards tuition fee and other fee.

Among various levels of education, higher education has pervasive and influential impact on development of the nation. National development should be in the form of both economic and human resources. Higher education empowers the individual with necessary skills and competence for achieving personal and social goals, which in turn contribute to the development of a country.

Household Expenditures for Higher Education in India

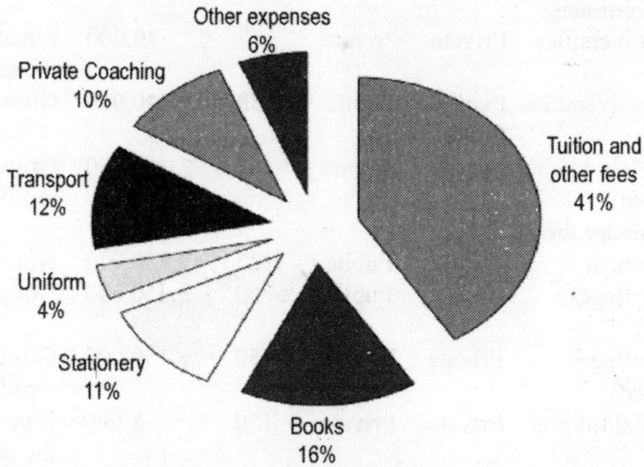

Fig. 14.1. Pie diagram showing Household Expenditure for Higher Education in India

Accessibility of Higher Education

By the end of March 2009, there were 428 Universities including 21 Central Universities, 109 Deemed to be Universities, more than 25000 colleges, 1.19 crore students and 4.91 lakh teachers in India. When India attained independence, there were just 19 Universities, 516 colleges, 2.28 lakh students and about 25 thousand teachers. Though there is improvement in the expansion of higher education, when compared to 1947, this is not adequate. The enrollment of 1.19 crore students looks to be huge but it accounts only for less than 1 per cent of total population of India. In other words, more than 99 per cent population of our country is yet to be brought into the fold of higher education. The reasons could be either no access or inability to afford. It is time to explore how best more population can be brought into the orbit of higher education. If one provide education, it is as good as empowering people. The major trends in growth of higher education institutions is given in Table 14.1

Regulatory Bodies

A regulatory body, in the context of higher education, is an external organisation that has been empowered by legislation to oversee and control the educational process and outputs germane to it.

TABLE 14.1: Trends in Growth of Higher Education Institutions

Types of Universities/ Institutions	*Owner-ship*	*Financ-ing*	*No. of Institutions*	*Number of Students*	*Growth trends*
Universities under the Government	Public	Public	240	1,000,000	Not growing
Private Universities	Private	Private	7	10,000	Emerging on the scene
Deemed Universities (Aided)	Public/ Private	Public	38	40,000	Growing slowly
Deemed Universities (Unaided)	Private	Private	63	60,000	Growing rapidly
Colleges under the Government	Public	Public	4225	2,750,000	Not Growing
Private Colleges (Aided)	Private	Public	5750	3,450,000	Not growing
Private Colleges (Unaided)	Private	Private	7650	3,150,000	Growing rapidly
Foreign Institutions	Private	Private	150	8,000	Emerging on the scene
Total			18,123	10,468,000	

University Grants Commission (UGC), Distance Education Council (DEC), All India Council for Technical Education (AICTE), Medical Council of India (MCI), The Council of Architecture, Pharmacy Council of India, Indian Nursing council, Dental council of India are some of the regulatory and statutory bodies that decide the direction and speed of higher education in India. Apart from these, there are several other regulatory bodies at the apex level but good governance based on transparency and disclosure norms is missing largely. The recent AICTE episode is a manifestation of this. The regulators need to act as a true facilitator, and an enabler. There is a need for both-way communication between government and the education providers for every kind of regulation, governance and financial affairs to make the functioning of the regulatory bodies should be participatory with all the stakeholders. This is the first step to ensure fair play, transparency and accountability. There is a need to provide adequate space for innovation and experimentation and facilitate growth of private sector in Higher Education.

Fund Allocation to Higher Education

It is a good sign that the overall plan expenditure for Budget 2009-10 to ₹3.25 lakh crore, up 34 per cent from the previous year. Even within higher education, the overall Plan allocations have increased by ₹2,000 crore or 26 per cent over the previous year's Budget amount of ₹7,600 crore. Among initiatives in higher education, it is proposed to allot ₹2,113 crore for IITs and NITs, which includes a provision of ₹450 crore for the new IITs and NITs.

The education sector as a whole received ₹41,978.21 crore against ₹37,366.57 crore in the revised estimate of budget allocation of 2008-09, showing a hike of ₹4,611.64 crore. The higher education has been allocated ₹13,179 crore in the Budget. On the higher education side, the University Grants Commission has been given an additional ₹1062.75 crore in the interim budget. A total of ₹6,545.11 crore has been earmarked for UGC against ₹5,482.36 crore in the revised estimate for 2008-09.

To promote a greater enrolment in higher education, fee reimbursement scheme has been introduced in Andhra Pradesh in the year 2007-'08 and it has been showing good progress in terms of enrolment into colleges including engineering and medicine.

Foreign Direct Investment (FDI)

To consider higher education as a trade in services, there has been strong argument that foreign direct investment should be allowed in India. Foreign Direct Investment (FDI) in education, including higher education, is allowed in India under the automatic route, without any sectoral cap, since February, 2000. In the current system, an international institution can offer courses in India with a local partner.

The number of foreign universities showing interest to set up campuses in the country has been on the rise. To make a significant progress in this direction, there is a need to simplify the regulations and guidelines under which they will have to operate. FDI up to 100 per cent is allowed on automatic route in the education sector. The number of collaboration agreements and MoUs between Indian and Foreign universities also has been rise.

Education Policy in India

In India, education has always been governed by the tenets of accessibility, quality and social inclusion. In plain speak this translates to low tuition fee. Accreditation by governmental authorities and reservation quotas on caste-basis restrict the opportunities for higher education to many. In India where the number of higher education institutions (358 universities and about 200 professional colleges of repute) is so scarce, the common student finds himself at a loss due to the quota system, as qualifying for these examinationss becomes more a matter of elimination than selection.

Some recommendations of the Knowledge Commission:

- Increase expenditure from the current 4 per cent to a minimum of 6 per cent of GDP on education.
- 1500 new universities and institutes of higher education required.
- Creation of one single Indian Regulatory Board of Higher Education (IRBHE) doing away with the multiple regulatory bodies trying to do each other's job. Thus: UGC to only manage funding universities, AICTE to act only as an expert advisory body on curriculum designing etc, NAAC and NBA to be streamlined under the IRBHE for accreditation.
- Allow foreign education providers to set up off shore campuses.
- Look for alternate funding mechanisms such as Public-Private-Partnership (PPP) institutions.
- To achieve this in phased time frames: Limits of 2010 and 2025 set.

Industry and services sectors say that only a miniscule number of graduates are readily employable and that they incur heavy expenses on retraining the youth to acquire skill sets required for employment. The industry academia divides needs to be addressed and for this liberalists advocate reforms as set forth by the knowledge commission.

Impact of Globalization

Education is viewed as one of the ways to upward social mobility, a stepping-stone to high-flying career. Education system looks quite paradoxical in India. We have world class and top ranking institutions such as IITs and IIMs on one side and the other side, we do not have basic infrastructure for large number of schools in our country. Why does this happen? Universal Literacy is still elusive despite the fact that we attained independence 63 years ago and our literacy rate is as low as around 52 per cent. Low literacy rate and low rate of employability among the graduates and postgraduates are the major issues that are catching the attention of the policy makers in the recent years.

The universities need to focus on higher levels of teaching and learning through contemporary pedagogical tools. This will ensure that the learner is able to handle the challenges with maximum efficiency by suitable application of knowledge and understanding, problem solving ability, creative thinking, practical and productive skills, attitudes and values. Education is the process of human empowerment. Ineffective delivery of education system is one of the reasons why the socio-economic development of the society is skewed and till remains incomplete.

The impact of globalization on education system has been very visible. People have started speaking about quality education and realizing that mere increase in numbers does not mean that we are progressing. Unless we have quality manpower, we will not be in a position to compete with the developed nations.

Ever since India has joined WTO, there has been a clear shift in the mindset of people how they perceive about education. If one is educated, they can move all over the world, they can take up assignments across the continents. General Agreement on Trade and Services (GATS), one of the WTO Agreements, focuses on removing all the barriers, internationalise education and provides for mobility of capital and people all over.

National Knowledge Commission Report (2007) pointed out that the Government of India must provide large volume of additional funds required to ensure the 'Right to Education'. This is not in line with GATS regulations. The Commission explained the need for setting up of 1500 new universities and 50 National Universities to achieve the enrolment target of 15 per cent by 2015. It also recommended setting up an Independent Regulatory Authority for Higher Education (IRAHE) thereby marginalizing the existing monitoring bodies. These recommendations are unique in nature though partly in disagreement with the GATS regulations. UNESCO, quite some time back, emphasized that higher education should be internationalized but should not commercialized. It emphasized that Education in a globalized society, should assure equity of access and respect towards cultural diversity as well as national sovereignty. What is happening in India in the field of education is not a happy phenomenon: the numbers of private players are increasing and the control has been nominal to the extent that ineffective controls have been damaging the entire system. Whether we like or not, GATS is going to continue and the teachers, teacher-educators and educationists need to use their intellect, skills and values to revitalize our conscience so that we can act rightly at right time for the sake of our meaningful existence.

GATS has opened up more challenges to our education system. Though it has brought in more discrimination and inequality among those who can afford and who cannot, it has paved way for increased marketisation of education programmes all over. Indian universities are likely to face a severe threat from the top ranking world-class universities such as Harvard, Sloan and Cambridge, which are capable of offering their off-campus programmes. The regulating bodies such as AICTE or UGC have nominal role and service implications for quality assurance. Developing market-relevant syllabus with appropriate technology base, pedagogy, course structure and course delivery mechanism continues to be a major challenge for many of the Indian universities.

Today, educational institutions in India have been focusing on ICT infrastructure for net working Open Distance Learning (ODL) institutions. The Open Education Resources (OERs) are increasingly becoming popular. Universities have come forward with innovative strategies such as course credit system, supporting research activity in ODL, offering training programmes for distance educators and increasing access for the learners with special needs.

To avail the benefits of the open education market, appropriate measures needs to be initiated. Some such may be:

1) The Corporate is invited to come forward with their educational projects and also to join policy-framing bodies in the universities and other educational institutions. This is intended to
   a) bridge the gap between the desired academic programmes in a given context and what exactly are being offered by the conventional universities.
   b) Create better infrastructure to ensure quality in the process of teaching and learning environment and
   c) develope the trained cadre at different levels of management to manage the operations of a given organization.
2) Foreign universities are being invited to set up their campuses and study centers to attract the students from our country.
3) Modes like consumption abroad, free movement of qualified teachers, virtual learning and twinning of institutions, which are already in the process, are encouraged.
4) Promotion of Distance Learning programmes to offer undergraduate and postgraduate programmes.
5) Collaborations with different international organizations like UNESCO, SAARC, Commonwealth of learning and other UN bodies.
6) Creation of UNESCO chairs in universities in India
7) Providing admission to foreign students in Indian universities.
8) Up gradation of infrastructure of Indian institutions to compete with elite institutes of national and international level through TEQIP grants from World Bank
9) Strengthening of institutional fund through internally generated savings and management consulting assignments.
10) Appointment of qualified teachers on contractual basis and thereby reducing the burden on the government exchequer.
11) To offer self financed market relevant courses emphasizing on privatization
12) Leveraging on technology focusing on ICT and Educational Technology to improve the quality of delivery of teaching-learning processes.

Shift in Focus

1. ***Increasing private participation*:** Private universities have been paying a major role in Japan, South Korea, Taiwan, Taipei, Indonesia, and the Philippines. In these countries, up to 75 per cent of students attend private institutions. Private higher education is reported to be rapidly growing in China, Vietnam, Cambodia, and other central Asian republics as well. Generally, private post-secondary institutions are found to be at the lower end in terms of prestige, though there are some high quality private universities, such as Waseda and Keio in Japan, De La Salle and the Ateneo de Manila in the Philippines, Yonsei in South Korea, and Santa Dharma in Indonesia. These universities are among the oldest in their respective countries and share a reputation of training the elite class.

2. ***Focused specialization*:** There are some relatively new private institutions specializing in fields such as management, technology, or education, with the sole aim of offering high quality academic degrees having market acceptability. The Asian Institute of Technology in the Philippines and the National Institute of Information Technology in India fall in this category. Besides private universities and colleges serving the mass higher education market on a massive scale, there are some non-selective institutions run by individuals or families. There are also some institutions sponsored by private, non-profit religious groups or ethnic organizations.

Many Asian countries already have considerable experience in managing private higher education institutions on a large scale, whereas other countries have picked this up during the last 25 to 30 years. Whereas we find a long tradition of private higher education in Asia, we find dramatic changes in terms of the public-private mix in Eastern Europe in the last few years. There are 91 private business schools in Poland, 29 in the Czech Republic, 21 in Armenia, 18 in Romania, and 4 in Bulgaria. In the Cote d'Ivoire, professional training is exclusively in the private domain, and in Gambia 44 per cent of skill-based education and training is privately provided. About 75 per cent of tertiary education in India is supposed to be under private management (Patrinos, 2002). Whereas most of the private colleges are affiliated with the open schools or public universities, we also find examples of new private universities being set up under the Private Universities Acts passed by some of the newly emergent states in India such as Chhattisgarh or Uttarakhand.

China has more than 1200 private higher education institutions today, though not all of them enjoy official government authorization. By the end of 2002, only 4 private colleges had been authorized to award the bachelor's degree and 129 were authorized to grant degrees below the level of the bachelor's. The private sector accounts for 10 per cent of the total enrollment in post-secondary education in China (Yan and Levy, 2003). The public-private educational institutions in Shanghai and Beijing enjoy reasonably good reputations; the schools in Shenyang are not doing so well. These *Minban Gongzhu* (owned and supported by the government through property and infrastructure) are seen as breeding corruption, sacrificing quality for the sake of profit, and putting unnecessary pressures on students and their families.

Collaborations

Today, JNTUH has many collaboration agreements with foreign universities. Some of the prominent ones include collaborated MBA programme with Central Michigan University and MSIT with Carniege Melon University. It also offers double degree programmes with University of Sweden. Another case can be Management Development Institute which has collaborations with 40 universities abroad—spread over Europe, US, China including ESCP-EAP, France, University of North Carolina, Chapel Hill, University of International Business and Economics, Beijing, Chinese University in Hong Kong. It is imperative that such collaborations will open up the minds of the faculty and administrators how best the quality can be integrated into the delivery of academic programmes. The success stories of universities such as Cambridge, Oxford, Stanford and Harvard can be taken as model to ensure sustainable growth through teaching, research, consulting and training.

Another exciting development is that Indian universities are going global. BITS, Pilani has its operations in Dubai, Amity has campuses in the US, UK, Germany, Singapore and Dubai for all the courses. China also has been inviting foreign universities to set up their establishments in addition to creating different universities to cater to different needs for sustained growth. Malaysia invites foreign universities to set up campuses.

International Council for Higher Education

With offices in Bangalore and Zürich, the International Council for Higher Education (ICHE) is an association committed to advancing the cause of Christian scholarship all over the world, particularly in countries where educational opportunities are restricted, and to helping its members develop sustainable and integrated models of higher education that reflect biblical faith through learning and service.

The ICHE was officially established in 1997 in Switzerland by concerned educators joined together on vital issues facing Christian higher education across the world. Since its founding, ICHE has addressed these wide ranging educational concerns by networking and partnering with educators, specialist agencies, and institutions worldwide. Through these relationships, established colleges and universities have been able to make significant contributions to institutions in the developing world through strategic service and program partnerships.

Present Scenario of Higher Education in India

There has been strong presence of Private participation in Higher education in India. While some private universities such as Manipal University are known for quality education, there are also some private institutions, which are money-oriented, and with these, the quality of education is jeopardized and even deteriorated. These modern educational institutions are running on contract teachers who are mostly underpaid and in some cases the teachers are not qualified to teach. Such proliferation of private institutions made the job of even the regulatory agencies very complex in terms of quality checks and compliance of regulations. The multi-regulatory system of higher education with overlapping functions has also made the system much more complex.

Gaps in Higher Education

Higher education in India faces several challenges and gaps. Because of lack of focus on problem solving in many universities, education in India is often criticized for being based on rote learning rather than problem solving. The Indian curriculum is often denigrated as it follow rote learning. There are many gaps but major ones have been outlined here:

a) ***Fake degrees***: Another problem is with fake degrees. As many as 1 lakh of fake degree certificates were found in one raid. There is a list of institutions in the websites of AICTE and UGC and the degrees awarded by these institutions are not considered valid. In February 2009, the University Grant Commission listed out 19 fake institutions operating in India.

b) ***Lack of appropriate skills in communication and Problem solving***: It is estimated that over 16 per cent of manufacturers in India offer in-service training to their employees for nurturing skill, compared with over 90 per cent in China. Students from the tier 2 and tier 3 cities face this problem more often. Even those with good communication skills are not good at problem solving. Majority of the students score less than 25 per cent in problem solving and this makes them fall in the hard-to-train segment. Only through focused intervention across communication skills, problem solving and technical skills, they may be brought to the employable pool.

c) ***Shortfall in the faculty***: There is short fall in the faculty by 70 per cent at different levels. Indian engineering institutions require 60,970 teachers, and this was broken down into 8,710 professors, 17,420 readers and 34,840 lecturers—in terms of professional qualifications, what was required were 26,130 Ph.D.s and 34,840 M.Tech.s. What was available; were 5,862 Ph.D.s and 11,035 M.Techs., resulting a shortfall of around 70 per cent. This shortfall enhanced more than doubled over the decade. It is difficult to make-up this gap. The massive increase in the intakes in recent years adds fuel to the fire.

d) ***Spending on education***: According to NCAER survey, in places like Bihar and Uttar Pradesh, the state is hardly spending any money on education and the spending by private individuals is dramatically higher. There is need for larger allocation of funding for education.

Demographic Dividend Vs Demographic Nightmare?

India is known to be young country as 54 per cent of Indians are younger than 30 years. It is projected, as per Census Reports, that the proportion of Indian in the 15-to-64 age group will increase steadily, from 62.9 per cent in 2006 to 68.4 per cent in 2026. By 2020, the average age in India will be 31years, compared with 37 in China and 48 in Japan. Census reports say that India is entering the advantageous 'demographic dividend' phase just as China leaves it. If the universities turnout graduates without learning how to get things done, without complex problem-solving skills, without knowing how to put their theoretical education into practice, and with poor articulation, this demographic dividend may result into demographic nightmare. The Government and universities need to take adequate measures to develop skills of the youth.

It is quite heartening to see the corporate taking responsibility to train the teachers and students. For instance, in the past three years, Wipro, TCS, Honeywell, Infosys and many other organizations have created several funds to finance grants, research scholarships and sabbaticals for teachers in engineering schools.

There are cases where most industries are struggling to achieve their growth targets because of a shortage of skilled labor. There has been critical shortage of blue-collar workers and some companies have begun hiring skilled blue-collar workers from abroad.

It is time for industries to track data, set standards and design training curricula in association with the universities and government departments. One should note that skill is a currency-bankable, certifiable asset and universities should focus on skill building among the students.

Employability Skills

- The survey jointly carried out by the Federation of Indian Chambers of Commerce and Industry (FICCI) and the World Bank reveals that 64 per cent of the employers are 'somewhat', 'not very', or 'not at all' satisfied with the quality of engineering graduates' skills. There is a significant skill gap exists among Indian engineering graduates, making a strong case for the engineering colleges and institutions to focus more on employability and quality.

- According to this survey, *Integrity, reliability and teamwork* are the top three most important general skills identified, while the top three most important specific skills are *entrepreneurship, communication in English and use of modern tools and technologies.*
- In case of engineering graduates, the industry expects them to be able to formulate, analyze, and solve a real life problem using standard engineering techniques.
- Competencies vary from industry to industry. Even within industry, the companies differ in the kind of engineers they would like to hire. For instance, IT companies demand advanced computer skills and communication in English, while infrastructure firms want engineers with strong knowledge of mathematics and abilities to use modern tools and technologies.
- To enhance the employability skills for the graduates, the universities have to focus on reducing these important skill gaps through improvements in curriculum and teaching methods.
- The faculty and deans of each university/college have to closely interact with employers to design education programmes that respond to the specific skill/competency demands of the employers.
- There is need for colleges to focus on the skills of the graduates. Each college should define the set of skills that a graduate is supposed to have after each year or semester.
- Also the colleges have to plan for a shift in pedagogy from teacher-centric to student-centric, and include more assignments for students to independently analyze and apply tools on real life problems. Such initiatives ensure better quality in the teaching-learning process and we can ensure that the future engineers become more employable.

India can save a lot of resources, and perhaps also generate additional resources, by encouraging both for-profit and non-state actors in foreign collaboration to provide quality education in India itself. It can also take advantage of virtual, online, and distance education, particularly given its strengths in terms of the latest technology. Extensive integration of ICT with the course delivery mechanism will enhance the employability skills.

Educational Technology

Educational technology is the study and ethical practice of facilitating learning and improving performance. It is facilitated by creating, using and managing appropriate technological processes and resources applied in the context of development, application, and evaluation of systems and techniques. Educational technology includes systems used in the process of developing human capability facilitated through software, hardware, Internet applications and activities. Smartphones, online and offline games have been the latest tools that are being extensively employed as tools of educational technology to explore ideas and communicate. Educational technology refers to an array of tools that might prove helpful in advancing student learning.

Instructional Technologies

There are two active learning educational technologies: Problem-based Learning and Inquiry-based learning and these are extensively used to facilitate learning. Technology can be incorporated into project, problem and inquiry-based learning as they all have a similar educational philosophy. All three are student-centered. These provide the students an opportunity to engage themselves in critical thinking activities so that they can appreciate real-world scenarios.

Educational technology provides:

- Easy access to course materials,
- Motivation to students,
- Wide participation,
- Improved student writing, and
- Subjects made easier to learn.

Pre-requisites for ET

For effective deployment of Educational technology at certain place, one require special training that is involved with adding elements of educational technology to the classroom. With proper training, teachers and students can benefit from devices that will improve the quality of education. Also it is necessary that the teachers plan, when they use educational technology, they must come to the classroom prior to start time and set everything up and make sure it is all working. At times, the gadgets of educational technology may fail and the teachers need to prepare backups and alternate activities.

Educational Technology and the Teaching/Learning Process

There are two approaches for Educational technology: Inquiry approach and Project-Based approach, combined with a focus on curriculum, effectively supports the infusion of educational technologies into the learning and teaching process. There are many kinds of computer and non-computer technologies currently in use in traditional classrooms. Among these are:

- ***Computer in the Classroom***: The teaching process gets strengthened with the help of a computer in the class room. One can use it effectively for demonstrating a new lesson, presenting new material, illustrating how to use new programs, and showing new websites.
- ***Class Website***: Through class website, the student's work is displayed, teachers can post homework assignments, student work, famous quotes, trivia games etc. Students may eventually become authors once they focus on contributing actively to the content of the website.
- ***Blogs***: Blogs facilitate for a dialogue on current or contemporary issues. Students can compile their thoughts, ideas as also invite comments from experts.
- ***Wikis***: Wikis, like Wikipedia, is a group initiative that allows multiple members of the group to edit a single document and create a truly collaborative and carefully edited finished document.
- ***Wireless Classroom Microphones***: These dispense with the noise in the class room. With the help of microphones, students are able to hear their teachers clearer. students learn better when they hear the teacher clearly. This also ensures that the strain on the vocal chords of the teachers is minimal, they need not stress any more.
- ***Mobile Devices***: Mobile devices such as Smartphone, digital cameras, video cameras, interactive whiteboard tools, document cameras, or LCD projectors have proved indespensable for better learning environment. These are used to enhance the learning experience in the classroom by providing the possibility for teachers to get instant feedback.
- ***Electronic Portfolios***: An electronic portfolio, also popularly referred to as 'multimedia portfolio, e-folio, webfolio', which are similar to paper portfolio. It is a combination of media tools such as audio or video recordings, multimedia programs, database, spreadsheet and word processing software as well as CD-ROMs and the world-wide-web (www) with hyper-media links. The objectives of the course and program schedule will determine the extent and depth of coverage of these tools.

An electronic portfolio has many advantages: it increases in the technology knowledge and skills, simplifies the process of distribution of classroom teaching material distribution, facilitates the storage of many professional documents, and provides increased access to database. One can showcase the best work with the creation of electronic portfolio and thereby exhibit the knowledge and skills in using technology.

Mobile Learning

Mobile Learning (M-Learning) is a relatively new pedagogical tool that supports students and teachers in the process of distance learning. M-Learning involves the use of small, portable computing devices such as smartphones, personal digital assistants (PDAs) and similar handheld devices. These facilitate display of content and/or lessons in small, manageable formats that can be utilized particularly when laptop or fixed station computers are not accessible. It is currently being used in a variety of educational, governmental and industrial settings.

Educational Technology—An Assessment

It is a fact that computers are useful in developing certain kinds of cognitive patterns. But there are certain limitations, which disqualify computer as general educational tool. Increasing use of computers in all kinds of curricula like languages and sciences is just another example of growing dependence on technology for education. Such an approach is based on behaviouristic model of learning, which views a student as a perfectly rational. Computer-like mechanism expected to respond in a systematic and predictable way whenever appropriate educational stimuli are impinged upon him.

Another aspect of learning through computers is that it reduces the learner to 'information process system.' Human learning is a process, which involves whole psyche. There is interplay of the imagination, value system and the unconscious of the learner and the wisdom and intuition of the teacher. The personality impact and the personalized touch make the teaching and learning process human. Imitation, effort and freedom of will results in such a personalized situation. Interpersonal warmth the learner lacks in computer-oriented education and fails to develop value system and value judgment, which are so vital in all human goals, process and institutions. The learners are alienated from their social environment.

New Role

Educational Technology has a very important and vital role to play in the development of participatory process of social change. The important prerequisite for using computers is the habit of logical reasoning.

Educational Technology delimited to computer awareness or literacy reduces its vast potential. The new computer culture can be a boon or a curse depends upon how we adopt it. It is a truism that expansion and application of microelectronics has invaded services and industries in the West, which has become predominantly information-based. The majority of the workforce in these countries is engaged in jobs involving creation, processing and dissemination of information. In these societies production of new information, production of equipment to store this data and use of this information has become a necessity. But we are far from being an information-based society. Technology has yet another area where it can be best utilized. Differently abled students, for example, the blind and the deaf could be benefited by computer-assisted instructions. The Telidon and Telematique, the sophisticated devices developed in telecommunication system were displayed at a Workshop of Educational Technology organized at Jamia Milia Islamia, Delhi. The Concept of Telematique is an integrated system of computers, teleconferencing and office technology. The Telidon is a system of presenting audio-visual message via telecommunication. In this system the audience can communicate with the instructor who is present electronically. Here the technology has the scope of being used as a teaching supplement. The scheme of instruction through audio-visual aids introduced in Andhra Pradesh is worth nothing in this context. The video sets are prepared for imparting instructions, which are also useful for adult and non-formal educational programmes. It was realized that if the educators have to reach their targets they have to produce programmes in a language and culture that could be easily understood by the students. It was felt that there is need of increasing the understanding of the entry-level skills or present state of knowledge of the target audience, develop step-by-step curricula, and provide a feed-back for the future.

Information and Communication Technologies

Irrespective of the background and professional status, one needs to know with regard to information and communication technologies (ICTs) and appreciate the techno-pedagogical ability with which these technologies can be integrated into their teaching practice. IT can extensively support the core activities of the institution of higher learning: i.e., the task of teaching, learning and research and manage both front-office and back-office operations.

To ensure optimization and ensure judicious deployment of resources, technology is coming very handy. But, in the process of complying with the demands of implementing and maintaining systems like ERP [enterprise resource planning], security and e-mail, one should not lose sight of the goals of the academic institution.

For effective learning, the number of students both at the PG/UG levels possessing personal computer (PC) or desktop or notebook, computer needs to increase. This will increase only when the course work is planned in such a way that the assignments are given or course materials of say 40-50 pages are sent through email. There is a need to change our course delivery that demands the use of PC. The premier academic institutions, including B-Schools and Technological Universities, are characterized by:

- Classrooms are equipped with wired Internet connections.
- High-speed Internet.
- Wireless Internet connectivity.
- Add the databases dedicated to research results.
- Courseware for faculty.
- Multimedia applications for Webcasting lectures.
- Hardware/software that facilitate the learning-teaching processes.

These are the secrets for the success of the premier institutions. There is equal focus both on the research and deployment of appropriate technologies (through continuous interaction between the teachers and the IT providers) that enhances the teaching-learning process. The ultimate effect is an extraordinarily rich technology environment, manifested by high quality of interaction and presentations, both individual and team, by students. To achieve this, the following are the ICT strategies need to be crafted and well executed:

a. Provide and expand easy, integrated access to IT services: Through wireless network for the entire campus, the teachers and students will be free to teach and to learn. How to use the technology to get to resources will be no more issue. By providing an access point for hardware, networks and applications, a campus wide login system will be set up, also build a portal to unify applications. One can use E-mail, courseware, learning tools, library catalogs, the grading system and many more applications can also be made available through a single window on a 'simple and clean' interface tool.

b. Align between pedagogy and IT initiative: One can address the immediate need of faculty and students by ensuring effective IT for higher education as reference points in a larger context. Let there be rational assessments of technology, understand how it impacts the teaching and learning processes at the institution and measurable goals to assess the progress.

c. Forge communications links with faculty, students and administrators: IT departments in the academic institutions should listen and talk to the stakeholders, i.e., faculty, students and administrators to identify the right tools for supporting the pedagogy. Let there be meetings, committees and advisory groups for continuous interaction. Even informal get-together will help to gather information and ideas and speak about the technology. It is always suggested that there should be an IT committee comprising all the representatives of the students, staff and administrators apart from the IT specialists to plan from early planning to implementation, and has real decision power.

d. Try out new technology in the faculty labs and classrooms: New Technology can be tried in the faculty labs and class rooms and identify tech-savy faculty who can test the technologies and share their experiences. Involving faculty and students in real testing of technology has both specific and far-reaching benefits. First, the practice provides answers to questions: Does it perform as promised? How difficult it is to use the hardware or software? Does it improve the quality of classroom delivery? A hands-on partnership with faculty members will strengthen the connection between IT and pedagogy. When the IT department, the educator and students share perspectives on the value of particular technologies, the understanding of what's further needed to support and improve teaching and learning will be better. This is one way of addressing the passion of some tech-savy faculty who wish to test new tools and technology ahead of others.

e. Enable meaningful measurement in educational programs: What cannot be measured cannot be controlled. To ensure better accountability, every one including trustees, parents, taxpayers, politicians, and even faculty and students themselves want to know what's working in education and what's not. IT departments, often in partnership with assessment specialists, are increasingly asked to collect, aggregate and analyze data that can be used to evaluate the impact of technology in the academic environment. IT departments can find and use the most sophisticated and flexible technology available so that the resulting measurements yield insights rather than snap judgments. The reporting of results can be fast and also individualized and this will support the teaching and learning process. The embedded evaluation and feedback tools can be implemented to understand how close we are to real time environment.

Modes of Learning: ICT All Pervasive

There are two modes of learning—Open learning and e-learning approaches have been advocated that enable to address the contemporary issues in the learning process. ICT Resources have strong role to play in all these modes of learning.

a) Open Learning: The term Open learning is generally used to represent the flexible learning. Both the terms are used to express an approach, which provides students with the opportunity and options to take greater responsibility for their learning with provisions to meet individual needs. The analysis of the processes and approach suggests that in open learning 'autonomy' and 'choice' plays an important role. In the specific context of technical education open learning could be interpreted as an approach to promote students' learning priorities. It is about reorganizing teacher's role as collaborators and promoter of learning autonomy for optimal learning experiences. These experiences are achieved through the provision of well-thought, pre-designed course material, negotiating of objectives, mentor-support and group tasks. Open learning can be applied to technical education in the following learning situations.

- Conventional lecture situation
- Small group unsupervised work
- Laboratory classes
- Independent study on/off site support
- Group learning, and
- Industry learning.

b) E-learning: An open learning environment enabled with Information and Communication Technologies (ICTs) can be called e-learning environment. Benefits of e-learning are anytime, anywhere learning, access to more information, enhance the retention, consistent delivery, and enabling knowledge management. The wide use of Internet is an effective medium for delivery of education and related services. Developments in Internet applications such as email, list-serves, discussion groups, voice-mail, chat-groups and video-conferencing have further enhanced the utility in the learning process.

Broadly, ICT application can be used in the open learning environment in the following:

1. Course delivery or access to learning material
2. Tools for laboratory training
3. Evaluation tools: assignments, tests and quizzes
4. Tools and technology for development of learning material
5. Interaction, collaboration and development of learner communities for counseling and discussions
6. Library and information services: digital libraries
7. Assistive technologies for physically challenged, and.
8. Educational administration

A typical e-learning model will include delivery of courseware in a web environment, from a repository using tools for enrolment, evaluation, counseling and peer networking. A faculty can create a virtual class, hosting interactive course material, schedule, learning plans, assignments etc, on a web server and providing access to the class participants enrolled for the class; all assisted by a single web based tool. The site would be supporting other applications such as user groups, student groups' work, and links to learning helps etc. A student will need to access the resources using an Internet enabled PC either from home, work or a service centre. e-learning need not necessarily be used only for distance learners. In a large number of universities around the world, e-learning application is used for in-campus programmes.

Opportunities for ICT in Higher Education

There have been many new challenges for Institutions of higher technical education in delivery and access of education, due to a variety of factors and each of these constitutes an opportunity. The ever-changing technologies, globalization and changing demand for new skill sets in the job market have been demanding a shift in the teaching and learning paradigm. It is good to think to make, in a democratic society, higher technical education accessible to all without any barriers such as time, space, gender, and class. But in reality, many critical issues such as policy, finance, role of state and institutional management have to be addressed to develop a sustainable model of education.

There are three major issues while we discuss about higher education: funding, access and delivery. When compared to funding, access and delivery are more critical factors. The access and delivery can be strengthened, as per the guidelines of UNESCO, by focusing on

a) ***Contents*** to ensure updated knowledge,

b) ***The types and paths (systems and structures)*** of education that can influence the life of individual

c) ***The pedagogy of learning***, particularly for practical tasks. The access and delivery also get restricted due to the following limitations:

- Geographic and time inequality
- Unsuitability for lifelong learning
- High cost of infrastructure
- Shortage of faculty
- High cost of staff
- Inefficiency in assessment system
- Cost of teaching materials.
- Lack of flexibility and customization
- Failure to use analytical and exploratory capability of the students.

Key Triggers

The following are the key triggers that have been driving unprecedented changes in the educational institutions and these can be addressed only by ICT:

- The metamorphic changes in the society as knowledge society
- Increasing realization for life-long learning

- Globalization and privatization
- The state becoming a facilitator than funding agency
- Emphasis of Quality in delivery of educational services
- Growth potential for delivery of education due to advancement of information and communication technology.
- Demand for different skills due to the emergence of new jobs and frequent changes in job requirements in one's life time

The New Learning Paradigm in the Globalized Era

To foster and make higher education widely accessible, a new paradigm may be taken into account with flexible, open, self-paced, student centered learning based on collaborative two way processes. In a learning society, the facility for learning should be accessible to everyone, everywhere and at all the time. The contents should be guided by the needs of the society and also the frequent changes impacting the dynamics of the society. Therefore, there should be a gradual shift from standard education to customized service. Flexibility would permit the students to learn at a convenient time and place.

The outcomes of both the traditional and contemporary learning models are depicted in the following table:

Focus: Traditional class rooms	*Focus: New Learning Environment*
Teacher-centered instruction	Student-centered learning
Single sense stimulation	Multi-sensory stimulation
Single path progression	Multi path progression
Single media	Multimedia
Information Delivery	Information exchange, Knowledge development
Isolated work	Collaborative work
Passive learning	Active inquiry based learning
Factual thinking	Critical thinking & decision making
Reactive response	Proactive planned action
Isolated, artificial context	Authentic, real-world context
Classical method of assessment: Testing of bookish knowledge	Test of knowledge, skills, problem environment
Geared to predefined jobs	Adaptable to new job requirement in a rapidly changing knowledge economy

E-Learning: Concerns and Challenges

Major challenges in developing e-learning are — technological infrastructure development, policy making, human resources development, contents development, and managerial and socio-economic issues.

a) Technological Challenges: Appropriateness, accessibility, handling, maintenance and information management have been mentioned as some of the technological challenges. Technological challenge may relate to development of infrastructure, coping up with fallouts of too much use of technology, technology for learning material development, particularly for engineering and technology subjects, and technologies for educational management. Development of communication and computing infrastructure, such as local, national and international networks, hardware, peripherals and support services is the foremost issue that needs to be addressed by the country. Technology is double-edged sword. Technology offers us visions of hell as well as the more widely promised glimpses of heaven.

b) Infrastructure Development: Apart from ICT infrastructure, in the specific context of technical education, development of laboratory infrastructure for open and distance learning for the purpose of wider access is an issue of utmost importance. A suitable strategy that enables replacement of laboratory training with virtual modules, automation and networking laboratories, and development of laboratory kits may facilitate spread of technical education to masses. Another aspect of infrastructure development is support services such as access-centers, learning-centre (Libraries), particularly digital libraries.

c) Socio-economic Challenges – The Digital Divide: Other concerns in technology enabled open learning are socio-economic, political and cultural consequences, if the virtual class becomes the dominant mode of instructions. In a vast country like India, a dual reality scenario is predicted, where two different generations will be living at the same time. Information being the most strategic weapon in the era of global economy, two new social classes of 'haves' and 'have-nots' will emerge; the former with good access to information and the latter with poor or no access to information. Therefore, spread of technology is an essential prerequisite for widening the access to education in the new learning paradigm. It is heartening to note that India has undertaken several initiatives to develop ICT infrastructure at the national level by the government as well as through public-private-partnerships (PPP). Through schemes such as village information kiosks and Simputer, the ICT will be within reach of common man. In the higher education sector UGC and Project Implementation Unit have started programmes for assisting institutions of higher educations in strengthening ICT infrastructure.

d) Content-Development: Content-development is another major concern in ICT enabled open education. The relevant issues are technology for courseware development, quality assurance, and suitability of the contents for an open and flexible learning environment. Several institutions have embarked upon web based courseware development. Most of the available courseware is little more than digitized printed material. There are some commercially available software suites for contents development and delivery of courses. Therefore, there is a critical need for development of learning materials, educational management software, electronic information/libraries, and teaching and research databases.

e) Managerial and Policy Challenges: The costs, access and quality are the major issues for e-learning and are some of the issues that confront the institutions of higher education in implementation of e-learning. Assessment and accreditation, demand and supply, employability, relevance of open learning, management of access, transparency, human resource development, institutional management, funding, and management of change are some of the policy and managerial issues that need to be addressed. A fresh framework of qualifications needs to be evolved at the policy level. Teacher's role should include gradually more and more as content developer and facilitator rather than deliverer of the instruction. Introduction of collaborative learning style will require intensive HR efforts.

Action Plan: To overcome some of the above mentioned challenges the following three strategies are suggested:

a) Synergistic and scalable use of technology for distance education as well as in-campus courses: It is an approach to make virtual education concept operational internally initially i.e. for in-house or regular courses and then externalize the concept by extending it for distance learners. By using available proprietary or free tools and online learning objects, ICT can be implemented in a gradual and phased manner within the existing programmes. For example curriculum may have a combination of online modules and quizzes, assignments and tutorials that can be taken by a student at a time and place of his choice; classroom lecture and laboratory based learning. Collaboration and discussion forum tools are used for class management, group work and interaction among the class participants, and thus developing an online learner-community. Efforts could be made to gradually increase the amount of online or electronic contents and its quality to make it more interactive and suitable for self-learning.

One major problem in implementation of open distance learning in technical disciplines is laboratory training. This will require a different approach. Initially, distance education programmes in an open learning model could be started for non-laboratory courses, just as many institutions have already done it in IT related disciplines. Laboratory based courses can be covered as and when networking is in place and advance based learning material that can replace some part of laboratory training become available. However, ultimate aim should be to make open learning as preferred mode of delivery, in both distance as well as in-campus programmes, rather than supplemental to the traditional learning model.

b) Hybrid model for delivery of distance learning programmes: In order to address the problem of digital divide a hybrid model is suggested for delivery of distance education programmes. Depending upon the access to computer and Internet a flexible mix of online-delivery and offline-delivery of course material, submission of assignments and interaction can be introduced along with a differential fee structure. For those who do not have reliable access at home, access at work place may be allowed by the employers for upgrading their skills and qualifications. Shared resource centers for distance learning at various places may be set up with high speed internet connectivity, where students enrolled in different institutions can come and use the facilities. Even the village information kiosks may be upgraded for this purpose.

c) Networking and sharing of resources: This approach is useful for fast implementation of ICT in open learning at less cost, and can be used for content-development, and reusability of knowledge and information. Facilities such as libraries and laboratories can be opened for use by multiple institutions. For example rather than investing in setting up of new library or laboratory by the institutions, the existing ones can be upgraded and made available for a consortium. Development of learning material is a highly time consuming and cost-intensive work. A cooperative approach may be adopted where standard core modules can be developed by a facilitating agency that can be customized by various institutions using some standards tool for a quick implementation. This will reduce the per capita cost of implementation.

Government Initiatives for Promotion of ICT

Dr. Vikram Sarabhai, one of the prominent physicists, India ever produced, was committed to adopting of advanced communications technology in India. Communications technology, which manifests itself through random, print technology, television, satellites, computers and microprocessors, through the merging of these technologies, constitutes the communication revolution. During the last five years many educational production centers have been set up in India. The preparation of educational video programmes for children is in full swing following the Government's declaration to provide second channel for education by 1991-92. The Central Institute for Educational Technology and the NCERT are coordinating the programmes. The CIET set up in 1984 is aided by State Institutes for Educational Technology in Six States. The Development and Educational Communication Unit of the Indian Space Research Organization and International Agencies like the United Nations Development Programme, UNESCO, and the Asia Pacific Institute for Broadcasting Development are all working for promotion, understanding and utilization of educational technology for the spread of education. The CIET provides the entire hardware to the SIETs, and finances and training are made available through it. Most SIETs have started producing their own programmes in their own languages and culture. These programmes are beamed for six hours daily in these States. DECU formed in December 1983, is engaged in aiding CIET in the production of programmes, adaptation of video hardware, communication research and training. The science programmes for SIETs are produced by DECU.

With the population of 1230 million, India is faced with the stupendous task of educating its people, having 36 per cent of literacy. Besides, all our developmental programmes were oriented towards urban population, three-forth of our population which resides in rural areas, remain yet uncovered. Statistics also show that 40 per cent students reach class V and 8 per cent reach the high school class and only two per cent of the youth population reach the door steps of temples of higher learning. With these realities before us, it was realized that we would have to rely on the modern technology to reach the vast population.

SIET has reached nearly 45 million people spread over the six States. These programmes had specific targets namely: out of school Adults, school children and teachers. The satellite, INSAT-IB was used for education in 1983. This was followed by INSAT-IC and INSAT-2. The central department of Electronics has introduced computer education and by end of Seventh Five-Year plan some 16,000 Higher Secondary Schools was catered for computer education. Further, this project was extended to some 45,000 Secondary schools during the Eighth plan. The 900 BBC-Acorn microcomputers purchased from UK under Computer Literacy and Studies in Schools (CLASS) project were given to schools and 42 resource centres were established in the country to monitor this project. The purpose is of making the young generation computer literate and preparing the ground to introduce computers as the medium of instruction for traditional school subjects, like, Physics, Maths, Chemistry, Biology and Languages.

Future

Educational Technology in general and ICT in particular have come as panacea for all educational ills. The electronic future in this country seems to be very positive and bright in the field of education. Nowhere else the attempt to force the pace of development is visible than in the field of educational technology. The educationists and technocrats of all hues extol the virtues of computers as the ultimate teaching aid that will revolutionize education. The spokesmen of educational technology proclaim that it has a liberalizing influence on education. It is rightly observed that, 'use of computers for scheduling classes, advanced techniques for planning and control, technological advances in media and mechanical and automated laboratory equipment all portend significant change in how educational institutions will be operated.' It has become increasingly clear that educational technology will improve the quality of education by replacing the traditional teaching modes and supplementing the teacher-student interaction.

REFERENCES

Scenario of Technical Education in India. *University News*, 47(45) November 09-15, 2009.

Altbach, Philip G. (2002). The Private Sector in Asian Higher Education. *International Higher Education,* Fall.—, ed. 2000. *Private Prometheus: Private Higher Education and Development in the 21st Century*. US: Greenwood Publishing Company.

Blumenstyk, Goldie (2003). "For-profit Colleges Attract a Gold Rush of Investors." *The Chronicle of Higher Education,* March 14.

Bollag, Burton (2003). "In Chile, A fast-growing University, Owned by Sylvan, Produces Profits and Scorn." *The Chronicle of Higher Education,* June 27. http://chronicle.com/free/v49/i42/42a02301.htm.

Brender, Alan (2003). 'Japan's Private Universities Awash in Red Ink.' *The Chronicle of Higher Education,* February 14: A41.

Douglass, John (2005a). 'All Globalization is Local: Countervailing Forces and the Influence on Higher Education Markets.' CSHE Research and Occasional Papers Series, CSHE1.05.

Geiger, Roger L. (1990). 'The Dynamics of Private Higher Education in the United States: Mission, Finance and Public Policy.' *Higher Education Policy* 3(2): 9-12.

Gupta, Asha (2005). 'Judicialization of Education: The Fee Cut Controversy in India.'

Gupta, P.V. Virtual University in the Indian context. University News. Vol. 41 No. 37 (September 15, 2003) p. 7.

Hariharan, R. Information technology for teaching and learning. Indian Journal of Technical education. Vol. 24, No. 4 (Oct-Dec 2002). p. 30.

Humphries, Jennifer (2002). "Canadian Universities: Private Linkages, Public Trust." Presented at *Globalization: What Issues are at Stake for Universities?* University of Laval, Quebec, Canada. September 19.James, E. 1993. 'Why do different countries choose a different public-private mix of educational services?' *Journal of Human Resources* 28(3): 571-92.

International Commission on Education for Twenty-first Century. Report: to UNESCO: Learning the treasure within. Paris, Unesco Publishing, 1996.

International Higher Education 38, Winter.—(2004). 'From a Learning Community to a Community of Learning.' *Higher Education Policy and Practice.* New Delhi: Amity Foundation.—. 2000. *Beyond Privatization: A Global Perspective.* IPSA-Macmillan Series in Advanced Studies. UK: Macmillan.—. 1994. *Changing Perspectives of the Welfare State: the Issue of Privatization.* New Delhi: Pragati Publications.—. 1987. *Socialism in*

Theory and Practice: Narendra Deva's Contribution. New Delhi: Gitanjali Publications.

—. January. 2005b. 'A Transatlantic Persuasion: A Comparative Look at America's Path Towards Access and Equity in Higher Education.' In David Palfreyman and Theodore

Kapoor, M.P. (2002). Technology enabled flexible education and development. In ICT enabled education, edited by K.B. Powar, M.D. Tiwari, and H.P. Dixit. New Delhi, Association of Indian University, p. 82-94.

Killedar, Manoj. Web based education in India. Paper presented at competition, collaboration, continuity, change- Conference on Open and Distance Education, held at University of South Australia, Adelaid September 11-13, 2000. http://www.com.unisa.edu.au/cccc/papers/non-refereed/killedar.htm

Laurillard, Diana, (1997). Recommendation of National Committee of Inquiry in Higher Education (UK) In *IT and Dearing: the implications for the HE: Colloquim proceeding*, edited by Helen Beetham. London, CTI Support service, University of Oxford.

Natarajan, R. Promise and prospects of e-learning. *Indian Journal of Technical Education*. Vol. 23, No. 3 (Jul-Sep 2002), pp. 1-11.

Rajasingham, Lalita. The virtual university in India. In Education India: the next millennium-report of the World Conference-New Delhi, 12-14 November, 1997, edited by Marmar Mukhopadhyay and other. Udang, Howrah, Institute of Education, Rural studies and Development, 1998. pp. 475-481.

Shukla, Jyoti Kiran. Open learning in technical education: Some conceptual issues. In Education India: the next millennium-report of the World Conference-New Delhi, 12-14 November, 1997, edited by Marmar Mukhopadhyay and other. Udang, Howrah, Institute of Education, Rural studies and Development, 1998. pp. 510-517.

Tapper, eds. *The Politics of Access to Higher Education.* Routledge: Falmer Press.

15.

The Foundation for an Engaged and Secure Campus Community by Mobile Technology

Maganlal S. Molia

Prologue

Montclair State University, a public New Jersey institution with more than 17,000 students enrolled, has harnessed the cell phone and cellular broadband technology to foster a stronger sense of community and provide students with a safe, secure, and rich learning environment. This chapter discusses the potential for new technologies to foster development of a virtual campus. With this goal in mind, it also provides a case study of the application deployment at Montclair State University, and a glimpse into the future of mobile technology at higher education institutions across the globe. The chapter is based on Keywords which includes broadband, cellular broadband, cell phones, digital natives, higher education, location-based services, mobile technology, social networking, student engagement, virtual campus.

Introduction

When reflecting upon creative uses of technology for the Montclair State University (MSU) campus, the author reminded of an inspiring story told by Dr. Rene Dubos in his classic work, "A God Within", which explores humanity's stewardship of the planet (Dubos 1972). He tells of the Inuit people of the far North who are known for carving very intricate and beautiful figurines from the ivory extracted from whales. When Dubos inquired of these artists how they decide what to carve from the pieces of ivory they worked with, he was surprised to learn that they do not make a decision about what to carve at all. Rather, they see the figurine that will result from their carvings as latent in the raw media, and their artistry is to remove the excess to release the 'god within'. These artists have a unique insight about their media. In some way, they comprehend all the facets and nuance of the undifferentiated material in hand, and with precision and care, they are able to fully realize its potential. What a fitting metaphor for our efforts to introduce new technologies into the fabric of the living and learning environment that is a university campus. We would do well to remember that the campus is a delicate ecosystem. We should take care to consider the multitude of subtle forces that define a campus community and treat technology as the carving knife, so to speak, that refines the campus environment in a way that helps all members of the community to fully realize their potential.

Quest for a Virtual Campus Experience

In today's higher education environment, campuses face multiple challenges and opportunities – keeping students safe, building stronger campus communities, and designing technology enriched courses that improve learning and are sensitive to the various ways in which people can learn. Technology has accelerated the pace of change at colleges and universities throughout the nation. Historically, colleges and universities kept in touch with students with landline and voice-mail technology, or more recently with campus e-mail. Over the past decade, the communication landscape and students' preferences is changed dramatically. This latest generation of students, referred to by many as 'digital natives', adopt technologies at a furious pace (Prensky, 2001). The proliferation and adoption of cellphones and the Internet lead to today's college student selecting them as their main communication gateway. Universities face the unique challenge of communicating with students using their preferred method of communication: the cellphone. In addition, social networking technologies have enabled students to forge strong communities that are entirely removed from the campus community utilizing sites such as Facebook and MySpace. These developments make it even more difficult for colleges and universities, especially institutions with a large enrollment of commuter students, to create a strong on-campus community that encourages student collaboration and provides a seamless learning experience.

Mission, Strategy, and Technology

Technology initiatives should support the mission of an organization. This is the case in any organization, regardless of whether it is an institution of higher learning or a Fortune 500 company. Unfortunately, many technology projects are conceived and executed in a vacuum. Often, these projects do not align with the basic purpose of the institution or with the audience they aim to serve. In higher education, technology deployments can be difficult. Building consensus and budgetary buy-in is a long process. In combination with an affordability mandate, it becomes even more important to 'work down' during the application concept, planning, and execution stages. Successful solutions must begin with a thorough understanding of the mission of the institution. For example, Montclair University is the second-largest and fastest-growing university in New Jersey with more than 17,000 students, of which 75 per cent are commuters. The university strives to graduate people on the bachelor's and master's level who have had sound education in the arts and sciences and relevant, specialized, training built upon that base. The mission of MSU as a multipurpose public institution is to '*... develop in students the ability to discover, create, evaluate, apply, and share knowledge in a climate characterized by tolerance and openness in the exploration of ideas. Curricular and co-curricular programs will cultivate the ability to think critically, to act ethically, and to become informed citizen participants prepared to assume leadership roles in a democracy. Recognizing the increasing connectedness of the world, the University will ensure that all students develop an understanding of global issues and of their responsibilities as citizens of the world (MSU Board of Trustees 2002)*'.

In order to effectively support its mission, MSU is committed to using applications and technologies that foster and encourage a strong campus culture. Because many students have lives that focus off-campus, the university strives to keep them engaged by providing technology enabled solutions that create a 'virtual campus'. This environment encourages student participation in campus activities, creates a safe and secure learning environment for all students, and provides easy access to faculty and educational tools regardless of the student's location. Most higher education institutions have realized that landlines are now obsolete. Students forego using the shared telephone installed in the residence hall and rarely check their voice-mail. Instead, they utilize their cellphone to manage the various facets of their lives. Applications that take advantage of the pervasive networked access to students and student cellphone behaviors – text messaging, internet access, and pushalerts – are more likely to be adopted by the student body as well as foster a stronger sense of community and student engagement in the campus environment. Those of us charged with managing telecommunications in the enterprise must not become frustrated by the rapid and high-adoption rate of cellphone use and the manner in which these consumer products have insinuated themselves into the fabric of our students' lives. Rather, in order to be successful in our organizational missions, we must view today's cellphone proliferation as an opportunity. When used effectively, mobile groups, e-mail, and academic communications allow the university to maintain a lifeline with the student and implement revolutionary academic applications that promote the well being of the student and provide timely access to available resources. The objectives of this innovative approach to student communications are increased academic participation, improved student retention rates, and stronger student participation in a more well-defined campus culture.

MSU Campus Connect: An effort to create the Virtual Campus

In 2005, the MSU administration began looking at new ways it could harness today's ubiquitous cellphones to communicate with students. This action was precipitated by the reality that landline usage on-campus has become obsolete. The university was failing in its efforts to communicate effectively with our student body, and these challenges, if left unchecked, threatened to fracture the sense of community across the campus. Montclair's implementation of mobile applications shows that the university recognizes the need to stay one step ahead of student technology adoption. Because students were opting to use their personal cellphones as their primary mode of communication, without even sharing their mobile phone numbers with the university, it became increasingly difficult to reach students for basic messaging, whether it was cancellations, grade postings, or other academic and community information. Rolling out mobile applications designed around trends, emerging in the consumer market space, was a significant departure from our normal methods for the design and launch of new Information Technology (IT) initiatives for the university. Like most of our peer universities, the typical approach to technology projects often perpetuated and accepted a linear approach to new technologies. Most back-end system deployments were transactional, data-driven, and feature-functional, yet not designed to be accessed in a way that fits the on-the-go lifestyle of today's students. The university had invested in many valuable systems, but it had not cracked the code on optimizing delivery of that value to its consumers: the students. The University sought assistance in developing the Campus Connect program from Rave Wireless, an innovative, start-up company, that was building its business around the untapped potential of broadband cellular networks. We also partnered with Sprint/Nextel, a tier one cellular carrier company, that offered specific technologies aligned with the features and functionality envisioned for our virtual campus solution. After extensive market research and industry scanning efforts, the first iteration of the MSU Connect program was launched. It included core phone based mobile applications for communication, collaboration, safety, and academics. The application suite features broadcast text alerts for campus-wide communications, including emergency security situations, severe weather, and class cancellations. There are also mobile group collaborations and opt-in text messaging and alerts for clubs and academics, in a format similar to Facebook. Students can also access campus-based e-mail, the Web, and browse campus directories, events calendars, and dining menus. The heart and soul of the program is the integration of the mobile phones with our academic resources through the Blackboard Learning System; so students can receive alerts for class cancellations, homework updates, and other relevant coursework. Students are also able to access pod casts and video casts of course content, homework assignments, course schedules, syllabi, and grades and can participate in real-time classroom surveys and polls related to their studies and utilize a flash-card-like learning reinforcement service outside of class. The recent tragedy at VirginiaTech certainly heightened awareness of campus safety issues and underscored the need for a persistent and reliable mechanism for ensuring the safety of our students and campus employees. In today's volatile world, campus safety and security is a top priority for students and parents. The MSU deployment of the Rave Guardian application enables students to activate GPS tracking on their phone if they feel uncomfortable or unwell and need special services. The GPS-enabled application provides a direct lifeline with the campus police force and enables real-time emergency aid if requested. A student profile that lists physical description and critical medical data for first responders is set up along with the application, so students can rely on emergency services in the unlikely event that it is needed. This feature is opt-in only and can be turned off or on via the student's handset. The mobile guardian capability along with our robust SMS textbased alerting and notification applications has earned MSU recognition for its leadership in the area of campus safety. In 2006, MSU was awarded the Jeanne Clery Campus Safety Award by nonprofit advocacy group, Security on-campus, Inc. In addition, the university was the recipient of the 2007 Innovators Award from Campus Technology magazine for the MSU Campus Connect program (Campus Technology, 2007). The large commuter population at MSU relies heavily on shuttle buses and the New Jersey Transit system to transport them back and forth from campus. University administration wanted to provide shuttle bus, train, and transit information to students to reduce wait time for students and free them to spend more time engaged in activities and academics while on-campus. The Rave Wireless deployment provides transit schedules and maps, so students can see where the campus shuttle buses are in transit, thus providing more efficient transportation services and planning. The Campus Connect mobile phone program also gives student access to the Rave Wireless Web console, where students can opt-in to group collaborations, course alerts, and personally configure desired features of the applications.

Evolution of the Campus Connect Programme

The rollout of the Campus Connect mobile applications began in 2005 and occurred in four phases. Over the course of the rollout, Montclair contracted with Sprint/Nextel to design and deliver a custom network installation on-campus that would ensure that any coverage and capacity gaps on-campus were bridged. The performance standard required that students should enjoy land line quality signal and service throughout every square inch of the campus and that the network should be robust enough to handle many thousands of simultaneous connections. The Sprint/Nextel team erected five additional towers and infrastructure in key locations throughout the campus to achieve this objective. The first phase of the application rollout established a voluntary pilot program to incoming freshmen. The second phase issued mandatory phones to incoming on-campus freshmen. The third phase expanded the mandatory program to all incoming freshmen, whether the students were commuters or on-campus boarders. And the final phase required every entering undergraduate student to own and operate an MSU Campus Connect capable mobile phone. The mandate to utilize the Sprint/Nextel handsets and network has been relaxed as the technology in the cellular carrier market space has evolved to accommodate most of the Campus Connect program capabilities. Today, nearly 5,000 phones are in use across campus. Over the next 3 years, as the rollout continues, all matriculated undergraduate Montclair students will be outfitted with Campus Connect compatible phones and applications. The university charges students a telecom fee, which is tax-free and can be paid with financial aid to support the applications development aspect of the Campus Connect program. The students contract directly with the carrier for their calling plan and handset. The vast majority of Campus Connect participants are using the Sprint/Nextel plans, which include the base Sprint/Nextel phone as well as an inclusive voice and data plan for mobile Web access, text messaging, location-based technology and push-to-talk and voice services. The students have the choice of six phones and can upgrade the phone or the standard plan. They can even keep their favorite phone number when they join the Campus Connect program, making the switch from their old cellphone an easier proposition. The initial pilot program allowed the university to test the system and make changes to the overall deployment plan. This enabled Montclair to ensure that the rollout would achieve its goal and help support the mission of the university. Lessons learned and key actions for the success of a campus-wide wireless application deployment follow.

Select the Right Carrier

Solution success depends on selecting, partnering, and maintaining close relationships with the right telecommunications carriers. Every institution needs to take a close look at their individual requirements and benchmarks for application deployment success before selecting a carrier or multiple partners. At MSU, there were several key requirements that led the university to select Sprint/Nextel as their partner to launch the Campus Connect program. These requirements included the need for additional infrastructure build-out on-campus in order to bridge coverage gaps, the need for location-based services to support safety applications, push-to-talk capability, and a willingness to establish reasonable group plan and hardware pricing. Rave Wireless facilitated negotiations and assisted in managing the relationship with Sprint/Nextel. This helped MSU achieve its pricing and network coverage and capacity goals quickly.

Mandatory Program verses Voluntary

Depending upon the goals of the program, universities need to decide whether to make the mobile phone program voluntary or mandatory. After the initial pilot, MSU decided to make its student phone program mandatory. The university was committed to the success of the rollout and had clear goals in attaining the solution. The goal was to foster a stronger sense of community and provide a universal learning experience facilitated by technology. If the program were voluntary, those goals would be compromised. In addition, the safety solution provided by Rave Guardian requires certified and secure Location Based Services (LBS)-enabled handsets. Without a university Sprint/Nextel phone, students would not be able to take advantage of the safety applications. Therefore, mandating the program afforded the university the economies of scale to provide a complete communications infrastructure and student solution at minimal cost.

Achieving Buy-in from key Constituents

Another key to success is to achieve buy-in from key constituents. Traditionally, higher education governance structures are disparate. The university has a core mission, but each colleges and departments has their own goals and budgets. In order to achieve consensus, IT must lead the way and establish the vision for the project. In addition, IT must also keep costs down and provide affordable options in order to achieve buy-in from budgetary contributors. Parental buy-in is also critical to the success of a mobile phone program. Clear marketing messaging is needed to promote understanding of the program. Parents need to recognize that the university-provided cell phone is not just a phone; rather, it is a mobile device that enables the student to maintain safety on-campus and fosters an improved learning experience. Once parents understand this, they are generally very supportive of the program and are accepting the associated costs in exchange for the safety and wellness capabilities, as well as the integration to the social and academic fabric of the university environment. They want their children to be safer, to make lasting friendships, and to succeed academically, and they realize that the Campus Connect program helps make that happen. Lastly, students are the essential ingredient in the recipe of success. Today's students are technologically savvy and have a well-established track record of being fickle consumers. If the university is able to provide affordable and compelling applications that improve their quality of life, aid in the learning process, and facilitate social life, students will adopt the technology eagerly.

Critical Path Elements of Success

Real success takes time, and universities need to start executing the vision of their campus mobility program early. If coverage gaps need to be filled through infrastructure build-out, begin working with the selected carrier as soon as possible. Negotiations and building can drag on for months. In addition, achieving consensus and budgetary approvals from internal communities can also take months to solidify. Marketing to key audiences like parents and students should be started as soon as possible. Lastly, when laying the roadmap for application development and deployment, look closely at turn-key application providers. Custom applications built by internal IT organizations are often characterized by delays and failures. Also, custom applications are always more expensive in the long run and involve exorbitant and skyrocketing cost of ownership and maintenance dollars. MSU determined early on that it was preferable to work with a software solutions provider who's core mission was to offer a solid base of mobile applications with the opportunity for MSU to further innovate on the platform, and its off-the-shelf delivery method enabled rapid rollout and limited maintenance responsibility for its IT staff.

What's on the Horizon?

The Horizon Report, a project co-sponsored by The New Media Consortium and EDUCAUSE, identifies emerging technologies that are likely to change the way in which we conduct the business of higher education and for two consecutive years, has focused, on the rich media, social networking and pervasiveness of cell phone technology as a force that will influence higher learning over the next several years (Horizon Report 2007, 2008). Part and parcel of the expected influence of the technology is the furious pace with which it is evolving and changing. In the few years since the MSU community launched the Campus Connect program, so much has changed in the commercial space and on college campuses that we should expect characteristics of the virtual campus to change dramatically over the next few years. Today, the university has created a mobile interface to its core information systems, including Blackboard and e-mail. As new technologies emerge and become standard practices in higher education, the university will continue to utilize cellular technology to foster a stronger sense of campus community and culture as well as expand its academic and learning experiences. Over the next 5 years, dual-mode phones will become more pervasive. Phones that are outfitted with Wireless Fidelity (Wi-Fi) and Wide Area Network (WAN) radios will provide the university an opportunity to enable seamless roaming between private and public networks and the deployment of Voice-Over IP capabilities. This enhanced capability will save the students money and enable access to multiple systems that are not currently available over Wide Area Networks. In addition, seamless multiple network roaming provides an opportunity for student and faculty interactivity. Intelligent phones will enable more intelligent applications, such as enhanced directions and safety services. Eventually, the campus could be a person-aware community. The standardization of Global Positioning Systems (GPS), Radio Frequency Identification (RFID), and LBS will enable interactivity between persons and different pieces of equipment. Permission-based applications managed through a student Web console can provide access control, point of sale, and other commerce-driven applications. For example, the cellphone can be used as the student's ID and key card for residence halls, dining halls, and commerce. In addition, applications that provide integrated video and GPS with tours, campus history, and services can help aid in student recruitment. Seamless Wi-Fi and WAN modal operation offer an increased opportunity for more academic-based applications. In-class surveying and polling will become standard practice in classrooms. Although this can be done over WAN, the implementation of Wi-Fi classrooms enables individual configurations that are automatically pushed to student devices when they enter the room or lecture hall. These configurations can be established based on faculty learning styles and teaching techniques. In-class learning tools will enable students to participate more extensively in the classroom learning process. In addition, faculty and staff can take advantage of improved monitoring and reporting on teaching techniques and group learning activities.

'Entheos' and the Virtual Campus

Entheos, a Greek term meaning 'god within', is the root of the word enthusiasm. Dubos (1972) argues that it is the force that drives us into ever-new ventures and greater creativity. It is axiomatic that today's college students and the campus environments they inhabit are dramatically different than they were half a decade ago. We as technology managers must redouble our efforts to elicit from our students and induce from the myriad components of the living and learning environment the most fitting technology innovations. Students are technologically savvy and prefer their cellphone as their primary mode of communication. Universities need to harness the power of the mobile device to foster a stronger sense of community and to establish virtual campuses. When deployed effectively, student-focused mobile applications can ensure that students are in constant real-time connection with the university, keeping them safe and secure, academically and socially engaged and, therefore, better able to succeed in their academic pursuits. MSU has enthusiastically embraced mobile technology to enrich the living and learning experiences of our students. We have every expectation that this compelling technology will continue to transform the ways in which we service their administrative, academic, and social needs for many years to come.

REFERENCES

Boulos, M.N.K., Maramba, I., & Wheeler, S. (2006). Wikis, blogs and podcasts: A new generation of web-based tools for virtual collaborative clinical practice and education. BMC Medical Education, 6(41), 1–8.

Campus Technology (2007, August). Campus technology innovators. Campus Technology (pp. 36–39).

Briggs, L. (2008). Emergency notification: Penn State stays on message. Retrieved June 9, 2008 from http://campustechnology.com/articles/52868/.

De Avila, J. (2008). Teachers tap video-sharing in the classroom. Retrieved June 9, 2008 from http://online.wsj.com/article/SB120649011463564023.html.

Denton, G.D., Williams, R.W., & Pangaro, L. (2003). Core problems reported by students in a palm OS and Internet-based problem entry system predicts performance on the third-year internal medicine clerkship. In AMIA Annual Symposium Proceedings (p. 827). Bethesda: AMIA.

Dubos, R. (1972). *A God Within*. New York: Charles Scribner's Sons.

Embi, P.J. (2001). Information at hand: Using handheld computers in medicine. Cleveland Clinical Journal of Medicine, 68(10), 840–842.

FCW Staff. (2008). SMS does SOS. Retrieved June 24, 2008 from http://www.fcw.com/print/12_11/ news/92790-1.html.

Ferenchick, G., Fetters, M. & Carse, A.M. (2008). Just in time: Technology to disseminate curriculum and manage educational requirements with mobile technology. Teaching and Learning in Medicine, 20(1), 44–52.

Fischer, S., Stewart, T.E., Mehta, S., Wax, R., & Lapinsky, S.E. (2003). Handheld computing in medicine. *Journal of the American Medical Informatics Association*, 10(2), 139–149.

Fontelo, P., Liu, F., Muin, M., Tolentino, H., & Ackerman, M. (2006). Txt2MEDLINE: Text-messaging access to MEDLINE/PubMed. In AMIA Annual Symposium Proceedings (pp. 259–263). Bethesda: AMIA.

Ganger, A.C., & Jackson, M. (2008). Wireless handheld computers in the preclinical undergraduate curriculum. Retrieved June 9, 2008 from http://www.med-edonline.org/pdf/t0000031.pdf.

Grasso, M.A., Yen, M.J., & Mintz, M.L. (2006). Survey of handheld computing among medical students. Computer Methods and Programs in Biomedicine, 82(3), 196–202.

Honey, M., Culp, K.M., & Spielvogel, R. (2008). Using technology to improve student achievement. Retrieved June 9, 2008 from http://www.ncrel.org/sdrs/areas/issues/methods/technlgy/te800.htm.

Horrigan, J. (2008). Pew Internet: Mobile access to data and information. Retrieved June 16, 2008 from www.pewInternet.org/PPF/r/244/report_display.asp.

Issenberg, S.B. & Scalese, R.J. (2008). Simulation in health care education. Perspectives in Biological Medicine, 51, 31–46.

Kho, A., Henderson, L.E., Dressler, D.D. & Kripalani, S. (2006). Use of handheld computers in medicaleducation—A systematic review. *Journal of General Internal Medicine*, 21(5), 531–537.

Kullman, J. (2008). "Wii" bit of technology aids medical education. Retrieved June 9, 2008 from http://asunews.asu.edu/20080222_wiistudy.

Lee, J.S., Sineff, S.S., & Summer, W. (2002). Validation of electronic student encounter logs in an emergency medicine clerkship. In Proceedings of the AMIA Symposium (pp. 425–429). Bethesda:AMIA.

Mackenzie, I. (2008). Social networking on the move. Retrieved June 16, 2008 from http://news.bbc.co.uk/1/hi/technology/6767593.stm.

Mehta, N. (2008). Op ed: An S.O.S. for SMS. Retrieved June 24, 2008 from http://www.imedia connection.com/content/7088.asp.

Montclair State University Board of Trustees (2002). Mission Statement. (Adopted 10/31/2002). http://www.montclair.edu/welcome/msumission.html. Retrieved 13 July 2008.

New Media Consortium, NMC (2007). 2007 Horizon report. http://www.nmc.org/horizon/2007/ report. Retrieved 13 July 2008.

New Media Consortium, NMC (2008). 2008 Horizon report. http://www.nmc.org/horizon/2008-horizonreport. Retrieved 13 July 2008.

O'Hear, S. (2008). e-Learning 2.0: How web technologies are shaping education. Retrieved June 2, 2008 from http://www.readwriteWeb.com/archives/e-learning_20.php.

Prensky, M. (2001). Digital natives, digital immigrants, Part II: do they really think differently? On the Horizon, 9(6), 1–6.

Raboteau, A. (2008). Tech looks to tap into text messaging. Retrieved June 9, 2008 from http:// www.roanoke.com/news/nrv/wb/wb/xp-81392.

Rosenblatt, R. (2008). Using technology to address change in medical education. Retrieved June 2, 2008 from http://www.bidmc.harvard.edu/prospective/vol1/ver1/tech_changes.asp.

Sandars, J. & Schroter, S. (2007). Web 2.0 technologies for undergraduate and postgraduate medical education: An online survey. *Postgraduate Medicine Journal*, 83(986), 759–762.

Schonfeld, A.R. (2008). Podcasts bring medical education to ears of the millennial generation. Retrieved June 2, 2008 from http://www.acphysci.com/aps/resources/PDFs/Feb_07_Feature.pdf.

Tinkelman, R. (2008). Podcasting comes to med school curriculum. Retrieved June 9, 2008 fromhttp://focus.hms.harvard.edu/2006/012706/med_ed.shtml.

Torre, D.M., & Wright, S.M. (2003). Clinical and educational uses of handheld computers. *SouthernMedical Journal*, 69, 996–999.

Valdez, G. (2008). Technology: A catalyst for teaching and learning in the classroom. Retrieved June 2, 2008 from http://www.ncrel.org/sdrs/areas/issues/methods/technlgy/te600.htm.

Waters, D. (2008). Why the future is in your hands. Retrieved June 9, 2008 from http://news.bbc.co.uk/ 1/hi/technology/7250465.stm.

PART D
Social Perspectives of Educational Technology

16.

Sustainability and Educational Technology

Alberto Arenas

Vignette # 1: In 2009, the scientist heralded as the father of modern agriculture, Norman Borlaug, died at the age of 95. According to the *New York Times* obituary, Borlaug "did more than anyone else in the 20th century to teach the world to feed itself and whose work was credited with saving hundreds of millions of lives" (Gillis, 2009). An agronomist by training, Borlaug directed meticulous scientific studies in Mexico starting in the 1940s that eventually led to the development of high-yield, disease-resistant varieties of wheat. These new varieties, along with synthetic pesticides and fertilizers, large-scale irrigation, and mechanized agriculture, increased wheat production several fold and made countries such as Mexico and India self sufficient in wheat. The resulting movement, dubbed in the 1960s the Green Revolution, was exported worldwide and it allowed food production to outpace population growth, and some believe that such a revolution was responsible for averting possible worldwide famine (Thurow & Kilman, 2009). The criticisms waged against the Green Revolution that it assisted in the displacement of small farmers, impoverished the soil and diminished biodiversity, contributed to the loss of local knowledge related to natural ways of farming, made farmers more dependent on agro-chemicals, and led to increased corporate control of agriculture, were dismissed by Borlaug and other defenders of the Green Revolution by arguing that organic agriculture by itself was insufficient to feed the world's population, and that high-yield industrial agriculture, with its higher production per acre, had prevented increased loss of virgin forests. As Borlaug said, 'Without high-yield agriculture either millions would have starved or increases in food output would have been realized through drastic expansion of acres under cultivation – losses of pristine land a hundred times greater than all losses to urban and suburban expansion' (as cited in Easterbrook, 1997, p. 79).

Vignette # 2: In 2010, the 70th anniversary of the publication of *An Agricultural Testament* (1940), penned by Sir Albert Howard who is deemed the father of modern organic agriculture, took place. The book was published a couple of years before Borlaug started his experiments in Mexico. Unlike Borlaug, however, Howard was not interested in universal, single solutions that could be applied everywhere, regardless of bio-cultural differences across countries and regions. Howard, who traveled to India as an agricultural expert with the original intent of teaching locals about Western agricultural techniques (and just as Borlaug to help mass produce wheat), soon realized that he had more to learn than to teach. He understood that he would do better to learn from local traditional farming techniques that saw culture and land as intertwined (Perkins, 1997). The central tenet of his work came to be that soil, flora, fauna, and humans were deeply inter-connected, and that to view plant diseases as isolated phenomena in need of a cure as did the Green Revolution, was a profound misunderstanding of nature as a supreme teacher and of the intrinsic connections between nature and culture (Howard, 1940). Ultimately, Howard was advocating for focusing less on technology and more on the social relations of agriculture, a deep departure from the Green Revolution, which became popularized after Howard's death.

These two vignettes, based on the work of Borlaug and Howard, offer opposing views on the role of development and technology in society. In many ways these two towering figures of the 20th century represent archetypes of modernism versus post-modernism, universalism versus localism, quantity versus quality, fragmentation versus holism or, as I will call them in this chapter, productivism versus ecologism. While it is the contention of this chapter that in the long run the ecologist paradigm offers a more sensible set of answers on the forms of technology to be used to address problems currently facing our planet than the productivist one, this chapter advocates for a gradual transition towards a development model that truly respects diverse cultures and bioregions by means of technologies that place human communities and the natural environment at the center of the equation.

These two development paradigms have strong implications for technological education (TE) in terms of purpose, process, and outcome. Although TE has popularly been defined as the form of education that uses computer literacy to enhance learning, for the purposes of this chapter I will define TE as the form that modifies the physical world by manipulating tools and materials, which may include but is not limited to, computer instruction. In this sense, 'technology' will be assumed in its broad anthropological conception, which includes not only material objects such as machines, utensils, hardware and software, but also non-material realities such as systems and methods of organization (Ember & Ember, 1988, p. 108). In both its material and non-material manifestations, TE will be understood as the form of education that seeks to understand and solve a real-world economic, social or environmental problem.

In this chapter a case has been made the ET should have a clear and overriding purpose of supporting the goals of sustainability in its economic, social and environmental dimensions. Whatever technologies are employed in and outside the classroom, they should be ones that foster knowledge, care and competence in the direction of protecting and enhancing human communities and natural habitats. Knowledge, care, and competence are tied to thought, feeling, and action, which should not be separated from one another. They are all vertices of the same triangle. These elements must be combined in a certain direction, one that was eloquently chosen by Robert Bellah and his colleagues when they wrote, 'however pluralistic in its forms, education can never merely be for the sake of individual self-enhancement. [Education] pulls us into the common world or it fails altogether' (1991, p. 176).

Exploring Sustainability

Not since the Industrial Revolution has a movement emerged on the world scene that promises to make such profound changes as those professed by the Sustainability Revolution (Edwards, 2005). Although the concept of sustainability originally started as an extension of the environmental movement and it is generally associated with it, it in fact encompasses a broad range of issues that also include economic and social dimensions. The emergence of sustainability in its modern form came as a result of the World Commission on Environment and Development, created by the UN in 1983 and headed by Gro Harlem Brundtland. The most famous quote from the report that the commission elaborated stated (1987, p. 43), [Sustainability] is development that meets the needs of the future without compromising the ability of future generations to meet their own needs.

While this definition has served as a lighting house to policy makers and researchers, it has been expanded and refined over the last two decades to better explain the interaction of four interrelated dimensions: Ecology/environment, economy/employment, equity/equality, and education. Let us explore briefly the four Es (Adams, 1990; Edwards, 2005; UNESCO & UNEVOC, 2004):

1. Ecological/Environmental Sustainability: This dimension calls for making educated choices in three crucial areas:

(a) Short-term verses long-term gain;
(b) Piecemeal verses comprehensive change; and

(c) Unlimited use of natural resources verses built-in limits that constrain their availability.

An ecological perspective seeks to address the long-term viability of resource use, especially in areas of resource extraction, such as mining and agriculture, and to increase the ecological literacy of citizens to help them appreciate the importance of and engage in actions that defend such basics as clean and safe water, air, and food. This dimension stresses a new set of attitudes, skills, and values that cultivate a respect for the Earth in all its diversity, and a sense of care for the Earth's community in a way that secures its bounty and beauty for present and future generations.

*2. **Economic/Employment Sustainability***: This dimension, the one that generally separates environmentalists from industrialists and free marketers, calls for secure, long-term employment that does not jeopardize the health of ecosystems. It assumes that the economic system is a subset of the larger environmental system, and as such, economic principles need to be subservient to the larger principle of a limited availability of natural resources and of the importance of a wholesome nature. In general terms, it seeks to promote economic literacy (how to ensure that a business remains alive over the long term) in tandem with sustainable production (how to provide goods and services that address basic human needs and offers a better quality of life while being accountable to social and environmental costs) and sustainable consumption. This latter theme is especially true for the developed world, which has only 20 per cent of the world's population but consumes 75 per cent of the world's energy and 80 per cent of its resources, while generating 75 per cent of its pollution.

*3. **Equity/Equality Sustainability***: This dimension calls for the inclusion of the individual and community into the mix of ecologically-based, long-term economic development. It advocates, first and foremost, for poverty alleviation, with an emphasis on the equitable and equal access to such resources as safe and nutritious food; clean water, air, and soil; decent housing; universal health care; and dignified work. It also calls for respect for cultural diversity, gender equality, and inclusion of groups that have been historically marginalized. It promotes the use of ecologically based traditional forms of knowledge and experience that are considered 'backward' and 'useless' by individuals who have bought the agenda of modernity, rather than viewing them as part of the cultural wealth of communities considered 'poor' based on the standards of the developed world.

*4. **Educational Sustainability***: This last dimension is the one that concerns us the most for the purposes of this chapter. Education is the catalyst that brings the other three together. It is education that helps to bring together knowledge, care, and competence. Our schools tend to do a better job at fostering knowledge (but even then, it tends to be highly fragmented and not systemic), but it does a poor job at ensuring that students learn to care for the environment and human community, and also be competent at addressing key issues at their developmental level. The challenge for schools today is to bring thought, feeling, and action in the direction of sustainability. One example of ET that has the potential to do this is vocational and technical education.

It should be noted that 'sustainability' is not without its contrarians—see, for instance, Arturo Escobar's *Encountering Development* (1995). At the basis of much of the critique is the idea that sustainability is used in such divergent ways that it can mean everything from Howard's well tendered land to Borlaug's industrialization in which there is a careful management of natural resources but that still engages in severe overexploitation and ecological damage. While the polysemous nature of the concept of sustainability constitutes a challenge for users of the term, it nonetheless offers a respite to the false dichotomy of people versus environment that so often clouds the debate surrounding development. With its triple emphasis on the economy, environment, and culture, it allows for formerly antagonistic camps to sit down at the same table to air their differences, and just as importantly, attempt to find common ground.

One Example of ET: Vocational and Technical Education

Historically, the form of education most directly tied to technology has been Vocational and Technical Education (VTE). Unlike general academic education, in which until the advent of the personal computer, technologies in the classroom were limited mostly to pens, notebooks, blackboards, textbooks and audiovisual equipment like television and movies, VTE has enjoyed a plethora of technologies at its disposal, including those from agriculture, husbandry, carpentry, welding, nursing, auto mechanics, and construction, just to name a few of those vocational courses found in schools worldwide. VTE has traditionally also been the form of education most directly tied to the world of work because it has provided students with the knowledge and skills to become economically productive members of society. Given this reality, VTE is worth exploring in detail because currently the main push for TE in schools is highly vocational in nature, that is, it supports computer literacy as the main vehicle for preparing students to be the knowledge workers of tomorrow.

Just as the Green Revolution was gaining popularity worldwide starting in the 1960s, VTE started to gain traction worldwide around the same period, thanks to national and international education policies that emphasized the development of human capital to increase economic productivity in both rural and urban areas (Heyneman, 1986). It was assumed that through VTE youth and adults would acquire a new set of skills and attitudes toward work (and modernity in general) that could help impoverished societies attain a higher standard of living. International organizations and ministries of education and labor became engaged in labor forecasting that would help mold VTE programs in accordance with the economic needs of the country 5, 10, or 15 years down the road. But as soon as implementation of these policies started, several publications emerged criticizing the alleged benefits of VTE (e.g., Blaug, 1973; Foster, 1963). Essentially, these studies pointed out that VTE did not confer the pedagogical, social, or economic benefits that national education planners were promising: Students' attitudes towards manual work did not improve; teachers often used manual work as a form of punishment; students, parents, and teachers perceived the vocational track as inferior to the academic one; VTE did not halt the migration to urban areas or prevent vocational education graduates from pursuing a university degree; and it did not alleviate unemployment or increase the salaries of vocational graduates. Moreover, it was concluded that needs for human power could not be forecasted with any degree of certainty; in fact, VTE programs based on the employment predictions put forth by planning agencies ended up yielding widely inaccurate results because graduates from these programs were pursuing either a higher status university degree or a different line of work altogether (Heyneman, 2003). More recent research on the role of VTE in specific countries (e.g., India: World Bank, 2008) or internationally (World Bank, 2005) have supported the premise that the social rates of return on VTE are too low to warrant its continuance as an independent curriculum strand in secondary schooling, and as a result international funding for VTE was slashed and many programs were discontinued. Nonetheless, it has continued to be maintained in many schools as individual courses, and now it is more common that VTE students also take the more mainstream technical Education (TE) curriculum related to computer literacy to make them more competitive in the workplace.

A collective analysis of these various studies reveals that the bulk of the research and discourse on VTE has concentrated on how to increase the employment prospects and lifetime earnings of individual graduates and, simultaneously, how to improve the economic productivity of the society as a whole. These raisons d'être of VTE have been inscribed directly into a development paradigm that supports industrialization, rationality, homogenization, and growth economics, while paying scant attention to developing local economies that reaffirm local culture and foster self-sufficient communities that protect the environment (Anderson, 2009). To be fair, the impetus behind vocational education has always been to reduce poverty, but the strategies have been mostly focused on introducing students to what Damon Anderson (2009, p. 36) called 'productivism', that is, a geopolitical space in which 'economic growth and [labor] are [viewed as] permanent and necessary features of human existence, regardless of their adverse impact and consequences, social, cultural and environmental'. In general, the practice of VTE and its mainstream discourse have had little regard for how they can address issues of social and economic justice, and far less for how they can improve ecological integrity. Productivism has been a key rationale behind VTE since its inception, and has been and continues to be vital in its reproduction. The same logic can be applied to educational technology (ET) in general. While ET does not seek to provide skill training for a specific occupation (like VTE does), it nonetheless has a tendency to prepare students for the world of employment, and it does little to distinguish between the jobs of a chemical engineer who wants to help purify a contaminated river versus one who wants to build biological weapons.

Countering productivism, a new discourse in VTE has emerged that strongly advocates a form of development that fosters a responsible economic system that is highly responsive to social and environmental issues, what Anderson (2009) called 'ecologism'. This trend became evident starting in 1999 with the UNESCO-sponsored Second International Congress on Technical and Vocational Education, held in Seoul, and the subsequent establishment in 2000 of the UNESCO-UNEVOC International Centre for Technical and Vocational Education and Training in Bonn. The Final Report of the 1999 Congress made explicit statements regarding the relationship of VTE to social and environmental stewardship (UNESCO, 1999, pp. 1, 27):

> *The VTE of the future must not only prepare individuals for employment in the information society, but also make them responsible citizens who give due consideration to preserving the integrity of their environment and welfare of others. An integral component of life-long learning, [VTE] has a crucial role to play in this new era as an effective tool to realize the objectives of a culture of peace, environmentally sound sustainable development, social cohesion and international citizenship.*

Other international organizations have issued statements that echo this new orientation, as demonstrated by these joint recommendations from UNESCO and ILO on the purposes of VTE (2002, p. 9):

1. Contribute to the achievement of the societal goals of greater democratization and social, cultural, and economic development;
2. Lead to an understanding of the scientific and technological aspects of contemporary civilization...while taking a critical view

of social, political and environmental implications of scientific and technological change;

3. Empower people to contribute to environmentally sound, sustainable development though their occupations and other areas of their lives.

Implicit in these statements is the rise of a new philosophy surrounding the notion of development. This new social and environmental discourse surrounding VTE was captured by Rupert Maclean, UNESCO-UNEVOC's founding director, when he wrote (2005, p. 270),

> *All countries want development, since this implies improvement; and they also want development that is long-term, and therefore sustainable. But communities increasingly want development that not only stresses economic matters but which also pays greater attention to important social, cultural, political and environmental considerations. Increasingly, countries are not willing to accept economic development at any cost and expect the benefits of development to reach all sections of the community.*

This new discourse, based in a human-in-nature focus, has several common themes across socio-cultural, environmental, and economic strands (Fien & Wilson, 2005). From a socio-cultural perspective, it includes human rights, peace, gender equality, cultural diversity, health, and democracy. From an environmental perspective, it addresses natural resource conservation, climate change, urban and rural sustainable development, and disaster prevention and mitigation. And from an economic perspective, it involves poverty reduction, corporate responsibility and accountability, a critique of unregulated market economies, and sustainable production and consumption.

One reform common to both forms of discourse is a push for a comprehensive curriculum that combines academic and vocational education. Advocates of both forms of discourse realize the importance of having all students, regardless of their socioeconomic background, engage in VTE as a means of providing relevance, context, and concreteness to academic learning. The convergence of academic and vocational education has the potential to challenge the individualistic nature of today's schooling and to give students the opportunity to learn collectively for a reward other than a grade. Many schools worldwide have come to recognize that curricular convergence is worth considering, as a 2005 World Bank report concluded:

> *Curriculum-based reform of secondary education in the 21st century is prioritizing skills and competencies that go beyond and cut across the traditional general-vocational divide. The frontier between*

> *general and vocational curricula is shifting and fading, and the heretofore hard-to-strike balance between vocational and general education is becoming increasingly irrelevant (p. xxi).*

This curricular convergence has particular implications for TE in general. More and more computer instruction is being considered indispensable in most forms of VTE, and as a result it is helping to weaken the barriers between academic and vocational education.

Expressions of Technical Education (TE) with Sustainability

Although it has become fashionable to talk about 'environmental jobs' (Renner, 2000) or 'employment for sustainability' (Edwards, 2005), the truth is that all forms of employment, regardless how 'green' they purport to be, include expressions that could be considered unsustainable. Such is the intrinsic condition of living in a modern society. For example, a person installing a wind turbine is considered to have an environmentally friendly job, yet a wind turbine consists of more than 8,000 parts, everything from screws to generators to blades, parts that tend to be manufactured under less-than-sustainable conditions. Or consider the receptionist working at a solar panel manufacturer who is paid a miserly wage. Or the solar panel distributor who discriminates against employees of a minority background. Clearly, many jobs wear many hats, and although the push should be toward truly sustainable employment that simultaneously addresses the needs of people, nature, and the economy, a dogmatic opposition to industrialism or to livelihoods that fall short of completely green or sustainable ideals would be counterproductive (Lehmann, 2008).

TE faces a similar predicament. Take agricultural education, for instance. The dilemma presented in the introduction regarding the type of agriculture that should be promoted – the high-input industrial agriculture advocated by Borlaug, or the more organic one supported by Howard – does not allow for an easy answer in schools. Historically, most agricultural schools have taught their students industrial agriculture with a strong reliance on synthetic pesticides and fertilizers, large-scale irrigation, monoculture production, and heavy machinery. Only until recently have some alternative schools offered organic farming as a choice, and even then it is only on a limited basis. In any case, the best-case scenario would be to teach organic farming and all that it implies along the lines suggested by Howard (1940) – using composting, minimal tillage, crop rotation, green manure, biological pest controls, and the knowledge that has been developed over the centuries by farmers around the world – but the reality is that many agricultural schools in rural areas teach conventional methods of farming that use synthetic pesticides and fertilizers, plant growth regulators, and even genetically modified organisms. Nonetheless, even in such schools, students are learning skills and values related to social and environmental sustainability, including the importance of manual labor, of working in nature, of producing a basic need, and of becoming self-reliant. Thus, the reality of the day-to-day practices of VTE carries within it a combination of sustainable and unsustainable practices.

Having said this, VTE practitioners and researchers would do well to adopt a set of sustainability principles that can guide the creation of new VTE programs (or revamp already constituted ones) to address social and environmental costs. Such sets of principles already exist, four of which are the Ontario Round Table on Environment and Economy Model Principles (to assist local communities to define their sustainable development goals); the Natural Step (created by Karl-Henrik Robert and others in Sweden, and based on systems principles); the Principles of Ecological Design (by John and Nancy Todd, which provides a biological framework that places nature at the center of the design process); and the Earth Charter (completed in 2000 and highlighting basic values of sustainability such as respect for life, protection of the environment, social justice, and democracy; for a review of these and other sets of sustainability principles, see Edwards, 2005).

Attempts to operationalize these principles in the context of VTE at the local level can be found in the work of Anderson (2009), Arenas (2001-03, 2008), and UNESCO (1999). As espoused by Arenas (2001-2003, p. 82),

In terms of environmental responsibility, VTE programs should:

- Establish meaningful and productive relationships with firms that engage in 'green' practices. Encouraged by a system of tax incentives and breaks, other firms may join in.
- Assess needs of locality first, instead of establishing standardized vocational models with pre-packaged answers for a whole country or state. 'Needs' should be understood, not in the modern sense of wants that are shaped by industrial commodities, but as the mixture of basic material and non-material needs that promote physical, emotional, and spiritual welfare.
- Strive for usage of local and organically grown resources. It is more economically sensible (lower transportation costs and lower costs associated with externalities), and it also helps to ensure soil fertility, less erosion, more forests, and cleaner air and water.
- Emphasize products that are durable, repairable, refurbishable, and that make use of renewable energy and/or that are energy efficient.

- Push for product life-cycle analysis at school to help unveil hidden externalities.
- Promote the conversion of all waste into a resource. Just as in any mature ecosystem all waste is incorporated into the system and recycled, vocational programs must seek to convert all waste into resources. This way, the energy and material cycle would make a complete loop.

In terms of social responsibility, VTE programs should:

- Ensure an equal concern for imparting adequate skills alongside a critical analysis of the social and political history of vocational education.
- Promote horizontality and ample dialogue in the decision-making process regarding the process and purpose of production.
- Ensure that the product or service addresses a social or environmental need. Do not create a product that is intended to harm humans or the environment, that has a built-in obsolescence, which is built on false needs, that deceives or manipulates, or that uses resources obtained by exploiting the labor of others.
- Avoid unnecessary job specialization. Allow all students to engage in as many activities of the production process as possible.
- Ensure that students are exposed to alternative forms of economic production (e.g., worker-owned businesses; cooperatives; unions) to promote collective associations, and, if possible, put them in practice.

Expressions of these principles in secondary schools can be found in the following examples (e.g., Arenas, 2008; Delisio, 2000; Practical Action, n.d.; Schreuders, Salmon, & Stewardson, 2007; Soledi, Sorial, McNerney, & Husting, 2007; Wolf, 2001):

- Green construction, including integrated design systems, low-impact and energy-efficient materials, rainwater harvesting, and compost toilets.
- Organic and integrated farming and animal husbandry, organic urban gardens, and native-plant landscaping.
- Environmental engineering, including the prevention of water, air, and soil pollution and restoration of polluted areas.
- Repairing automobiles and home appliances, such as old computers.
- Furniture-making with sustainably harvested materials.
- Creating and rehabilitating urban and rural parks.
- Rescuing non-commodified and ancestral knowledge and skills, such as those of indigenous groups, related to healing, construction, food, clothing, recreation, and other basic needs.

- Tapping onto alternative and low-impact energy sources, such as solar and wind.

The actual manifestation of these types of training will vary from school to school in terms of who benefits from the vocational program (do all students take the courses or only those in a vocational track?); the school's organization (is the school organized around vocational clusters or limited to a vocational course that students take, or is it an after-school or summer program?); or the school's curriculum (is there a vocational track per se or is it part of the regular academic courses, or is it considered part of service-learning or community service?). These differences are less important than the fact that students have the opportunity to provide a product or service that benefits the community as a whole and the environment. In each one of these examples, some form of technology is the common denominator, and in all cases they share, or should share, such attributes as reparability, durability, affordability, simplicity, environmental friendliness, community care, and promotion of self-autonomy.

Example of a Curricular Unit: Wind-Power

The following curricular unit was adapted from the British-based group Practical Action, whose project, 'Sustainable Technology Education Project' is geared towards VTE and general academic teachers who want to use technology in ways that recognize the environmental and social impacts of the technologies they employ (Practical Action, n.d.). The unit starts by asking students a series of questions related to the origin of their home electricity: Where does it come from? What are the original sources that give rise to the electricity? Are workers who create the electricity paid fair wages? Are the working conditions safe? Once a problem has been identified (for instance, people living in rural areas in developing countries who do not have easy access to electricity and as a result need alternative sources that are reliable and do not hurt the environment or community.

The unit then shifts to Sri Lanka, were Practical Action engages in appropriate technology. It presents teachers and students with four criteria whenever new technologies are adopted: (a) It should be easy to install and maintain; (b) it should be affordable; (c) it should be manufactured locally whenever possible; and (d) it should support social and environmental goals. These criteria are discussed with the students, and compared to criteria used in evaluating other technology. This includes having students analyze the pros and cons of installing such a system with the help of life cycle analyses. In the specific case of wind power, some of the pros are that the conversion of energy would not require fossil fuels; wind is a renewable source that is inexhaustible; if components are created locally it would lead to local job creation; it would allow the community to be more self-reliant; and it would be less expensive in the long run to generate electricity. Some of the cons include that wind powered systems are expensive in the short-term, they require extensive tracts of land for their installation, and it may affect migratory birds.

After the philosophical and technical aspects are discussed, teachers and students set themselves the task of actually building a wind power turbine. It can be installed in the school, at the home of one of the students, or in some other location. Once the installation takes place, then students are charged with evaluating the progress of the wind power unit, and teachers charged with incorporating its lessons in various subjects, such as mathematics, design, natural sciences, and the social sciences. This curricular unit exemplifies the type of work that is directly connected to the ecologist development model described above. The wind power system created and installed in a poor community with the participation of youth exemplifies what Ivan Illich called 'convivial tools' (1973). These are tools, or technologies that share such qualities are reparability, durability, affordability, and other qualities mentioned above. Practical Action, originally founded by E. F. Schumacher, the author of "Small is Beautiful (1973/1989), embodies the adoption of technologies that provide real and sustainable improvement to people's lives.

Conclusions

In devising a new philosophy that connects sustainability to TE, several words of caution are in order: First, there needs to be a recognition that we live in a society that is so infatuated by technology that it assumes it offers solutions to all problems, regardless if they are technological, political or social in nature. While technology may be useful in some instances, it has for the most part been transformed from being a support system for a culture's traditions, to creating a new order that disposes of tradition completely, a transformation particularly nefarious for poor communities around the world whose main wealth is constituted precisely by the traditions that are being marginalized.

Second, in an effort to 'green' TE programs, there is a danger of displacing or not giving equal import to social and cultural concerns. Becoming 'green' has become fashionable in contemporary society, and firms, big and small, have jumped on the environmental bandwagon. It is easy to fall into the belief that the solution to environmental problems is simply a matter of improved technologies and better pricing systems. Although these strategies are often part of the solution, just as important is the need to address issues of oppression and injustice inside schools and places of work. Thus, it is imperative that educators do not lose sight of the importance of working on both environmental and social concerns simultaneously. The focus on appropriate technologies

Third, academic educators sensitive to sustainability issues are becoming increasingly aware of the importance of joining forces with VTE educators, and with TE educators more broadly. They are realizing that it is no longer enough simply to talk about the importance of organic farming if the student (or the teacher) does not know how to farm organically. This issue calls for new curriculum development and teacher training (both pre- and in-service) that imparts new knowledge and skills to all teachers and includes a permanent dialogue among teachers to create cross-disciplinary and experiential learning. It also requires the constant support of school administrators and of new educational policies that allow for a more flexible school schedule and a performance-based system for grading students. Ultimately, a philosophy linking sustainability to TE needs to ensure that teachers foster knowledge, care, and competence whenever new technologies are adopted.

And fourth, educators must be aware that the form of TE outlined in this chapter clashes head-on with industrial economies that are characterized by incessant material growth that is undifferentiated and unqualified. As Schumacher wrote, in the context of modern economies it has become nefarious to consider 'the idea that there could be pathological growth, unhealthy growth, disruptive or destructive growth' (1989/1973, p. 51). In rejecting this notion, educators must be steadfast in the belief that the goal of TE should be to maximize human satisfaction through the optimal amount (not the maximum possible amount) of production and consumption. The opposite of growth should not be non-growth, but rather sufficient growth, less material growth with regard to wants but more with regard to basic needs (including services such as health, housing, mass transportation, clean water, and so on). In essence, there needs to be a recognition that the new approach to TE redefines the current concept of well-being, from one that stresses material accumulation to one that focuses on the development of solidarity in a harmonious relationship with nature.

REFERENCES

Adams, W.M. (1990). *Green Development: Environment and Sustainability in the Third World.* London: Routledge.

Anderson, D. (2009). Productivism and ecologism: Changing dis/courses in VTET. In J. Fien, R. Maclean, & M. Park (Eds.), *Work, Learning and Sustainable Development: Opportunities and Challenges* (35–57). Dordrecht, Netherlands: Springer.

Arenas, A. (2001–03). Vocationalism for social and environmental responsibility. *La educ@ción, 136-138,* 77–92.

Arenas, A. (2003). School-based enterprises and environmental sustainability. *Journal of Vocational Education Research,* 28(2), 107–124.

Arenas, A. (2008). Connecting hand, mind, and community: Vocational education for social and environmental renewal. *Teachers College Record,* 110(2), 377–404.

Bailey, R. (2000, April). Billions served: Norman Borlaug interviewed by Ronald Bailey. *Reasononline* [online version].

Bellah, R., et al. (1991). *The Good Society.* New York: Alfred A. Knopf.

Blaug, M. (1973). *Education and the employment problem in developing countries.* Geneva: International Labor Office.

Bowers, C.A. (2001). *Educating for Eco-justice and Community.* Athens, GA: University of Georgia Press.

Delisio, E.R. (2000). School gardens sprouting in Chicago. *Education World.* Retrieved May 20, 2009, from http://www.educationworld.com/a_curr/curr313.shtml

Easterbrook, G. (1997). Forgotten benefactor of humanity. *The Atlantic Monthly,* 279(1), 75-82.

Edwards, A. (2005). *The sustainability revolution: Portrait of a paradigm shift.* Gabriola Island, Canada: New Society Publishers.

Ember, C.R. & Ember, M. (1988). *Cultural Anthropology, 5th edition.* Englewood Cliffs, NJ: Prentice Hall.

Escobar, A. (1995). *Encountering Development: The making and unmaking of the third world.* Princeton, NJ: Princeton University Press.

Fien, J., Maclean, R. & Park, M. (Eds.). (2009). *Work, learning and Sustainable Development: Opportunities and Challenges.* Dordrecht, The Netherlands: Springer.

Fien, J. & Wilson, D. (2005). Promoting sustainable development in VTET: The Bonn Declaration. *Prospects, 35*(3), 273–288.

Foster, P.J. (1963). The vocational school fallacy in development planning. In C. A. Anderson & M. J. Bowman (Eds.), *Education and Economic Development* (pp. 142–166). Chicago: Aldine.

Gillis, J. (2009, September 13). Norman Borlaug, plant scientist who fought famine, dies at 95. *New York Times* [online edition].

Hautecoeur, J.P. (2002). *Ecological education in everyday life: Alpha 2000.* Toronto: University of Toronto Press.

Heyneman, S.P. (1986). *Investing in education: A quarter century of World Bank experience.* Washington, D.C.: World Bank.

Heyneman, S.P. (2003). The history and problems of making education policy at the World Bank, 1960–2000. *International Journal of Education Development, 23*(3), 315–337.

Howard, A. (1940). *An Agricultural Testament.* London: Oxford University Press.

Illich, I. (1973). *Tools for Conviviality.* New York: Harper & Row, Publishers.

Kincheloe, J.L. (1995). *Toil and trouble: Good work, smart workers, and the integration of academic and vocational education.* New York: Peter Lang.

Lehmann, C. (2008, November/December). What about the dirty jobs? *Mother Jones,* 55–56.

Maclean, R. (2005). Orienting VTET for sustainable development: Introduction to the Open File. *Prospects, 35*(3), 269–272.

Perkins, J.H. (1997). *Geopolitics and the Green Revolution: Wheat, genes, and the Cold War.* New York: Oxford University Press.

Practical Action. (n.d.). *Sustainable Technology Education Project—STEP.* Retrieved September 5, 2009, from http://www.stepin.org/?id=home

Renner, M. (2000, September). *Working for the Environment: A growing source of jobs.* Washington, D.C.: Worldwatch Institute.

Schreuders, P.D., Salmon, S.D. & Stewardson, G.A. (2007). Temporary housing for the homeless: A pre-engineering design project. *The Technology Teacher,* 67(4), 4–10.

Schumacher, E.F. (1989). *Small is beautiful: Economics as if people mattered.* New York: HarperPerennial, originally published in 1973.

Shor, I. (1988). Working hands and critical minds: A Paulo Freire model for job training. *Journal of Education,* 170(2), 102–121.

Simon, R.I., Dippo, D., & Schenke, A. (1991). *Learning Work: A critical pedagogy of work education.* New York: Bergin & Garvey.

Soledi, S.W., Sorial, G., McNerney, P. & Husting, C. (2007, October). *Work in progress: Creating high school student environmental engineers.* Paper presented at the 37th ASEE/IEEE Frontiers in Education Conference, Milwaukee, WI.

Sollart, K. (n.d.). *Framework on indicators for education for sustainable development: Some conceptual thoughts.* The Netherlands Environmental Assessment Agency, unpublished manuscript.

Thurow, R. & Kilman, S. (2009). *Enough: Why the world's poorest starve in an age of plenty.* Washington, DC: PublicAffairs.

UNESCO. (1999). *Final report of the Second International Congress on Technical and Vocational Education, Seoul.* Paris: UNESCO.

UNESCO & ILO. (2002). *Technical and vocational education for the twenty-first century: UNESCO and ILO recommendations.* Paris & Geneva: Authors.

UNESCO & UNEVOC. (2004). Orienting technical and vocational education and training (VTET) for sustainable development: A discussion paper. Bonn: Authors.

Wolf, J.E. (2001). Building green: Creating environmentally friendly trade programs in vocational-technical schools. *Green Teacher, 66:* 14–18.

World Bank. (2005). *Expanding opportunities and building competencies for young people: A new agenda for secondary education.* Washington, D.C.: Author.

World Bank. (2008, January). *Skill development in India: The vocational education and training system, Report No. 22.* Washington, D.C.: Author.

World Commission on Environment and Development (1987). *Our Common Future.* London: Oxford University Press.

17.

Revisiting Educational Technology: Past, Present and Predicted Future

Dulal Mukhopadhyaya

Eric Ashby (1967), a noted educational thinker identified four revolutions in education. These are:

- The shifting of responsibilities from family to school
- The adoption of written word instead of verbal communication
- The invention of printing press
- The development of electronics

Exactly all of these have tremendous impact on education and changed methods and methodologies of education.

During 20th century, the changes were quite visible due to the rapid growth and development of information technology (IT) and we are now passing through the fifth revolution, the information revolution. In the days of information revolution knowledge is the best and most important asset in personal and social lives.

David Moore (1993), a theorist of Distance-Education opined that higher education has entered in to its third generation:

- The first generation was based on *brick and mortar technology*. Because a specific university awarded degrees, face-to-face teaching was given importance; examination was conducted on scheduled place, date and time.
- The second generation was partially place free. Because of introduction of Open and Distance learning; *distance delivery was gaining ground.*
- The third generation education is developing a virtual mode of education. Due to the development and continuous reshaping of IT, building of information, super highways, Internet and virtual lab *universities are rapidly transforming in to virtual mode.*

The third generation education of the 21st century is now using educational technology (ET) in different forms and ways through different technological devices.

But interestingly, long time ago the most illustrious philosopher, Plato criticized the medium for its inability to recreate the give and take of spoken discourse. He strongly agreed with Socrates that writing is analogous to painting. Plato had accepted argue of Socrates in *The Phaedrus,* which reads:

> *'The painters' products stand before us as though they were alive, but if you question them, they maintain the most majestic silence. It is the same with written words; they seem to talk to you as though they were intelligent, but if you ask them anything about what they say, from a desire to be instructed, they go on telling you just the same thing forever'.*
>
> (Socrates in *The Phaedrus*, as quoted by Feenberg, A., 2006)

Dimensions of Educational Technology

The Webster Dictionary (1988) defines education in the following ways:

1. The process of training and developing knowledge, skill, mind, character, etc. especially by formal schooling, teaching, training.
2. Knowledge, ability, etc. thus developed.
3. Formal schooling at an institution of learning or a stage of this.
4. Systematic study of methods and theories of teaching and learning.

And it defines technology as:

1. The science or study of the practical or industrial arts, applied sciences etc.
2. The terms used in science, etc. technical terminologies
3. Applied sciences
4. A method, process etc. for handling a particular technical problems.
5. The system by which a society provides its members with those things needed or desired.

So 'Educational Technology' can be seen as both a study and an application of methods and/or processes for handling the problem of education, in the light of what society needs or desires to train and develop students' knowledge, skill, mind and character.

Callahan (1962) observed it in a different way. According to Callahan, *Educational Technology is not a set of machines or device, it is actually a means or a way of structuring thought and action; it is a system rooted in positivism and empirical science, social engineering, and the social discourses related to vision of progress, economic interest and control.*

Educational Technology (ET) has two dimensions: *Technology in Education* and *Technology of Education.* Along with the two dimensions stated above, another two terms are also important in ET: *Hardware* and

Software. Though these terms are used in engineering and technology, but they are now used in education also, and ironically, without having basic idea of knowledge-formation or 'technology of education'. Before proceeding to discuss the basic issues, it would be wise to present a synoptic view of these terms.

Technology in Education

It includes most of hardwares that are the contributions of engineers and other experts mainly outside the education field. Projected and non-projected aids and modern technologies fall into this category.

Technology of Education

It includes various teaching learning processes, which can be designed to enhance the learning processes of the learners. In the 20th century 'teacher determined processes' are emphasized. It was considered that the teacher should control the process of teaching learning only.

But from the last stage of the 20th century it became evident that the process of teaching learning should not be the discretion of the teacher only but it should be 'learner centered'. Technology of Education has rapidly been progressed by the advancement of cybernetic systems.

ET is classified in the following three categories:

i) Hardware Approach,
ii) Software Approach, and
iii) Systems Approach

These three types of approaches accords two types of teaching aids: *Hardware devices* and *Software materials.*

Hardware Devices

This term is used in engineering and technology. But now it is extensively used in education too. Hardware devices are based on Hardware approaches. Hardware approaches are based on engineering principles used to develop electromechanical instruments for instructional purposes. Naturally these devices are the result of the growth and development of scientific and technological know-how. This approach deals with the mechanism of the 'teaching-learning process', abbreviated as TLP. Hardware approach based teaching devices are called 'hardware devices'.

Software Materials

A software material develops from software-approach. These are mostly uses the principles of psychology to modify the behaviour of learners. It generally uses behavioural psychology in teaching and learning. Software approach is used for:

- Task-analysis, preparation of objectives, development of TLP and

- Task-selection and development of appropriate evaluation systems etc.

Thus like Hardware devices, teaching learning materials that are developed by the use of software approach are called Software materials.

Hardware devices include all sorts of teaching machines including devices like projectors, tape-recorder, OHP, TV, Radio, Computers and the like.

Again Software materials are used to operationalise Hardware devices. The Software materials are written-matters, instructional-materials, self-learning modules, programmed-instructional materials, films, slides, OHP transparencies or the like. Some Hardware devices and Software materials are shown below for convenience.

The relationship between *Technology in Education* and *Technology of Education* can be described by the diagrammatic sketch as depicted in Fig. 17.1.

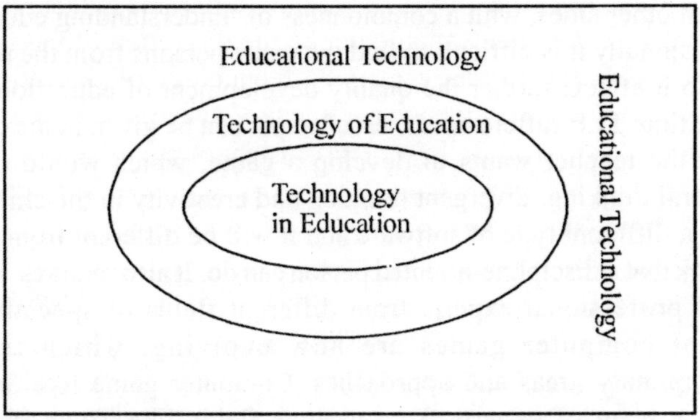

Fig. 17.1. Relationship among domains of ET

Educational Technology as an Interdisciplinary field of study with a mandatory orientation of Education

Technology optimizes human learning and development of technology increases the capacity and capability of human knowledge. The development of new technologies has enhances the changes of methods and methodologies of teaching-learning process. Till the first half of the 20th century, teacher was at the center stage in education system, and whatever helped the teacher in controlling the TLP was put in to the fold of ET. But a paradigm-shift took place in the scenario since after 2nd world war. Then onward, the learners came to the center stage and they are given more priorities than the teachers in the process of TLP, and the scenario continues. In the last few decades, new systems of teaching learning processes have evolved and 'systems-approach' from

'Cybernetics' has taken the dominant place in education. Computer-system evolved from 'Cybernetics' and has influenced and thereby changed education systems and the learning processes simultaneously.

Sometimes it was found that a small innovation creates ripples and influenced other related fields. Educational technology has also faced similar effects due to the advancement of cybernetic systems. But scientists, psychologists, technicians and researchers also have contributions in the advancement of ET.

Most of the teachers in the present days are discipline-oriented. Teachers and educationists are experts in their own field of studies and remain in their closed-door compartments. Thus a teacher of Physics or Chemistry hardly know anything about methods and methodologies of Education and in the same way a teacher of pure Psychology or Education knows little about development of software required for the application in the TLP. Thus in most of the occasions, one compartment requires the help from other sides, with a commonness of 'understanding education'. But occasionally it is difficult to find out exact persons from the required fields. So it affects further the quality development of education and at the same time TLP suffers much. An example can be given in the context; suppose the teacher wants to develop a game, which would develop multilateral thinking, divergent thinking and creativity in the children. It requires a different type of software and it will be different from writing a textbook that a discipline-oriented person can do. It also requires different types of professional experts from different fields of specialization. Different computer games are now evolving, which requires interdisciplinary areas and approaches. Computer game like *Sim City* requires a team of experts from various fields like Town-Planning, Psychology, Sociology, Engineering, etc.

In old days a teacher had to depend only on one-way communication like lecturing. Thus the learners could know the one side of the problem. But nowadays, due to the possibility of developing Virtual Reality, the rigid concepts are slowly breaking. It is now becoming reality that teachers, experts and educationists will also change there thinking styles slowly, but it will require time to arrive at the expected level. The future development of ET as an interdisciplinary subject is shown by Figure 17.2.

Reigeluth, C.M. and Beaty, B.J. (2004) characterizes the fundamental changes of different paradigms in the knowledge society. Some of these are shift from:

- A concern for standardization to a concern for customization.
- Central, bureaucratic control to autonomous, team-based management.
- Adversarial relationships to collaborative relationships.

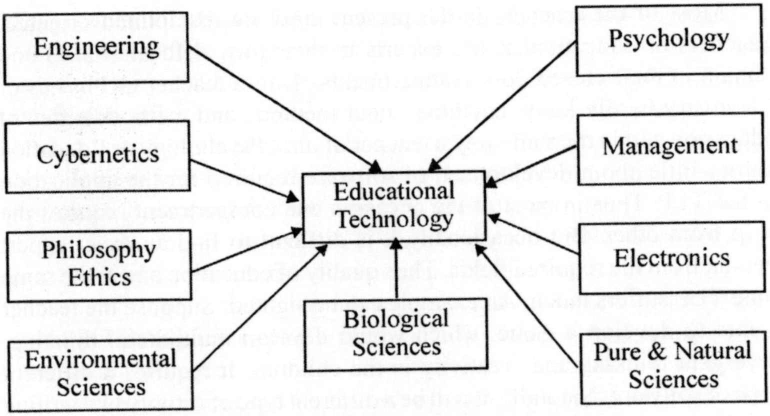

Fig. 17.2. Interdisciplinary aspects of ET

- Autocratic decision-making to shared decision-making.
- Valuing compliance to valuing initiative.
- One way communication to networked communication.
- Compartmentalization to integration.
- Product-orientation to process-integration.
- Teacher-centered instruction to learner-centered instruction etc.

Teachers are the managers of TLP. Their duties are to prepare a total man suitable to fulfill the needs and demands of the future emerging society. This requires the balanced development of cognitive, affective and psychomotor domains. Future ET would help teachers, students and experts of different subject areas alike. Technology optimizes human learning and development of technology increases the capacity and capability of human teaching and learning. The development of new technologies has enhances the changes of methods and methodologies of teaching learning process. Till the first half of the last century, teacher was at the center stage and whatever helped the teacher in controlling the teaching learning process (TLP) was put in to the fold of ET. But things changed after 2nd world war. Learners now come to the center stage and learners are given more priorities than the teachers. In the last few decades, new systems of teaching learning processes have evolved and systems approach from Cybernetics has taken the center place in education. The computer system evolved from Cybernetics has influenced education systems, learning processes in different ways.

Sometimes it was found that a small innovation creates ripples and influenced other related fields. Educational technology has also faced the similar effect due to the advancement of cybernetic systems. But scientists, psychologists, technicians and researchers also have contributions in the advancement of ET.

Most of the teachers in the present days are disciplined oriented. Teachers or educationists are experts in their own field of studies and remain in their closed-door compartments. Thus a teacher of Physics or Chemistry hardly know anything about methods and methodologies of education and in the same way a teacher of pure Psychology or Education knows little about development of software required for the application in the TLP. Thus in most of the occasion one compartment requires the help from other. But occasionally it is difficult to find an exact expert person from the required fields. Thus quality of education and at the same time TLP suffers much. An example can be sighted. Suppose the teacher wants to develop a game, which would develop multilateral thinking, divergent thinking and creativity in the children. It requires a different type of software. Naturally, it will be a different type of activity like writing a textbook that a disciplined oriented person can do. The future trends of ET are to synthesize both the streams.

Different computer games are now developing which requires the knowledge of interdisciplinary areas. Computer games like Sim City requires a team of experts from various fields like Town Planning, Psychology, Sociology, Engineering, etc. Now-a-days, this is possible due to the emerging trends of Technology of Education.

In the old days a teacher had to depend only on one-way communication like lecturing. Thus the learners could know the one side of the problem. But now due to the possibility of developing Virtual Reality, the rigid concepts are slowly breaking. It is now becoming reality that teachers, experts and educationists will also change their thinking styles slowly, because it will require time to arrive at the expected level.

Some Developing Issues of Educational Technology

A few years back Plotnick, E. (1996) made a detailed study on the trends of ET and its future prospects. Sources for the analysis included five leading professional journals in educational technology; papers given at annual conventions of three professional associations; dissertations from five reputed universities. The analysis was complemented by the examination of supplementary documents to confirm the trends indicated in the content analysis.The study has reported the following trends of ET:

Trend 1: Computers are pervasive in schools and higher education institutions. Virtually every student in a formal education setting has access to a computer.

Trend 2: Networking is one of the fastest growing applications of technology in education.

Trend 3: Access to television resources in the school is almost universal.

Trend 4: Advocacy for the use of educational technology has increased among policy groups.

Trend 5: Educational technology is increasingly available in homes and community settings.

Trend 6: New delivery systems for educational technology applications have grown in geometric proportions.

Trend 7: There is a new insistence that teachers must become technologically literate.

Trend 8: Educational technology is perceived as a major vehicle in the movement toward education reform.

Some recent advances in technology might help us to understand their stupendous impact on education and we can assume where we are moving in the near future. ET has gained a lot from this advancement of science and technology.

In his article 'The Future of Educational Technology' Dawson, J.M. (2005) has described it in a very lucid way.

According to Dawson (2005), 'The key to educational technology is software and what the students and teachers do with it. Judging the appropriateness, effectiveness, and capability of technology in the classroom is difficult. New classroom tools mean new opportunities for learning and teaching. Simple-to-use multimedia authoring applications, digital media collections, the Internet, and new, educationally valid curriculum-based software are all making the learning-centered classroom a reality'.

'Begin small and start promptly', is the best way to deal with the rapid change in technology. A few examples are given to understand how the changes are going on in our different walks of life.

Animators who used to spend months and even years hand painting cells for cartoons are being replaced by computers that can do the work possibly in a tenth of the time.

The electronic numerical integrator and computer (ENIAC), the first all-electronic computer, built in 1946, had 19,000 vacuum tubes, weighed 30 tons, took up 1800 square feet of space, and ran only five days without the need for repair. Efficiency of information technology (a scientific calculator has more power than ENIAC) has since jumped by more than 32 orders of magnitude, one hundred octillion times, the greatest improvement in productivity in human history.

It is very interesting to note that in 1972 there were only 150,000 computers in the world. By 1999 one company alone shipped almost 100 million computers.

Virtual reality is nearly as real as reality. Commercial pilots used to fly empty planes for practice; now they train exclusively in simulators. The first time they ever fly their actual plane filled with passengers.

There are now more than 50 million homepages on the Internet, with a new one added every four seconds. Some sites on the Internet are visited over 15 million times a day.

Emerging Trends of Educational Technology

Long time ago Peter Drucker wrote:

> *'In a few hundred years, when the history of our time will be written from a long-term perspective, it is likely that the most important event historians will see is not technology, not the Internet, not e-commerce. It is an unprecedented change in the human condition. For the first time - literally - substantial and rapidly growing numbers of people have choices. For the first time, they will have to manage themselves. And society is totally unprepared for it.'* — Peter F. Drucker

A few years ago David Thornburg (1999) and Aureo Castro (2001) wrote two articles: 'Reading the Future'(1999) and 'Learning in a Digital Age: Current and Future Trends in Educational Technology'(2001). Both the articles are thought provoking and important for the present discussion.

Even though David Thornburg's article appeared in 1999, the trends he writes about are still relevant today. David Thornburg lists seven 'trends and their consequences' (1999) while Aureo Castro mentions six. The former discusses the 'rapid increase in the growth of information, the collapse of the information float, increasingly global marketplace, computers continue to increase in power while dropping in cost, the computer chips continue to follow Moore's Law, bandwidth is becoming free and finally network power continues to obey Metcalfe's Law as future trends that will have 'implications for education' (1999).

On the other hand Castro's discussion about future trends include an increase in web enabled courses, more home scholars, new roles for teachers, a paradigm shift in primary education, new roles for schools and centralization of curriculum and instructional development' (2001).

According to David Thornburg, because the Internet is 'doubling in size every year, [and] the web is doubling in size every 90 days [there is need for] a complete rethinking of education'(1999). He suggests the need for 'technological fluency so that students can sit down at a computer and use it as easily as [they] can pick up and read a book in [their] native language' (1999).

Castro sees 'home schooling and more web-enabled courses' (2001) as future trends in 'rethinking education'. He predicts, 'new roles for teachers as facilitators who will concentrate on the teaching of social skills rather than [on] academic or technical expertise' (2001). Castro predicts that there will be an increase in online courses 'offered through the Internet' (2001). He suggests 'the only way to go with the fast increase in population and the physical constraint of the existing colleges and universities is in cyberspace' (2002). Castro focuses on the Internet and 'distance education' as a trend that will become even more popular in the future. He claims that future 'schools will cease to become like a mill where students undergo academic processing but will evolve into becoming community centers where students engage in a variety of activities and projects' (2001).

David Thornburg focuses on another trend for the future of schools. He worries about 'the lack of technologically fluent workers' and getting prepared for jobs that have not been invented yet (1999). Thornburg claims that educators 'must create an educational system that prepares students to work in fields that do not even exist' (1999). Thornburg doesn't predict how educators would deal with the educational trends of the future. However, he does claim that once 'technologies become commonplace with all students, the tools for lifelong learning will be in place, [adding that] the notion [of] lifelong learning is a survival skill' (1999). Future trends cannot be ignored. Thornburg claims, 'Schools that ignore the trends shaping tomorrow will cease to be relevant in the lives of their students and will disappear quickly' (1999).

Both Castro and Thornburg are educational futurists who have looked at future trends in technology and their impact on education. Technology can improve student learning and make teachers' work much easier. Educational technology will become 'powerful low-cost, off the shelf tool that can make learning more engaging and knowledge more accessible' (Snyder, 2004). Educators 'must work in partnership to break down the barriers of time, space, content and form so that learners can collaborate, communicate, and share ideas' (Mulcahy, 2003).

Future of ET depends on the persons who will use it, the ease of handle effective software and cost effective and time saving process.

Software is to be called effective if it has four important characteristics:

1. Presentability (P)
2. Accountability (A)
3. Customizability (C) and
4. Extensibility (E), or in short PACE. (Dawson, 2005)

Presentability is the software's overall appearance to the user. Accountability is essential for evaluation of student work and progress. Customizability is the third essential element of sound educational software. Programs should never be complex and should be adaptable to the users. Extensibility is the final component of the PACE and essential for sound educational software. Software that is extensible is easy to adjust, easy to take beyond its own environment, and can extend in the creation of new things. For example, if a geography program focuses on the teaching of map reading, it should be not only possible but also easy to integrate a local map in the lesson.

'Humanistic' education is possible if each learner is empowered with a greater role in his or her learning. The learner must start with a plan to learn and with a commitment to a continuing, effective learning process. ET has a penetrating impact in this case. In brief, emerging trends of ET in the changing society is summarized below:

a) Traditional classrooms to Twenty First Century Classrooms: The typical secondary or elementary school teacher in a classroom, the university or college professor in a lecture hall all share a number of common characteristics when it comes to traditional delivery methods and the use of established Educational Technologies. Each of them has experienced a number of these educational environments as they have moved through the formal education system. The classroom of the early 1800s had its standard collection of resources with the single most important being the teacher. This central figure, the teacher, was frequently the expert in all manner of subjects along with the other resources such as a small collection of books or the timetable.

Contemporary researchers viewed the last century as a time of transition. Toffler (1993) referred it as a move from the age of the 'smokestack' or 'rust bucket' technologies to the age to Information Technology.

Figure 17.3 presents a diagrammatic representation of traditional classrooms. Its most striking characteristic, as indicated by the inward pointing arrows, was its ability to attract and hold resources for use in subsequent teacher/learner interactions. Its most striking feature was the central position of the teacher who controls the entire class with the help of mostly lecture method and other simple technologies like Blackboard, Whiteboard, VCR and OHP etc. A telephone connection may sometime available for mostly office use.

Figure 17.4 is a diagrammatic representation of the type of classroom that is being evolved from the end of the last century and which is becoming the model for classrooms of the twenty first century. Its most striking feature is the central position of the learner and the two-way connections with 'outside' resources including not just the traditional resources of print or pictures or the like, but connections with other learners and teachers. Learners are everywhere and the place of teacher is not restricted in to the classroom or in the educational institutions.

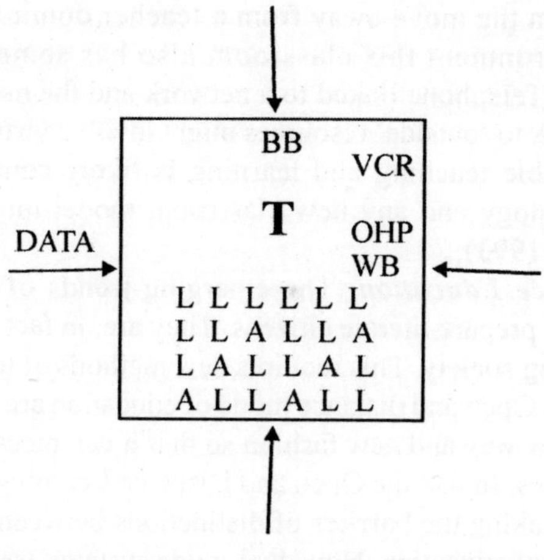

Fig. 17.3: Elements of the traditional classroom
(T= Teacher, L = Learner, A= Absent learner)

Equipments–Black Board, Whiteboard, overhead projector, VCR etc.

The overlapping second learner environment, and more of these could be included, is intended to emphasis the continuing role of face-to-face social interaction and learning for both teachers and students. Considerable teaching and learning is likely continued to occur without technology and any new classroom model must acknowledge this (Postman, 1993).

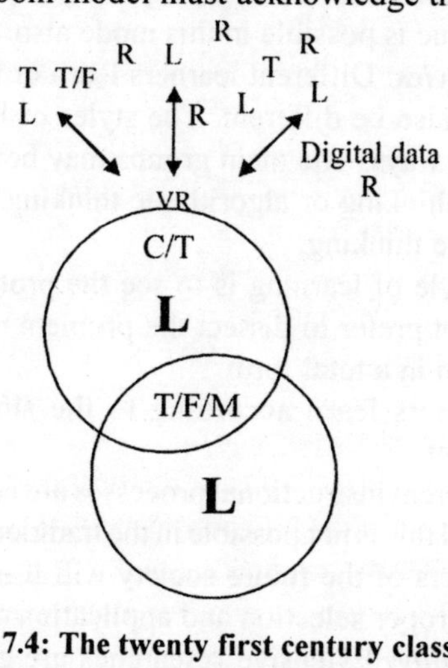

Fig. 17.4: The twenty first century classroom

L = Learner, **T/F/M** = teacher/ facilitator/ manager, **R** = resources (print, speech, music, pictures, animations video etc.), **C/T** = computer/telephone (network link)

Apart from the move away from a teacher dominated to learner-centered environment this classroom also has some new features. Computer and Telephone linked to a network and the notion that an element of this link to 'outside' resources might involve virtual reality (VR).

Considerable teaching and learning is likely continued to occur without technology and any new classroom model must acknowledge this (Postman, 1993).

b) Distance Education: The emerging trends of the future new societies are to prepare literate citizens. They are, in fact, new learners of the new learning society. This requires new methods of teaching learning process (TLP). Open and distance mode of education are now developing rapidly in a new way and new fashion so that it can meet the demands of the new societies. In fact the Open and Distance Learning (ODL) systems are rapidly breaking the barriers of distinctions between the regular and distance mode of education. Now dual-mode systems are effectively used in education system and it is assumed that it will replace the present on-campus education system. Due to rapid changes in communication systems, progress of ET is tremendously high and in future it will take the central stage in the development of study materials, dissemination and delivery of teaching–learning materials, change the role of teachers by the use of both technology and communication systems.

On-line distance learning holds tremendous promise in this regard. With the use of Internet educational technologies now supporting rapid and convenient communication and people have every reason to think that Socratic dialogue is possible in this mode also.

c) Learning Styles: Different learners learn or think differently and learning pace may also be different. The styles of learning may also be divided in different ways. The main groups may be:

i) Serialized thinking or algorithmic thinking. This type is similar to deductive thinking.

ii) Another style of learning is to see the problem in a total form. They do not prefer to dissect the problem rather try to consider the problem in a total form.

iii) Some learners learn according to the situation and learning environment.

Therefore different instructional processes are necessary for different types of learners and this is not possible in the traditional teaching–learning system. New learners of the future society will learn according to their own styles by the proper selection and application of appropriate ET.

d) Virtual Reality: Extensive researches are going on Cyberspace and Virtual Reality. Cyberspace technology is a vast thoroughfare where computer meets and exchange information. By adding other computers in on line process, practically an unlimited space can be used to collect and exchange information and are now used in education systems. Learners are now familiar with the term Virtual Education.

Virtual education is a term describing online education using the Internet. It refers to instruction in a learning environment where time or space or both separate teacher and student, and the teacher provide course-content through course management applications, multimedia resources, Internet and videoconferencing. Virtual courses are courses delivered on the Internet. 'Virtual' is used here to characterize the fact that the course is not taught in a classroom face-to-face but through some substitute mode that can be associated with classroom teaching.

A virtual program (or a virtual course of studies) is a study program in which all courses or at least a significant portion of the courses are virtual courses. Students receive the content and communicate with the teacher via the same technologies in a virtual classroom.

Cyber Media Creations defines the virtual classroom as 'A simulated classroom that allows students to interact using software such as live chat, forums or desktop sharing'.

Encyclopedia defines a virtual classroom as, 'a learning environment that exists solely in the form of digital content that is stored, accessed, and exchanged through networked computer and information systems'.

Sim City games are virtual reality games and are still in developing stage. This will help future learners to learn independently and design their own learning modes and styles. Practically now-a-days virtual universities, virtual libraries, virtual laboratories have come up in different ways. Learners can sit for the examinations through online methods and can have their degrees and diplomas in different subjects. In future, this will increase in many folds.

The explosion of the knowledge age has changed the context of what is learnt and how it is learnt – the concept of virtual classrooms is a manifestation of this knowledge revolution. Different instructional modes for Virtual Classrooms are:

- ***Hypertext courses***: Structured course material is used as in a conventional distance education program. However, all material is provided electronically and can be viewed with a browser. Hyperlinks connect text, multimedia parts and exercises in a meaningful way.
- ***Video-based courses*** are like face-to-face classroom courses, with a lecturer speaking and PowerPoint slides or online examples used for illustration. Video-streaming technologies is used. Students watch the video by means of freeware or plug-ins (e.g. Windows Media Player, Real Player).

- ***Audio-based courses*** are similar but instead of moving pictures only the sound track of the lecturer is provided. Often the course pages are enhanced with a text transcription of the lecture.
- ***Animated courses*** are enriching text-oriented or audio-based course material by animations is generally a good way of making the content and its appearance more interesting. Animations are created using Macromedia Flash or similar technologies.
- ***Web-supported textbook courses*** are based on specific textbooks. Students read and reflect the chapters by themselves. Review questions, topics for discussion, exercises, case studies, etc. are given chapter wise on a website and discussed with the lecturer. Class meetings may be held to discuss matters in a chartroom, for example.
- ***Peer-to-peer courses*** are courses taught, 'on-demand' and without a prepared curriculum. A new field of online education has emerged in 2007 through new online education platforms.

Now many other varieties of instructional are available.

e) Artificial Intelligence: Artificial Intelligence used in education systems is now called 'intelligent tutors'. It is a step beyond traditional computer aided instruction. The Intelligent Tutoring Systems (ITS) will be able to deduce a learner's approximation of the knowledge that he is being tutored for. The tutorial strategy must be intelligent in that the system can implement strategies to reduce the difference between expert and student performance.

The ITS must have definitive knowledge of the domain it intends to tutor the students. At this juncture help from human experts is sought to generate and store a knowledge base. Once a knowledge base is available, the systems will then make appropriate deductions and give directions to the student performance.

ITSs have a wide range of applications in different disciplines and subjects. Training related to tactical planning, business decision-making, and interpersonal communication is only a few examples of candidates for ITSs (Chrungoo, A. & Malviya, M. 2005).

Imagine that each learner in a classroom setting has a personal training assistant who pays attention to the participant's learning needs, assesses and diagnoses problems, and provides assistance as needed. The assistant could perform many of the routine instructional interventions and alert the instructor of learning problems that are too difficult for it. By taking on basic assistance tasks, the instructor would be free to concentrate on training issues that require greater expertise.

Providing a personal training assistant for each learner is beyond the capacity of most Institutions. However, a *virtual* training assistant that captures the subject matter and teaching expertise of experienced trainers provides a captivating new option. The concept, known as intelligent tutoring systems (ITS) or intelligent computer-aided instruction (ICAI), has been pursued for more than three decades by researchers in education, psychology and artificial intelligence. Today, prototype and operational ITS systems provide practice-based instruction to support corporate training, K-12 and college education or military training. The goal of ITS is to provide the benefits of one-to-one instruction automatically and cost effectively. Like training simulations, ITS enables participants to practice their skills by carrying out tasks within highly interactive learning environments. However, ITS goes beyond training simulations by answering user questions and providing individualized guidance.

Based on the learner model ITS's tailor instructional strategies, in terms of both the content and style, and provide explanations, hints, examples, demonstrations, and practice problems as needed.

Researches indicate that ITS-taught students generally learn faster and translate the learning into improved performance better than classroom-trained participants.

The intelligent tutoring system (ITS) also offers the following additional functions:

It can:

- Control the time of each student spends on each unit.
- Predict the grade (pass or fail) of the student.
- Design a revision lesson plan for the students.
- Analyze the difficulty of the course units.
- Register teacher and student access.
- Visualize evolution diagrams of the students
- Provide services such as e-mail, telephone, forum, messenger, video-conferencing and intelligent tutor.
- Offer an exclusive service for the teacher, which is the transfer of teaching material.

f) Life-long Learning: Due to rapid development of technology and communication systems we are rapidly moving towards a new learning society where everybody will be a lifelong learner. Continuous learning will be the key element of societal development in the new learning society. In the future learning society, technology will help learners in the new learning paradigm.

Digital reading and writing has permeated all aspects of daily literacy activity in the different countries of the world. Emailing, Internet access to information, and word processing are literate acts that employed by people for personal, professional, and business communications. How work is done is largely being recreated by computer-related technologies and requisite literacy including digital literacy. To be digitally literate, one will have to be able to navigate, locate, communicate on-line, and participate in digital, virtual and physical, communities. Literacy definitions in the future will relate to informatics abilities, a range of meaning, making strategies required to assemble knowledge in cyberspace (Labbo, 2005).

g) Multiple Learning Resources: Today computers can do multiple activities in TLP. Many new dimensions of computer applications are developing rapidly. The future learners will be able to use ET in different ways in education. The new learners of the future society will learn according to their time, interest and pace of learning. It is assumed that present classroom teaching learning system will get a new boost in the future society.

h) Future Education for Specially Challenged People: In future, individual educational plans for disabled students may be applied to all learners. Thus the true inclusion system in education will develop. This will create greater efficiency in all schools, enabling us to provide the human and computer resources needed to meet the educational needs of each child in the same form and same way.

Technology for the future includes *sensory prosthetic devices* too for disabled people. This may be one of the most significant factors in providing all children an equal and appropriate education. *Cochlear implants* are already providing many hard of hearing youngsters with functional hearing. *Speech synthesizers* give voice to mute individuals. New developments in *microelectronic lenses* may enable a large number of visually disabled people to read printed books. Already, *reading machines for blind* people open the vast world of print to them. Experiments with *computer-controlled muscles* in people with spinal cord disabilities have enabled them to walk across the stage to receive their college diplomas.

Educational Technology and Teachers in the Future Digital World

Question has been raised regarding place and functions of teachers in the newly developing digital society. Some technologists are of opinion that the technology will replace teachers and they are predicting a 'teacherless education' system in the future digital society. But others are visualizing a greater and important role of teachers in it.

Harasim (1995), Berge (1999) and many other experts have observed that computer technology has developed new forms of dialogic interaction among teachers and students.

Ability of Internet to transmit graphically exciting materials, programs and text made it more acceptable than earlier means of delivering information. It is now offering:

- Answering questions using FAQs (Frequently Asked Question lists) and 'Ask the Expert' help programs.
- 'Intelligent agents' can adapt computer-based programs to students' learning styles (Kearsley, 1993).
- To automate the grading essay, tests based on a technique called 'Latent Semantic Analysis' (Foltz, 1996) are on operation.

Is such future 'teacherless education' system really plausible? Probably not. Much of today's progress has its appeals to the potential of virtual universities, degrees and hints at the obsolescence of the traditional campus and its teaching methods, yet the importance of teachers will be far more than the present day education system, because the future teachers will have to bear new roles, new strategies and new instructional systems not known earlier. The most important part of the teachers will have an appeal forever; it is the human touch in the education system. Machines are machines only; it can never give the learners a human touch like the teachers.

Conclusion

The technology is advancing like the speed of a rocket and so educational technology. Consider the news item: 'Scientist has created the world's first human-sheep chimera – which the body of sheep and half-human organs. The sheep have 15 per cent human cells and 85 per cent animal cells. University of Nevada's Esmail Zanjani has spent seven years and £5 million for perfecting the technique,…' (*The Times of India*, 26 March 2007)

Thus this will has an impact on ET in one way or other and future teachers, learners and the society will have to consolidate and expand their experiences in more than one way: philosophical, psychological an sociological.

Educational technology in the present century can make a far greater reality than ever before with powerful, accessible databases, electronic learning communities and peer-reviewed portfolios on the Web. The future will bring access to the tools, people need to live the more examined life we all strive for.

Experts are predicting that direct brain wave input to computers will be possible by the year 2020. The digital world has the potential to equalize educational opportunities for everyone. More sophisticated and large databanks of educational information can be developed and thus educational plans and programmes might be formulated according to the need and demands of different fields of education and society at the same time.

Teachers in future classrooms will assume flexible instructional roles (Model, Manager and Counselor) that support effective computer-related literacy instruction. They will use software and Internet links to support children's traditional print-based literacy Development; however, they will also be well prepared to support children's digital literacy-development as well. A crucial part of digital literacy instruction will involve helping students acquire critical literacy and reasoning required for assembling and evaluating information from the Internet. There are many questions that remain to be answered about effective use of computers for digital literacy instruction in the classroom. However, the time has come when we must formulate a vision for effective computer-related literacy practices. There should be a 'symbiosis' of humans and machines, because the role and nature of education is changing very fast. In a paper this was also versioned by the UNESCO. It reiterates:

> *'One of UNESCO's overriding aims is to ensure that all countries, both developed and developing, have access to the best educational facilities necessary to prepare young people to play full roles in modern society and to contribute to a knowledge nation.'*
>
> —(Daniel, J. Assistant Director-General for Education, 2002)

Due to the inherent nature of technology the future teachers will have to perform as 'disseminators of knowledge to facilitators of learning'. But one unhealthy situation may develop due to the digital divide among the students. It should be carefully minimized so that all the people get equal chances in the future new world.

Feenberg, A. (2006) observes, 'If we can resist simplistic appeals to managerial efficiency and focus our efforts on sustaining the dialogue that has always been at the heart of the educational experience, then technology holds great promise; if not, then we face a great threat'.

REFERENCES

Bostingl, J.J. (1996). Schools of Quality: An Introduction to Total Quality Management in Education. Columbia: The Center for School of Quality, Maryland.

Cross, K.P. (1986). *Adults as Learners: Increasing Participation and Facilitating Learning*. London: Jossy-Bass.

Ellington, H., et.al.(1993). *Hand Book of Educational Technology*. London: Kogan Page Ltd.

Feenberg, A. (2006). 'Whither Educational Technology?'. San Diego State University, San Diego.

Gregory, G.H. and Chapman, C. (2002). *Differentiated Instructional Strategies*. London: Kogan Page Ltd.

Mukhopadhyaya, D. (2002).Teacher Education in the Cybernetic Age: A Challenge before the Developing World. Paper presented in the International Conf. Moradabad.

Mukhopadhyaya, M. (2004).*Educational Technology: Knowledge Assessment.* Delhi: Shipra Publications

Plotnick, Eric (1995). *Trends in Educational Technology 1995.* ERIC Digest. Syracuse NY.

Raggatt,P., Richard E. and Small, N. (Eds.) (1996). *The Learning Society: Challenges and Trends*. London: Routledge.

Schank, R.C. (2000). Future Perspective: A Vision for the 21st Century. T.H.E. Journal Online.

Shah, B. (Ed) (2003). *Information Technology and Education*. Allahabad: Kitab Mahal

The Times of India (Kolkata), 26th March, 2007; cit. in.

Tyler, W. (2002). Total Quality Management. *ERC Digest*, No. 73.

18.

Ukraine-specific Managerial Ethics: Its Structure in the Light of Educational Technology

Olena Vynoslavska and Mariya Kononets

As for *the importance of the professional managerial ethics in the activities of modern organizations,* it is important to note that during the last decade, in the process of development of the market institutions in Ukraine, under the conditions of amorphous post-Soviet economics, Ukrainian managers found themselves under the pressure to pull through both personal and social resistance. Among the social and psychological determinants that went through reconstructions are value orientations, thinking and behavioral stereotypes, orientation of social attitudes, motivation of economic behavior, style characteristics of consumer behavior (Fominykh). Such reconstructions are the result of the fact that professionals, formed outside of the market economy, *found it particularly hard to psychologically accept even the basics of the managerial culture.*

It is important to point to the fact that Ukrainian organizational psychology is just probing the ground in such sphere as managerial culture (Vynoslavska, 2002, *Etychni*; Vynoslavska, 2005, *Transition*). However, in the foreign sources these issues have been discussed since the 30ies of the 20th century, after E. Mayo (1880-1949), an American sociologist, grounded a human relations doctrine as a response to the psychological problems arising in the production sphere (Doroshenko). The main provisions of the doctrine are as follows:

Human Relations theory rapidly gained acceptance among the entrepreneurs and practice of application of psychological factors in management expanded just as rapidly. As a result, social psychology began developing very fast, as well as such related applied disciplines as labor psychology, organizational psychology, economic psychology etc. Success in development of psychological theory and practice stipulated gain in attention to development of the *professional managerial ethics* in the process of the professional training. Gradually, in all developed countries, serious ethical and psychological training became an essential component of staff development in the sphere of management and business while assessment of development of professional ethics became one of the key requirements in professional selection. Implementation of the Western experience became topical in Ukraine due to transition to the market economy.

Theoretical Consideration

The basic theoretical considerations, on which the present study hinges-on, includes professional ethics, ethical decision making in managerial practice as also the model of professional managerial culture.

What is professional ethics?: Going to the analysis of essence and specifics of the universal and professional ethics, we believe it is important to analyze the essence of culture first of all.

Culture, as a sphere of mental human life, includes the objective results of human activities, as well as individual specific traits, manifested through such activities, in particular, knowledge, skills, level of intellectual development, moral and aesthetic development, worldview, tools and forms of communication with other people.

Ethics, often called *universal ethics*, explores morality and various ethical systems, justifying it, grounds of this systems and logical system of terms describing the moral phenomena, collisions and situations. On the one hand, universal ethics is a reference point for *moral personal development*, a component of human spiritual culture; on the other hand, it is a *generalization of moral norms* that characterize conformity of human behavioral to the requirements of moral law and models of moral behavior, traditional for the society. It is necessary to stress that *universal ethics* generalizes the behavior norm that are obligatory for all individuals irrespectively of their professional background or social functions.

A separate set of ethics, *professional ethics*, which generalizes specific moral norms related to specific functioning of various professions, in particular, professions directly influencing the psychological reality of individuals, stands out in the framework of the professional activities.

Professional ethics often lays ground for positive influence on solving ethically moot points arising in the process of professional activities, in particular, in the *process of professional managerial activities* (Petrunin, 2004). For instance, a manager should take a decision whether he should or should not fire a lazy worker who is the only bread-earner in his family.

Ethical decision-making in managerial practice: It is important that a lot of ethical problems, which are thought of as related to the professional managerial activity, include a *certain type of contradiction between the universal and professional ethical systems.* When such conflict takes place, it becomes a serious ethical problem for a manager:

which obligations, universal of professional should he rely upon to take an ethical decision?

In the contemporary world, there are *two approaches to explain the process of taking ethical decisions – normative and descriptive.*

Normative approach discovered by the philosophers, opens up ways to taking ethical decision by an individual who is a conscious representative of morality and thinks of his/her moral choice in earnest. Moral norms were established in order to assist in talking the best ethical decision; however, it is known that people do not always take the best decision and the established norms are not followed.

Descriptive approach, on the other hand, is based on the results of the psychological research and describes the way through which people use to take ethical decisions in reality. In particular, it focuses on cognitive processes and limitations that often hold the managers back from taking the best possible decisions (Trevino, 1995).

One of the *most important aspects of a problem of taking an ethical decision is an issue of responsibility*, obligations, or necessity of an individual or an organization to report its actions and to take consequences of their possible outcomes. *Moral managerial obligation* is a correspondence of the ethical actions of a manager to his/her obligation which is evaluated by taking into consideration both personal abilities and external circumstances. Thus, moral responsibility for taking the managerial decisions and their outcomes are the important component of the professional managerial ethics (Belolipetskyi, 2004).

Professional ethics of a modern manager also includes his/her openness to the *ethical standards, traditional for the foreign economic and international activity.* In particular, *the following are the universal ethical principles and norms of the international activities: respect to personality, human rights and freedom, proper professional competence, conscience, and amiability.*

When analyzing general professional requirements to managers, D. Graham deduced a list of key individual characteristics of American, Japanese, Taiwanese and Brazilian professionals. Some of the skills overlap cultures and countries and include training, planning, listening, common sense, intellect, generating ideas, as well as honesty and respect to confidentiality of other partner (Raider, 1982). Besides, a qualified manager is expected to:

- Understand that there are four categories of values: universal, shared by all societies, similar, but open for cultural interpretation, somewhat similar, and incompatible (Trevino, 1995);
- Accept the cultural differences at all levels (be it individual, corporate or national);

- Be competitive in discussing differences prior to taking of the decision, which will satisfy both sides (Raider, 1982).

Model of the professional managerial culture: When talking about the professional ethics, it is also important to analyze it as a component of *the professional managerial culture and to analyze the basic elements of the professional ethics.*

Professional managerial culture is a 'specific subsystem of human culture' and merges the culture of professional labor and "a number of qualities, first of all, moral, also demonstrated by estimable professionals outside of their labor functions" (Ball, 2004). In other words, there are two interrelated substructures in the structure of the *professional culture*, in particular – *professional competence and spirituality of a professional* (Ball, 2004), or, according to Kohlberg, no-moral and moral elements (Antsyferova).

As for the professional managerial competence, it is important to analyze it on two different levels, namely, *managerial and psychological* (Karamushka, 1997).

The managerial level is an expert and high-quality performance of functions of planning, organization and control of operation of certain organizational activities. All corresponding knowledge and skills are developed as a part of the professional training of managers in the higher education institutions.

Psychological level of the professional managerial competence is an ability to take decisions, to create psychological conditions for productive activities, personnel management, and development of successful communications.

Spirituality of a professional, or the *managerial professional ethics*, is an *ethical background* to the managerial activities.

Figure 18.1 presents a *model of the professional managerial culture*. The model is presented as a triangle where the sides are the components of the psychological substructure of the professional managerial culture, namely, decision-making and delegation of the responsibility; personnel management; creating the productive work environment. On top of the model, there is a backbone component – communications and interpersonal relations between a manager and his/her subordinates and superiors that significantly influence both the psychological climate of a specific unit and organizational culture in general (Vynoslavska, 2006; Paleha; Samoukina, 1999). The core of the model is the *ethical segment*, which is manifested in taking the moral responsibility for managerial decisions upon oneself, evaluation of the work results, upholding the ethical norms in the relations etc., and can be regarded as the *professional managerial ethics.*

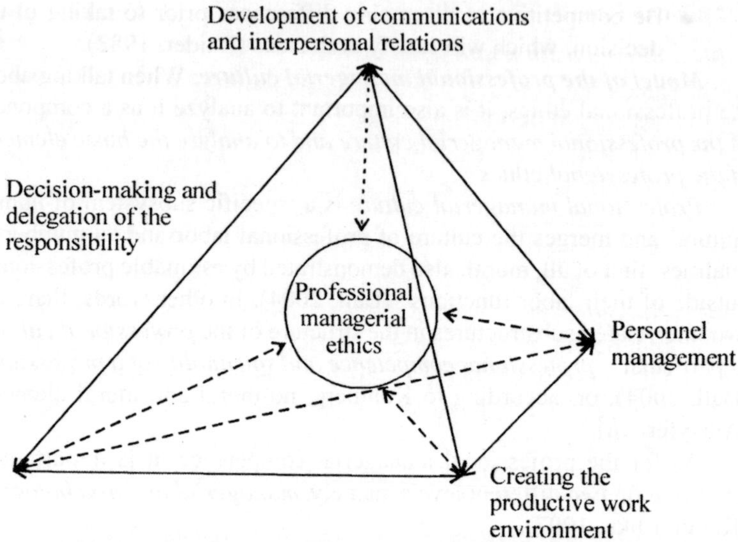

Fig. 18.1. Model of the Professional Managerial Culture

The following components are a part of the *structure of the professional managerial ethics*:

- *Ethical attitudes* (acceptability of unacceptability of decisions, ambiguous from the viewpoint of the morals, in the specific cases of professional activity);
- *Ethical behavior* (norm-conformative performance by a manager of the professional functions);
- *Striving to ethical relations* during the managerial communications (Ball, 2004).

Besides, '*openness to the world of the human culture*', or regard of ethical norms, rules and notions, which regulate attitudes, behavior and relations of business partners in the international relations, by a manager, is yet another important component of the professional managerial ethics (Ball, 2004).

It is worth noting that development of the ethical background of the professional managerial culture is officially and formally sounded out in the curricula of the higher education institutions of Ukraine, but lack of efficient technologies to develop its components prevents practical implementation of these intentions.

Empirical Results

Ethical dilemmas in managerial activity

At the same time, research that we have carried out in the framework of special research of the Organizational Psychology Laboratory of the H.S. Kostiuk Institute of Psychology, Academy of Pedagogical Sciences of Ukraine, clearly demonstrated that in their activities, managers deal with a number of problems that cannot be efficiently settled by them due to lack of necessary ethical and psychological training.

In order to study a *level of orientation of managers to solve the ethical and psychological problems*, we addressed the managers and top managers of the commercial organizations, operating in the sphere of small and medium business, with a request to fill out a special questionnaire (Wood, 1988). Seventy Ukrainian entrepreneurs from Dnipropetrovsk, Ivano-Frankivsk, Kyiv, Lviv, Kharkiv, and Chernivtsi (Vynoslavska, 2002, Osnovni, 2002) took part in the research as sample group and extended required data.

As for *the ethical dilemmas in the professional managerial activity*, it is important to stress that evaluation of intricate ethical situation is often used to evaluate ethical attitudes of managers, which forms an important component of the professional ethics. Such situations, when choice of one of the contradictory possibilities is equally complicated, are called ethical dilemmas.

Ethical dilemmas that managers face in the course of their professional activities can be divided into *two main groups*.

The first-group ethical dilemmas arise inside an organization and can be divided into two subgroups (Doroshenko, 1997).

The *first subgroup* is the ethical dilemmas that arise in the vertical relations of a manager. It includes two types of ethical dilemmas:

a) Ethical dilemmas that arise in the process of interaction between a manager and his/her superior;
b) Ethical dilemmas that arise in the process of interaction between a manager and his/her subordinates.

Ethical dilemmas arising in the horizontal managerial relations fall into the *second subgroup*, which also includes two types of ethical dilemmas:

a) Ethical dilemmas that arise in the relations with the colleagues;
b) Ethical dilemmas that arise in the relations among the subordinates of a manager. In such cases, the manager usually operates as a mediator.

The second-group ethical dilemmas may also appear in the process of cooperation between the organization and other institutions. They fall into the following three groups (Trevino, 1995):

a) Ethical dilemmas that arise in the process of interaction between the organization and other commercial structures;
b) Ethical dilemmas that arise in the process of interaction between the organization and non-profitable organizations;
c) Ethical dilemmas that arise in the process of foreign economic activity and international cooperation.

Content analysis of the answers demonstrated that all psychological and managerial problems named by the respondents fall in the following three groups:

1. Inherently managerial problems;
2. Problems arising in the relations;
3. Inherently ethical and psychological problems.

First of all, it is important to mention that the range of the problems, which the respondents deal with in the process of interaction with the subordinates and colleagues, is much wider than a range of problems arising in the interaction with the superiors.

1. ***Inherently managerial problems*** proved to be topical for 10.0 per cent of a total number of respondents.

Among the problems arising in *interaction with the subordinates and colleagues*, are the following:

a) Inability of the team member to take part in the decision making *('I am forced to take decisions myself')* – 1.4 per cent;
b) Failure to abide by rule of confidentiality of information *('Cases of dissemination of confidential information regarding the company occur')* – 1.4 per cent;
c) Need to fire employees *('Firing of an unskilled employer, who is unlikely to find another job, is a complicated moral problem', 'I always feel guilty when I fire and incompetent employee who supports a family')* – 4.3 per cent;
d) Need to fire an employee due to lack of work *('I feel uncomfortable when I am forced to fire somebody since there is no work')* – 1.4 per cent.

The first-group problems that respondents face when *working with top managers* also include rigid subordination *('Rigid subordination prevent from solving many issues')* – 1.4 per cent.

2. ***Problems arising in the managerial relations*** proved to be topical for 32.8 per cent of a total number of respondents.

Among the problems that respondents face in the process of interaction with the subordinates and colleagues, are the following:

a) Communication with partners *('There are misunderstandings with the partners')* – 1.4 per cent;

b) Working with the friends (*'Misunderstanding of a distance between a manager and a subordinate, if you work with friends or acquaintances', 'They do not accept career growth of a friend'*) – 1.4 per cent;

c) Lack of trust in financial issues (*'It is hard to work when there is no trust in financial issues'*) – 1.4 per cent

d) Dishonest attitude of subordinate towards a manager (*'cheating', 'plotting', 'low conduct', 'some employees are disposed to abuse intellectual property rights'*) – 11.4 per cent;

e) Need to be flexible (*'It is hard to always stay yourself'*) – 1.4 per cent.

The second-group problems that respondents face when *dealing with top managers* include:

a) Interrelations with the superiors (*'Trying to find understanding with the head of the company', 'Dishonest attitude of a top manager to the subordinates', 'conflict of interests'*) – 5.6 per cent;

b) Relations with friends of a top manager (*'Top manager's friends believe that abusing some rules for their good is okay'*) – 1.4 per cent;

c) Relations with relatives of a top manager (*'It is hard to explain to the top manager's wife that she is not my boss', 'Our director does not want to notice lack of professionalism and mistakes made by the employees related to him'*) – 4.3 per cent;

d) Difference in attitudes of a top manager to male and female employees (*'contemptuous attitude of a boss towards working women', 'Our boss is absolutely against hiring women with small children'*) – 2.8 per cent.

3. ***Inherently ethical and psychological problems*** proved to be topical for 10.0 per cent of a total number of respondents.

Among the problems that respondents face in the process of interaction with the subordinates and colleagues, are the following:

a) Need to keep up the obligations (*'it is very hard to keep the obligations, including towards the employees'*) – 2.8 per cent;

b) Complications due to lack of a set ethical code (*'Lack of any ethical norms in the state. The most precious thing is money; the cheapest is human being'*) – 1.4 per cent;

c) Legal and financial limitations regarding pay raise (*'It is impossible to raise salaries'*) – 1.4 per cent;

d) Dishonest attitude to work obligations of some employees (*"It is hard to explain to people that they are paid for working, not for 'attending a workplace' "*) – 1.4 per cent.

The second-group problems that respondents face when *dealing with top managers* include cases of bribery *('giving bribes', 'a need to bring presents')* – 2.8 per cent.

At that, it is necessary to mention that a process of development of a request by a client in the process of the psychological-organizational counseling is a three-stage process:

1st stage – realization of a problem;

2nd stage – realization of a need to seek psychological assistance;

3rd stage – making the request.

The research clearly demonstrated that unfortunately there was not a single client on the 2nd or 3rd stage of the request development. Approximately half of the of the respondents (52.8 per cent) realized there were psychological and managerial problems preventing efficient functioning of the organizations; approximately 4.8 per cent of respondents pointed to the problems unrelated to competence of a psychologist; the rest of the respondents either hesitated (1.4 per cent) or were unable to answer the question (41.0 per cent) (see table 18.1).

TABLE 18.1: Breaking down of the respondents based on realization of the psychological managerial problems in the organization

Level of realization of a problem	*Number of responses*
Named a psychological managerial problem	52.8%
Named a problem that does not fall in the competence of a psychologist	4.8%
Answered 'it is hard to answer'	1.4%
No answer provided	41.0%

Educational Technology for Improvement of Professional Ethics in Managerial Activity

On the basis of methodology of inte.active technologies usage for managers and personnel training in organizations (Karamushka, 2005) and also our own experience of managers' training, the educational technology for improvement of professional ethics in managerial activity was developed. This educational technology consists of three interconnected trainings, which carry out in sequence (Vynoslavska, 2005, Technologia).

1. *Training for development of managers' moral consciousness.*

The training purposes:

- to define how often the manager is directly or indirectly involved into the ethical dilemma decision;
- to estimate how it influences on a level of development of manager's moral consciousness;

- to find out the most difficult ethical dilemmas the managers face in their work with.

The basic results of training. As a result of participation in training the participants can:

- to define level of their moral consciousness and to compare their ethical attitudes with attitudes of other group members;
- to familiarize with the basic steps of moral choice making and to apply them to the decision of an actual ethical dilemma;
- to analyze changes in structure of ethical attitudes that happened in consciousness of group members during group discussion.

2. ***Training of manager's skills of ethical behavior in the organization.***

The training purpose:

- to estimate manager's behavior in typical situations of professional work;
- to interpret the esteem of manager's ethical behavior in the organization by special scale;
- to plan the program of individual development of the manager's skills ethical behavior in the organization.

The basic results of training: As a result of participation in training participants can:

- to estimate the manager's behavior in typical situations of professional work and to compare his/her results to results of other group members;
- to familiarize with the basic steps of an ethical act and to apply them to the decision of an actual ethical dilemma;
- to analyze changes in style of ethical decision-making that happened in thinking of group members during group discussion.

3. ***Training of manager's ethical relations with others members of the organization.***

The training purpose:

- To define the important ethical problems and obstacles, which arise in manager's relations with other people;
- To receive an expert estimation of the reasons of ethical problems occurrence from the close person;
- to plan optimum ways of building of ethical relations with other people.

The basic results of training.

As a result of participation in training participants can:

- To define the basic obstacles which interfere with building of ethical relations between a manager and his/her subordinates and superiors;

- To receive an objective estimation of the reasons of ethical problems occurrence from the independent expert (close person);
- To build of ethical relations with other people.
- Implementation of this educational technology in Ukrainian commercial organizations testifies to expediency of its use for improvement of professional ethics in managerial activity.

Conclusions

On the basis of the forgoing research it is possible to make the following *conclusions*:

1. Democratization of the political processes in Ukraine, it accession to the world economic space determine a need for the managers to master the professional ethics, in particular, universal ethical norms and international standards of the professional ethics.
2. Present-day ethical and psychological training of Ukrainian managers in a majority of cases is insufficient, which is a result of a number of external and internal reasons. Thus, it is necessary to conduct special training, aimed at understanding of a need to address the specialists in organizational psychology when the ethical and psychological problems arise, of managers and to promote them to file the requests.
3. Counseling on development of the professional managerial ethics is an urgent task of the present-day Ukrainian organizational psychology; in order to solve it, it is necessary to train the practical psychologists. Such training should include the following:
   - Reviewing the specifics of the psychologist-manager (top manager) cooperation;
   - Training in developing the normative and ethical grounds of the managerial activities in order to prevent the ethical and psychological problems in the organization or its department;
   - Mastering of the methods to diagnose a level of development of the ethical component of the professional culture of a manage;
   - Mastering the training programs which will promote development of the professional managerial ethics;
   - Mastering of the ethical grounds for organizational counseling (Vynoslavska, 2002, *Spetsyfika*).

Therefore, it is possible to conclude that today, on one hand, an issue of development of the professional managerial ethics and, on the other hand, an issue of analysis of diagnostic, correcting and developing elements of the activities of the organizational psychologists in this sphere are particularly urgent in Ukraine.

REFERENCES

Antsyferova L.I. "Sviaz moralnogo soznania s nravstvennym povedeniem cheloveka (Po materialam issledovania Lourensa Kolberga i ego shkoly)". *Pskhologicheskiy zhurnal*. Vol. 20 (3): 5-17.

Ball G.O. (2004). "Humanizatsia zagalnoi ta profesiynoi osvity yak spryiniattia rozvytku kultury osobystosti". In *Psyholohichnyi resurs prostoru vyshchoyi osvity: Zbirnyk naukovyh prats* (ed. by O.V. Vynoslavska). Kyiv: Vydavnytstvo "Politehnika", 7-17.

Belolipetskyi V.K., Pavlova L. (2004). *Etika i kultura upravlenia: Uchebno-prakticheskoe posobie*. Moscow/Rostov-na-Donu: IKTs "MarT".

Doroshenko V.Yu., Zotova L.I., Lavrinenko V.N. et al. (1997). *Psihologiya i etika delovogo obshcheniya*. Moscow: "Kultura i sport"/ YuNITI.

Fominykh V.P., Zakharova A.N. (2002). "Issledovanie sotsialno-psihologicheskih faktorov determinatsii ekonomicheskogo povedeniya predprinimateley". In *Sovremennaya psihologiya: sostoyaniye i perspektivy. Tezisy dokladov na yubileynoy nauchnoy konferentsii IP RAN, 28-29 yanvarya 2002 goda* (ed. by. A.V. Brushlinsky, A.L. Zhuravlev). Vol. 2. Moscow: "Institut psihologii RAN", 254-255.

Karamushka L.M. (1997). *Psyholohichni osnovy upravlinnya v systemi serednyoi osvity*. Kyiv: IZMN.

Karamushka L.M., Malygina M.P. (2005). "Vykorysnannya interaktyvnych tehnik u protsesi realizatsii tehnologichnogo pidhodu v roboti organizatsijnyh psychologiv". In *Technologii roboty organizatsijnych psychologiv: Navchalny posibnyk* (ed. by L.M. Karamushka). Kyiv: INKOS, 60-71.

Palekha Yu.I., Kudin V.O. (1998). *Kultura upravlinnya ta pidpryyemnytstva*. Kyiv: MAUP.

Petrunin Yu.Yu., Borisov B.K. (2004). *Etika biznesa: Ucheb. posobiye*. Moscow: Delo.

Raider E. (1982). "Strategy Assessment." In *International Negotiations*. Plymouth, Mass.: Situation Management Systems, 4-16.

Samoukina N.V. (1999). *Psihologiya i pedagogika professionalnoy deyatelnosti*. Moscow: "TANDEM"/EKMOS".

Trevino L.K. (1995). *Managing Business Ethics: Straight Talk About How To Do It Right*. New York: J. Wiley & Sons.

Vynoslavska O.V. (2002). "Etychni zasady rozvytku osobystosti menedzhera zovnishnyoekonomichnoi diyalnosti". In *Zbirnik naukovykh prats vykladachiv i aspirantiv fakultetu menedzhmentu i marketyngu NTUU "KPI"*. Kyiv: Vydavnytstvo "Politehnika", 363-371.

Vynoslavska O.V. (2002). "Osnovni zapyty upravlinskogo personalu komertsiynyh orhanizatsiy shchodo psyhologichnoyi dopomohy z problem upravlinnya". In *Aktualni problemy psyholohii*. Vol. 1 (*Sotsialna psyholohiya. Psyholohia upravlinnya. Organizatsiyna psyholohiya.*). Kyiv: Instytut psyholohiyi im. G.S. Kostiuka APN Ukrayiny, 182-186.

Vynoslavska O.V. (2002). "Spetsyfika zdiysnennia hrupovoho psyholohichnoho konsultuvannia kerivnykiv orhanizatsiy z problem upravlinnia". In *Osnovy psyholoho-upravlinskoho konsultuvannia: Navchalny posibnyk* (ed. by L.M.

Karamushka). Kyiv: MAUP, 76-86.

Vynoslavska O.V. (2005). "Tehnologia formuvannya profesiynoi etyky menedzheriv". In *Technologii roboty organizatsijnych psyhologiv: Navchalny posibnyk* (ed. by L.M. Karamushka). Kyiv: INKOS, 170-191.

Vynoslavska O.V., McKinney J.A., Moore C.W., Longenecker J.G. (2005). Transition Ethics: a Comparison of Ukrainian and United States Business Professionals // Journal of Business Ethics. – N61, ID BUSI3507-I J3AUT1 2178908. – p. 283-299.

Vynoslavska O.V., Malyhina M.P. (2006). *Liudski stosunky: Navchalny posibnyk.* 2-e vyd. Kyiv: Tsentr navchalnoi literatury.

Wood J.A., Longenecker J.G., McKinney J.A., Moore C.W. (1988). "Ethical Attitudes of Students and Business Professionals: A Study of Moral Reasoning". *Journal of Business Ethics.* Vol. 7: 249-257.

19.

Gender Equality through ICT in India

Yazali Josephine

Globalization is a controversial term being defined in different ways. It has come into use in the last ten years. In fact it makes us wonder what is this force that has emerged on planet Earth to attract such attention? It indicates that the world now is more interconnected than it was before. It is a result of changes in the global economy – notably rapid movements of large volumes of money and increased volume of trade as well as changes in communications and in information technology. These trends are related in turn with a variety of political, cultural and educational changes. Globalization integrates the world economy through more trade and intensified factor mobility. Movement of people from one country to another links them to distant localities in such a way that local happening are shaped and in turn shape events occurring miles away (Giddens, 1994). Globalization implies weakening of the restrictions imposed by or inherent in a nation state. The 19th century had seen the weakening of the national barriers, as the movement of goods services, capital, and labor are much easier. The 20th century saw progressive liquidation of the colonialism and corresponding rise in the powers of the Nation and state. We find that the mainsprings of globalization during this period were development in IT, which contributed more than anything else to the emergence of a 'global village'. The U.K. Government's white paper on globalization of December 2000 highlighted, making Globalization to work for the poor – aims to address – 'there is no alternative' to globalization and we must learn to live with it. Not only has that globalization created unprecedented new opportunities for sustainable development and poverty reduction. This paper also recognizes that globalization poses threats to employment and livelihood and more intensive impact on the weaker sections and to the human security in general. However we must have to learn how to live with it. The UNDP's Human Development Report further substantiates this point and states that the Public health has declined, it can be seen in the spread of aids, there is increasing environmental degradation, there is under-employment or unemployment which now accounts for one-third of the labor force of the world – one billion people according to ILO as the relevance of education, type of education in demand has changed drastically. Education is undergoing constant changes under the effects of globalization. The structure of education is being altered to enable it to compete in an open, global market, leading to the modification of education. Educational institutions around the world are being forced to compete globally, by engaging in entrepreneurial activities to sustain themselves in an uncertain and competitive world. The strongest arms of the globalization are privatization and Information Technology. As women education and gender disparity in education in developing countries are already a major problem this has added fuel to the problem. For women in Asia, given the skewed distribution of resources within households and communities, that makes not just access to health, but often-basic survival itself and struggle. Female literacy in many Asian countries has always been lower in enrolment of higher education than boys. Thus the gender inequality, is already exists in Asia. Privatization of higher education and the introduction of self-financed courses in colleges and universities can be seen as the major impact of globalization on women. A high fee structure in private institutes and self-financed course would be detrimental to women taking admission at the tertiary level education. The already existing gender inequalities have reinforced more forcibly. Thus entry of women in technical education is becoming much difficult as a result the job opportunities for them also shrinking.

Gender and ICT: Current Scenario

In the service industries of banking, finance, and insurance, women are concentrated at the lower and less skilled employment levels. In India, for example, women made up 70 per cent of the banking workforce by the middle of the last decade. Women's employment in the telecommunications industry in Malaysia reflects similar percentages. However, they tend to be data entry clerks, computer typists, or tellers. The percentages of women in electronic data processing and in management are low, ranging from one to 12 per cent in India. According to Nancy Hafkin and in their study entitled 'Gender, Information Technology and Developing Countries: An Analytical Study' although IT is a new field; a 'gendered' division of labor is already emerging. In general, women tend to be concentrated in end-user, lower skilled IT jobs related to word processing or data entry, comprising only small percentages of managerial, maintenance, and design personnel in networks, operating systems, or software development. In brief the impact on women is mixed i.e. The Trade openness increased the share of women's paid employment but they are also the first to lose their jobs when economic crunches occur.

Women predominate informal subcontracting, which is on the rise, but this is associated with low wages and poor working conditions. Thus, Women also predominately prefer home based, part- and tele-work that accommodates family care obligations but these jobs are precarious and poorly paid. But how to make this weakness into strength for the women is a major problem. In this context, in the following section the author tried to discuss the Asian scenario by focusing on Indian illustrations.

Globalization in Asia with Special Focus on ICT India

Globalization refers to the international flow of goods, capital, labor, services, information, which has occurred in response to, improved transport and limitless revolution in communication technologies, and the regulatory policies/economy restructuring policies adopted in many countries during the past two decades by realizing as the economy restructuring as a path for economic development. At first, the development paths adopted were just four Asian tigers. The next were South East Asian countries, which experienced very rapid growth of development and employment during last decade. Thailand, Indonesia, Malaysia and China also now join them. In the past few years the Philippines, and even Bangladesh have shown interest to follow them. This process of restructuring has made the nations to liberalized, and then privatized and globalized (LPG). The reforms in these countries are related to Information Technology, Trade, Industry, Financial, Fiscal, Agriculture Sectors. These reforms have made tremendous impact on education and training either directly or indirectly. Some cases, it had a lethal effect and in some cases, it has done miracles and experienced rapid economic growth. The Developing countries that has experienced rapid economic growth over the last decades in technology revolution were, Republic of Korea, Taiwan, Hong Kong, and Singapore. The sector of Information Technology (IT) has shown impressive results in these countries. The last decade liberalization and globalization have gone hand in hand. As a result, the information technology has spread quite fast. IT could simply defined as 'Technology to exploit information the most efficient way' it comprises computer science, telecommunications, electronics and computer applications. This also includes artificial intelligence, Robotics', numerically controlled Machines, and Computer Integrated Manufacturing (CIM) Computer aided designs (CAD) and the like. Now India is beginning to see the culture of innovations and magic in hi-tech. The IT magic after globalization has not only made the software sector as one of the high value-addition and net foreign exchange earning industries, but has created a history of sort in the Indian stock exchanges. The strengths of the capacity of IT to generate, foreign exchange and employment has already caught the imagination of Indian businessmen, citizens, economists, educationists, planners and politicians. Thus Globalization has made many changes in Asia in the last 10 years. It indicates that the world now is more interconnected than it was before. It is a result of changes in the global economy-notably rapid movements of large volumes of money, increased volume of trade as well as change in communication and information technology in each of these sectors. Last decade of economic reforms has touched different sectors, ranging from Agriculture to International Trade. Thus, there is an up rise of demand for IT related education. As a result e-learning centers, corporate universities, abundant Computer Coaching Institutions, Technical Institutions and Engineering Institutions have grown tremendously in many parts of Asia particularly in India. Moreover functioning of the government offices, in agriculture, education, Industrial and business sector has also drastically changed. Many innovative IT related changes were taken place in these sectors. These changes has yielded better results and led to digital empowerment. However, the process of globalization and the new technology movement aggravated the already existing gender inequalities in education and employment. Thus In this context to explore, how weakness of globalization can be made as strengths for women empowerment and reduce gender inequalities is discussed in this chapter. Few illustrations of India are discussed below.

The Indian IT Industry and Women Employment (Illustrations from India)

There are several employment opportunities in IT for young women who have had education and training in urban, English medium schools. The IT enabled service centres offer several opportunities to women. The IT enabled services require excellent verbal communication skills and pleasing personality. Data entry/data conversion needs typing conversion and strong written English communication skills. Medical transcription requires a good understanding of medical terminology, ability to understand English with different accents and good typing speed. Entry-level salaries range from ₹3,000-10,000 a month. After four to five years of experience, medical transcriptions can look forward to 14,000-20,000 a month. The same is true for other jobs in this field. The age of entry is between 19-24 years. The minimum qualifications required are generally XII standard. Call centres prefer women as they feel that women are better suited to voice-based projects.

A large number of women are joining the IT enabled services sector (Ramani, S. 2000). A large number of companies as GE, American Express, Standard Chartered Bank, Citibank, British Airways, Microsoft,

AOL time Warner, HP, Dell Computers, Prudential Insurance, Morgan Stanley, Mark & Spencer have call centres where a sizeable number of women are employed ranging from 35 per cent to 65 per cent (www.expressit-people.com). GE capital had 40 to 55 per cent women employees in their various centres (Sandhya Sule, 2002). A study of an international call centre at Pune (Dutta, 2003) showed that 59 per cent of employees were women.

As per Nasscom estimates, women comprise 20–25 per cent of total number of science and engineering graduates in the country. The number of software professionals has been rising continuously over the years. The number of software professionals increased from 6800 in 1985 to 650,000 in 2003-2004 (Nasscom, 2004). Women are joining the IT sector and their numbers are fast increasing in India.

In 1993, only 10 per cent of workforce was women. In 1998, 18 per cent of IT workforce was a woman, which was higher than the national average of 12 per cent. In 2003, the proportion increased to 21 per cent. The participation of women in IT is rapidly growing and is expected to go up to 35 per cent in 2005. Hence, women are now occupying a prominent position in the labour force.

Women in India are employed in IT companies located mainly in cities as Bangalore, Poona, Chennai, Delhi, Hyderabad and Mumbai. More women are employed in Southern regions of the country, where hiring of professionals was 41 per cent as compared to Eastern region at 6 per cent (Nasscom 2003). The women employed in IT belong to the younger age group. The overall median age of software professionals was about 25.6 years. 44 per cent of software professionals possessed over 3 years of work experience (Nasscom 2003).

Due to IT, women have employment options as flexitiming and work at home concept. Tele-tech India, a joint venture BPO Company between Tele-tech and the Bharti Group, gives its employees a choice of four-day weeks instead of the normal five, hourly rates with a minimum number of work hours in a week. There are incentives for housewives and other part-time workers for 30-hour weeks.

Mumbai-based Automatics Technologies, a BPO that processes data allow women to work from home, 20 hours a week. This facilitates employment for married women, especially with small children. The employee strength is over 800 part-time workers as compared to only 500 permanent employees. Tracmail, a Mumbai-based business process outsourcing (BPO) company employs 2,000 people of which roughly 45 per cent of them are women who work 8.5-hour shifts, attending calls from clients across the world. A BPO company, Infowavz International, has one third of its 800 employees as women. 24 × 7 Customer Service, a company based in Bangalore employs women in large numbers where the share of women employees increased from 25 per cent to 40 per cent in the last two years. ICICI one source, a company based in Mumbai has 2,400 employees, of which 60 per cent are women, in the age group of 22 to 27 years. There are more women employees in call centres in north and western India.

Workforce trends show that a large number of women are joining the ICT sector. What is the position of women in newly emerging areas of information technology? Has ICT provided suitable employment opportunities to women leading to women empowerment? The main objective of this paper is to examine the different ways in which in IT has benefited women in terms of employment. However, the extension of the market economy can have both positive and negative effects for women's situation and gender relations. Positive effects may include increased employment opportunities for women in non-traditional sectors, thus enabling them to earn and control income. This is potentially empowering and may contribute to enhancing women's capacity to negotiate their role and status within the household and society. Negative effects can include increased exploitation and dependency on direct engagement with the market, and particularly on the vagaries of the market. In the past two decades, the relocation of labour intensive industries from advanced market economies to middle income-developing economies has increased employment of women in the latter. Even though female employment remains concentrated mainly in low skill sectors and the gender wage gap shows no signs of disappearing, the rapid increase in the female labour force participation rate has a considerable positive effect on women's economic well being and that of their families. Nevertheless, the issue of the poor conditions under which many women enter the labour market needs to be consistently raised. The problem is particularly acute in sweatshops in the informal sector, which through arrangements such as sub-contracting and outsourcing became an integral part of the formal economy and has experienced an explosive growth in recent years. In the developed countries, on the other hand, as industries relocate elsewhere in search of cheaper labour and production, labour demand has been shifting towards relatively high-skill manufacturing, while employment growth in traditionally low skill sectors such as relatively low-skill sectors in textiles and apparel, where women workers predominate, has been declining. The impact of these trends as observed, in both developing and developed countries, on gender relations is still not too clear. Evidence from around the world on women's labour market participation and gender inequalities (e.g. wage gap, power relations, etc.) is still mix.

Importance of ICT for Women Empowerment

ICT, gender and the labor market: The present day is witnessing a rapid change from an industrial to a knowledge based global economy. A highly skilled labour force is the key to success in the knowledge economy (Skyrme 1997, Stiglitz 1999). In the knowledge era, 'information technology' serves an integrated factor of production. The Information and Communication Technologies have reduced the globe to a village. These technologies have created new opportunities for scientific progress, economic development, education and social change.

The IT industry has gained the status of the fastest growing industry all over the world. In Asia particularly India too, the IT sector has come to occupy a prominent position. The contribution of ICT is significant in terms of income and earnings, growth and employment generation (Nasscom 2002). An abundant pool of skilled manpower has facilitated the rapid growth of IT industry in India. Hence, the IT workforce has come to occupy an important role in the economy.

The IT sector has not only created a large number of jobs, but has also resulted in new types of challenging careers. In the IT sector, emphasis is on intellectual rather than physical resources. In the knowledge industry, work is the output of skills (Taylor 1998). Knowledge workers get fulfillment through their work (Drucker, 1999). As emphasis is on knowledge, the IT industry is considered non-discriminating. It is considered an equal opportunity employer for men and women, minorities and handicapped alike.

ICT has profound gender implications for both men and women in employment, education, training and other productive and personal development areas of life. What becomes clear from these discussions and case studies is that access for rural women will depend critically on where the technologies are located. The most efficient and beneficial use of ICTs is closely related to the kind of information produced and distributed, that is, information that directly supports women's activities and responsibilities. In order to facilitate access for women from various classes and sectors, ICTs will need to be located in places which women frequent and to which they have open and equal access, such as health centres, women's NGOs, women's employment centres and perhaps even places of worship. In this context, location also pertains to the practical, specific kind of information that women require as a result of the time constraints they face. When women can understand and experience the benefits of ICTs, they are quick to use such technologies. Establishing telecommunication canters in local communities is also a potentially useful strategy, if gender obstacles to access to them by women are taken into account. Information production and distribution strategies will also be an important consideration in order to make the most of each point of access. They will need to be flexible, mixed media and multi-technology systems in order to reach the greatest number of women effectively. Further consideration should also be given to the social background of women. For example, because girls in many developing countries tend to leave formal education earlier than boys, Technical education should be started at an early level of education.

There are several opportunities arising for women out of the Globalization of Technologies: one among is ICT and Biotechnology ICT can make some of the traditional farming role of women redundant leading to unemployment particularly among older and rural women. Imported bio-technologies are not always relevant to the needs and traditions of the communities but they can make it possible to codify and transfer some of the unmodified knowledge of local women to the global market. However if uncompensated, the move deprives women the economic gains and royalty they should be entitled to. *to make the most out of globalization, we must manage globalization better so that its downside is minimized and its benefits maximized.*

The second opportunity is Relocated service sector jobs from high-wage countries. A combination of personal computers, cheap software, and cost-effective connectivity has given rise to networking technologies. The Internet is the prime example, whereby it is possible to transfer digitalized information across local boundaries with ease. These networking technologies are bringing new job opportunities for women in vast numbers in the region particularly in English speaking countries, such as India and the Philippines. A wide range of service sector jobs (e.g., medical transcription, data entry, geographical information systems, back office clerical jobs, airlines ticketing, and customer care services) can be and are being located from high-wage OECD to low-wage Asian countries that have a steady pool of high quality women workers. These relocated jobs are called Remote Processing. Women are getting a substantial proportion (nearly 20%) of relocated software services in India, the figure is 20 per cent; the figure is comparable in the Philippines. As it takes up a smaller amount of capital to start up businesses in remote processing work, women find new opportunities in self-employment as sub-contractors of global corporations.

Opportunities arising out of the Globalization of Technologies

Imports of technology affect the local modes of production and employment. Internet technologies facilitate the way companies can locate and manage production away from the main site to geographically distributed centers. This expands employment possibilities of women who live away from metropolises, in suburbia, in rural areas – both in the manufacturing and services sector. To achieve this governance is the key, because governance is not just mere government, but includes the framework of rules, institutions and established practices that set limits and give incentives for the behavior of individuals, organizations and firm. Such technologies allow women to have possibilities of flexible location and flexible hours, through tele-working or with the use of neighborhood centers. It also allows women to have new forms of business: such as selling telephone services and Internet services through Internet and telephone kiosks or cellular phones. There are examples of such initiatives in India and Bangladesh. These potentials become reality only when the policy makers can create an enabling environment of access to infrastructure such as adequate connectivity and low-cost telephones. Institutional innovations, such as tele-centres, or Internet kiosks facilitate commercial and affordable use of new technologies. An adequate pool of skilled women workers with literacy in English and computing: in order to be employed in the new economy or be self-employed e.g., as an entrepreneur of telephone shops or Internet kiosks.

Conclusions and Policy Implications

The advent of globalization and IT one can change the concept of work, especially for women. It is expected that more women will enter this sector as the new emerging trend could allow women to work from home with Internet and telecom connectivity. Flexi timings and work at home would enable more women to join the labour force. It has been observed that companies like Datamatics have adopted this policy and it has proved to be a great success. Similarly, other companies should also use this policy. The concept of part time work will also go a long way in helping women. There should be provision of childcare support as day care centres and crèches also. All these factors will go a long way in benefiting women. Women also predominately prefer home based, part- and tele-work that accommodates family care obligations but these jobs are precarious and poorly paid. But how to make this weakness into strength for the women is a major problem. It can be by improving technical education facilities for women or introducing technical education/ICT related courses for girls at early stage might help to women certain extent. As we have seen in the case of India and Asian increase of women in IT related jobs and contributing to the family and national income. To reduce the gender disparities and empower the women, they should form a significant portion of labour force. To help women, policies should be undertaken as to increase women's access to computers and Internet. There should be provisions for setting up of more women's only access sites. Efforts should be directed towards improving women's skills and usage of new technology.

It is also found from the several studies that there is a wide gap between computer education and absorption in the labour market. This is due to the fact there is restricted mobility for women. Timings of work are also a problem for women. Factors as marriage, childbirth, childrearing and household responsibilities may prevent women from working fulltime. Policies should be made to subsidize childcare. Transport facilities should be provided to women. If women had a break from work, there should be provisions for retraining in industry.

Steps should be taken to encourage women employees. Noteworthy examples are companies as Infosys, Wipro and I-flex of India. The Infosys Women Inclusivity Network (IWIN) conducts networking and mentoring sessions along with initiating policies, benefits and training via the group and there is a similar initiative within Wipro, called Women of Wipro (WOW). I-flex Solutions ensures that women are encouraged to join i-flex by having a woman representative on most its employment panels and has also run women-focused recruitment advertising campaigns.

REFERENCES

Agarwal, R. (2000). *Educated Women in the urban Labour Market: A study of career mobility patterns of women professionals in Information Technology.* Ph.D. Thesis. Zakir Hussain Centre for Educational Studies, School of Social Sciences, Jawaharlal Nehru University, New Delhi.

Aamagaon Soochna Kendra: Rural upliftment through web services: A case of W. Godavri

Business Standard (2003). Calling on women, more and more, *Business Standard, 18 June,* http://www.tracmail.com/news.asp?

Dasgupta, S. (2003). Playing for keeps.

Dutta, (2003). A study of an international call center. www.tiss.edu / papers: Paper presented at the International Labour Press Conference, April 5 –7.

Dong-Sook S. Gills. *Economic Globalization and Women in Asia: Challenges and Responses* (http://www.isanet.org/noarchive/gills.html)

Economic Times (2004). India Ins hottest Geeks are women

Merchant K. (2003). Calling India for financial growth, Financial times

Ibef (2004): Workshop on ICT for poverty alleviation in India, IIM, A hmedabad, 26-27 Feb. http://www.ibef.org/eventsdisplay1.aspx?Event_id=30

Mishra, P. (2003). Call centre jobs are not monotonous, www.express it people.com.

Nasscom (2004). '*Knowledge Professional*', National Association of Software and Services Companies, www.nasscom.org.

NASSCOM (1999). *The Informational Technology Workforce,* India's National Association of Software and Service Companies, New Delhi.

Nasscom-Mckinsey Report (1999). *The Indian IT Industry*, Nasscom Mckinsey Study, Mckinsey and Company incorporation, Nasscom.

Nasscom (2000b). Nasscom for immediate Action to increase supply of knowledge workers, *Press Release*, 17 March New Delhi, National Association of Software and Services Companies.

Sule, S. (2002). Employee analysis with gender focus, www.iimahd.ernet.in. In/ itps/gender &ICT/ presentations/ppo.pdf

Solita Monsod Professor, University of the Philippines *Globalization: Challenges and Opportunities*

Sify (2003). "Internet usage in India," *Sify News*, 31 July.

Ramani, S. (2000). IT enabled services: Growing forms of Telework, *Economic and Politcal Weekly*, June 24.

UNESCO: Putting ICT in the hands of the poor http://inhome.rediff.com/money/ 2003/may/17spec.htm, http://ictpr.nic.in/seelampur/profile.htm, www.westgodavri.org/ICT/rajiv.doc, http://meaindia.nic.in/iimedia/2003/02/ iimv8.htm#khozem, http://www.bsnl.in/business.asp?Intnewsid=37200 &strdisplaystyle=block&intdaysbefore Digitalempowerment:http:// gyandoot.nic.in/gyandoot/outlook.html http://www.capwip.org/resources/ womparlconf2000/workshops.htm

Contributors

Arenas, Alberto, *Ph.D.*, is Associate Professor in the College of Education at the University of Arizona (United States). He specializes in Education for Sustainability, with particular focus on Environmental Education and Productive learning. His main scholarly interest revolves around the fostering of pedagogy of place that has as main foci cultural desalinization, the protection and revival of vernacular, non-commodified knowledge, and productive Education. Previously he was Professor at the University of Massachusetts, Amherst where he taught at the Center for International Education. Arenas obtained his Ph.D. degree from the University of California at Berkeley.

Arputharaj, Nilasco, *Ph.D.*, is a specialist in Human Resource, IT and Transport Management. As an employee of Southern Railways in the capacity of H.TE, Dr. Arputharaj is a recipient of CCM's Railway Week Award 2010 for meritorious services in Railways. His doctoral research was on performance appraisal system for Indian Railways. He has presented and published many papers in higher education too.

Calhoun, Emily F., *Ph.D.*, has a BA in English from Georgia College in Milledgeville, Masters in Early Childhood and Reading from Georgia Southwestern College in Americus, and a Doctorate in Education from the University of Georgia in Athens. Since 1993, she has been Director of the Phoenix Alliance in Saint Simons Island. Her work abroad includes conducting workshops in the U.K. at the University of Nottingham and Cambridge and in Hong Kong with the Institute of Education and the school district. She is the creator of the Picture Word Inductive Model for the teaching of reading and writing, K-3 and as the core of programs for struggling readers.

Chadha, Rajat, possesses Ph.D. in Education from Indiana University, Bloomington. His area of interest is Educational Measurement. Dr. Rajat was an Associate Instructor for a Doctoral level class 'Experimental Design for Educational Research' at Indiana University. At present, he is working as a Research Associate at Educational Initiatives, India in the Large Scale Assessments group.

Frick, Theodore W., *Ph.D.* has been Professor in the Instructional Systems Technology (IST) Department since 1984. Over the past three decades he has taught graduate-level courses in computer-mediated learning and research methods. During 1980s, he led development of curriculum for using computers in education and computer-mediated learning. During 1990s, he led efforts for use of the Web in Education and served as the Web Director for the School of Education at Indiana University from 1998-2005. Since 2000, he has developed and taught distance-learning courses over the Web. His early research focused on computer-adaptive testing, where he invented an expert systems method for making decisions on mastery of instructional objectives (EXSPRT). He is currently investigating methods of instructional design for complex learning, especially for Web-based educational simulations and games. Dr. Frick has recently invented research methods for Mapping and Analyzing Patterns and Structures Across Time (MAPSAT).

Hlynka, Denis, *Ph.D.*, is Professor of Instructional Technology and Curriculum theory in the Department of Curriculum, Teaching and Learning at the University of Manitoba. Dr. Hlynka has a major contribution to the McGraw Hill *Handbook of Research in Educational Technology* (1996, 2004). His current research deals with the intersection of instructional technology, culture, history, and philosophy. He is on the editorial boards of *Educational Technology* and the *Canadian Journal of Technology* and a well-known public speaker in business, military, education and community venues. He also served as Acting Director of the Centre for Ukrainian Canadian Studies at the University of Manitoba. Dr. Hlynka has been a long time member of the Board of Directors of St. Andrew's College, University of Manitoba.

Hlynka, Markian holds undergraduate and graduate degrees in Computer Science with specialization in Artificial Intelligence and Learning. He explores and critiques New Information Technologies from a socio-technical perspective, and is currently an Information systems analyst with the Office of the Registrar at the University of Alberta.

Hughes, Phillip, *Ph.D.,* is Emeritus Professor of Education from Tasmania and presently Professor at the Australian National University at CEDAM. He was the founder Head of the School of Teacher Education at Canberra College of Advanced Education, establishing the School of Education, now part of the University of Canberra. He was Professor of Teacher Education at the University of Tasmania and Dean of the Centre for Education. He also served as Chairman of the Professorial Board at the University and was Acting Vice-Chancellor. Dr. Phillip Hughes has had extensive international experience in Asia, Europe and America. He has also been active through UNESCO and in other international activities in Asia and the Pacific. His professional interests are in the areas of Curriculum development and program evaluation, in which he has taught in USA, UK, China, Hong Kong, Thailand and Australia and for international bodies such as UNESCO and OECD. He has published widely in the areas of evaluation, curriculum development, science and mathematics education and moral education.

Ignatjeva, Svetlana is a docent at Daugavpils University. Since 2010 she is the head of the Department of Information technology. Dr. Svetlana participated at number of international conferences and possess sizable publications to her credit.

Iliško, Dzintra, *Ph.D.*, is an Associate Professor at Daugavpils University, Faculty of Education and Management. Since 2009 she is the Head of the Institute of Sustainable Education. Her research interest is Teachers' research competency and Inclusive education. She was in the team of scientific organizators for a a number of significant international conferences organized by JTEFS/BBCC in Paris and in Latvia. She is a member of several internatioanl networks, such as *Baltic and Black Sea Consortium in Educational Research* (BBCC) and *International Seminar of Religious Education and Values* (ISREV). Dr. Dzintra is a national expert in UNESCO group '*Communities in Practice*' since 2008 and is active participant of implementing UNITWIN/ UNESCO project '*Reorienting teacher education towards sustainable development*' since 2001. She was an active participant in Comenius international projects: '*ICTime - as a Tool of Intercultural and Media Education*' and 'Children as Researchers in the Primary schools in Europe' as a national coordinator.

Josephine, Yazali is Ph.D. from Jawaharlal Nehru University with specialization in Economics of Education. Professionally trained in Educational Planning and Administration from IIEP (UNESCO), Paris, she obtained Post Graduate Diploma in Developmental Administration from International University for Cooperation, Rome, Italy. She conducted several impact research studies related to DPEP, Girls Education and Incentive Programmes at School level; Dr. Yazali presented several research papers in the national and international organizations like UNESCO, Oxford and the like and published several research articles related to educational resource planning and management. Currently Dr. Yazali is working in the area of Globalization, Education and Poverty.

Joyce, Bruce, *Ph.D.*, grew up in New Jersey, was educated at Brown University, and, after military service, taught in the Schools of Delaware. He was Professor at University of Delaware, University of Chicago; and Teachers College, Columbia University, where he Directed the laboratory school and the elementary teacher education program. Dr. Bruce's research and writing are focused on Models of Teaching and professional development and the social studies. He lives in Saint Simons Island, Georgia.

Koh, Joyce Hwee Ling, *Ph.D., is* an Assistant Professor in the Learning Sciences and Technologies Academic Group at the National Institute of Education (NIE) of Singapore. She teaches pre-service teacher education courses in Educational technology integration and graduate-level courses in Instructional design, e-learning, and Project management. Dr. Joyce's current research interests include *Teacher knowledge development*, *Online facilitation pedagogies*, and *Analysis of instructional patterns*. Prior to joining NIE, she worked in Instructional design and consulting positions at both private and public training institutions.

Kononets, Mariya, *Ph.D.*, is the teacher of Psychology and Pedagogics Department at National Technical University of Ukraine (Kiyv Polytechnic Institute) since 2005. She trains Managerial Psychology, Konflictology, Business Ethics, Human Relations and Business communications. With Dr. Mariya's effort, the discipline 'Business Ethics' is delivered as distance-learning course. Dr. Mariya is a member of Ukrainian association of work and organizational psychology. She authored around 30 publications on organizational and economic psychology, psychology of entrepreneur activity, coaching on ethical and psychological management problems. Her main direction of scientific research is psychological conditions of forming entrepreneurial professional ethics. The results of her scientific research were presented at International psychological congresses and conferences in Ireland, France, Check Republic and Ukraine.

Lal Kishore, K., *Ph.D.*, presently Professor of JNTU, has distinguished academic record and significant achievements in the field of Engineering Education. Having obtained Master's and Doctoral from Indian Institute of Science (IISc) Bangalore, he joined teaching in 1977 in JNTU Hyderabad. He held various administrative positions including Chairman, Board of Studies, Principal, Director (Academic & Planning), Director UGC-ASC and Registrar of JNTU. Presently, he is Rector-in-Charge of JNTU, Hyderabad. Dr. Lal Kishore possess to his credit more than 115 research papers in various international and national journals of repute, five books, several awards from Government of Andhra Pradesh, IETE, DEC Ethiopia, IETE and number of doctoral supervision. He is a member of IEEE, Fellow of IETE and IE as also Life Member of ISTE and ISHM.

Londoño, Fernando is a doctoral student in the department of Teaching, Learning and Soico-cultural Studies, College of Education at the University of Arizona (United States). He has a B.S. in Mechanical Engineering and a M.A. in Soicocultural Anthropology. His research interests include: socio-cultural variables in the implementation of solar technology, education for sustainability through environmental projects, and the mobility of knowledge.

Majumdar, Shyamal, *Ph.D.*, is presently holding the position of Director-General of Colombo Plan Staff College (CPSC), Manila, Philippines and Senior Research Fellow, UNESCO-UNEVOC. Apart he holds his substantive position of Professor at National Institute of Technical Teachers' Training & Research, Kolkata, India. Dr. Mazumder was the regional Vice President of Asia and Pacific Region of IVETA.

Mei, Lum Wai possesses Masters of Education in Learning Science and Technology. Presently she is teaching at Maris Stella High School, Singapore. Her research interest is focused over use of ICT and collaborative learning in teaching of Biology.

Molia, Maganlal S., *Ph.D.*, served Saurashtra University, India as Associate Professor in the Department of Education since 1998. He is having academic liaison with various universities and academic bodies. Dr. Maganlal is keen researcher and has published good number of research papers, articles and books. His areas of interest include Instructional Psychology, Statistical Methods for Analysis of Data, Advanced Educational Psychology, Methodology of Educational Research, Educational Measurement and Evaluation, Yoga and Mathematics.

Mukhopadhyaya, Dulal, *Ph.D.*, is senior most Professor of Education in the Faculty of Education of University of Kalyani and Visiting Professor of West Bengal State University, India. He has to his credit several books on Instructional Technology and Educational Management as also many papers in different journals of national and international repute. He is associated with many universities in India and served as expert member in his capacity. Dr. Mukhopadhyaya has attended many national and international seminars, conferences and workshops as expert member.

Nelasco, Shobana, *Ph.D.,* is a postgraduate in management and doctorate in Economics. Presently she is Associate Professor in Economics of Fatima College, Maryland, Madurai, India, teaching and guiding research scholars for last twenty years. She is a recipient of Malcolm's '*Best Teacher in Economics Award'*, Association of Economist of Tamil Nadu's *Young Economist Award* and *Lion's International Award.* She has specialized herself in the areas of 'Quality in Higher Education', 'international economics', 'Issues of Asian Countries', 'Women Empowerment' and in the issues of developing countries. She has published handful number of papers in international and national journals. She has also been a member of different associations, committees and academic boards, both in Indian and in foreign. Presently on capacity of Director, she is handling a UGC major project on 'External Debt between India and China' and for a Malcolm project on 'Women Empowerment in South Asian Countries'.

Paira, Anjana, *Ph.D.,* is a postgraduate in Education and Modern History and Doctorate in Education. Her present area of interest is zoomed over exploration of appropriate technology for dissemination of formal education to the ethnic women population group, residing in eastern Indian province states, apart from learning strategies of gender groups and women education.

Reddy, D. Narasimha, *Ph.D.,* the Vice-Chancellor of Jawaharlal Nehru Technological University Hyderabad, is a leading academician and is known for his affable and inspiring personality. Starting his academic career as a member of the faculty of Mechanical Engineering at Osmania University, he served universities at various capacities such as Principal, Dean Faculty of Engineering and Member Executive Council. Throughout he has been working closely with students, teachers, colleagues and university authorities to promote academic excellence and educational partnerships. Dr. Reddy is a postgraduate in Mechanical Engineering from IIT Madras and Ph.D. from IIT Delhi. He is the Life Member of many professional bodies.

Roy, Rajarshi, *Ph.D.,* a postgraduate in Education and Sociology and doctorate in Education, is actively associated with educational policy research. His specific contribution is in the arena of Ethnopedagogy, Environmental Education and Indigenous Technology for the life-improvement for the population at crisis. He was offered with professorship in a university in 2008. Presently he is associated with a National Research-cum-Training Institute under Ministry of Human Resource Development of Government of India, located in Kolkata, dealing with restricted sphere of Education. Dr. Roy possesses to his credit significant number of publications in journals of international and national repute.

Singh, R.P., *Ph.D.,* is a Fulbright Fellow, holds his master's and doctoral degrees from the University of London. He is one of the senior academicians in Education in India. A former Joint Secretary, MHRD, retired from the NCERT where he was Dean Research (Chairman, Educational Research and Innovation Committee, (ERIC) and Head, Department of Teacher Education. Singh has written numerous books including *Teacher Education Today* and *Dialogue with Teacher Educators* and won several awards.

Thomas, P.Y. is currently Online Instruction designer in the Educational

Technology Unit of Centre of Academic Development of University of Botswana. He possesses Masters in Physics, Science Education and Educational Technology and presently perusing Doctoral study in University of South Africa. His research interest is zoomed over web-based blended approach to learning in higher education. He is a reviewer of South Africa Journal of Mathematics and Science Education.

Tiwari, Rajiv, *Ph.D.*, graduated in Mechanical Engineering from Ravishankar University, Raipur; and M. Tech. in 1991 and Ph. D. in 1997 from IIT Kanpur. He worked as Lecturer in REC, Hamirpur and there from shifted to IIT Guwahati as Assistant Professor and became Professor in 2007. He worked as Research Officer at University of Wales, Swansea, UK in 2001. He has been the Head of Center of Educational Technology, and Institute Coordinator of National Programme on Technology Enhanced Learning (NPTEL) during 2005-2009, and National Coordinator of the Quality Improvement Programme (QIP) during 2003-2009. His main research area is Rotor Dynamics. He has authored over 70 journal and conference papers, apart from doctoral supervision. He has organized Symposium on Rotor Dynamics (2003) and National Workshop on Use and Deployment of Web and Video Courses for Enriching Engineering Education (2007) at IIT Guwahati.

Vynoslavska, Olena, *Ph.D.*, is Professor and Head of Psychology and Pedagogics Department at National Technical University of Ukraine (Kiyv Politechnic Institute) since 1998. Olena is a senior researcher of Organizational psychology laboratory at Georgij Kostiuk Psychology Institute of Ukrainian Academy of Pedagogical Sciences. She is also the member of International Association for Research in Economic Psychology and Ukrainian Association of Work and Organizational Psychology. Olena authored around 290 publications focusing on psychology of higher education, ethical-psychological and cross-cultural managerial problems, including 12 manuals for students. The results of her scientific research were presented at International Psychological forums in Ireland, Spain, Italy, Norway, Russia, the USA, Hungary, Finland, France, Check Republic, Sweden and other countries. She participated in international projects with North Arkansas Technical College (1994), Baylor University, Waco, Texas (1998, 2001-2005) and Norwegian Family Therapy Association (2000-2003).

Zhu, Chang holds a Ph.D. in Educational Sciences and is a senior researcher at Ghent University, Belgium. Her research focuses on the application and effects of e-learning in higher education, the influencing factors on teacher adoption of e-learning and educational innovations, and inter-cultural differences of student learning in online learning environment. Previously she was a lecturer at Communication University of China in Beijing.

Index